PARTNERSHIP AND PARTICIPATION:
COMMUNITY ARCHAEOLOGY IN IRELAND

Partnership and participation: community archaeology in Ireland

EDITED BY CHRISTINE BAKER

First published in 2020
Wordwell Ltd
Unit 9, 78 Furze Road, Sandyford Industrial Estate,
Dublin 18
www.wordwellbooks.com

Front cover image—Community excavation within
the walled garden at Bremore Castle, Balbriggan.

ISBN 978-1-9162912-1-8

British Library Cataloguing-in-Publication Data.
A catalogue record for this book is available from the
British Library.

Typeset in Ireland by Wordwell Ltd
Copy-editor: Emer Condit
Cover design and artwork: Wordwell Ltd
Printed by W.G. Baird

This volume was published with the financial
sponsorship of Fingal County Council; the National
Monuments Service, Department of Culture,
Heritage and the Gaeltacht; and the Heritage Council.

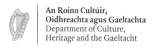

Contents

Foreword

This is a book based on innovation and partnership. I write this because one of the most interesting and satisfying developments in Irish heritage in recent years has been the development of community archaeology. By this I mean the participation and direct involvement of communities in investigating their heritage by working in partnership with archaeologists as well as with local and national government.

It has been really heartening for the Heritage Council to watch this develop and to have played a role in its emergence. Many of the projects described in this book received support from the Heritage Council. This is because partnership between the local government sector across Ireland and national organisations like the Heritage Council and the National Monuments Service is a key means of connecting local communities with heritage.

The real heroes of all this are the community groups who roll up their sleeves with a passion to learn about their heritage. Through adopting monuments, recording ogham inscriptions, learning new digital heritage skills, excavating archaeological sites and communicating their results, all of the projects in this book show the benefits of a strong partnership between professional archaeologists and community groups.

I want to acknowledge the leadership shown by Fingal County Council in employing the first full-time local authority community archaeologist in Ireland. This partnership between Fingal County Council and the Heritage Council has delivered valuable results: the projects at Swords Castle and Drumanagh as well as the work of the Resurrecting Monuments Group have continued to bring communities together to network and to plan for the future. I congratulate Christine Baker of Fingal County Council for having the vision and stamina to deliver this book.

The scope of this volume covers all of Ireland, North and South. The community projects shown here provide a compelling case for investing in heritage projects, thereby helping to protect this national resource by raising awareness and by creating links and connections within communities. In many ways, heritage is an enabler of such social connections, acting as a glue to bring people together.

The projects described illustrate how Ireland's heritage practice continues to evolve; this is still a developing field, but the processes and approaches presented here will be of interest to community heritage practitioners internationally.

Virginia Teehan

Introduction and acknowledgements

Over the past number of years there has been an increasing desire among communities to engage directly with the archaeology, heritage and traditions of their local area. The term 'community archaeology' is generally understood as the communities of today engaging with the people of the past through a variety of means—excavation, surveys, studies and dissemination. As can be seen in this publication, projects undertaken under the banner of community archaeology are varied and can include field-walking, building surveys, oral history projects, graveyard surveys, art projects, archive research, geophysical, landscape and topographic surveys, conservation and excavation. The common thread has been that of reconnecting people with their past and encouraging new communities to connect with their localities, thereby creating awareness and ensuring the protection of the archaeological resource.

An impetus for this publication was to highlight the quality of work being undertaken across the country. Dissemination of results is an important aspect of the archaeological process and, while many of the community groups have undertaken innovative and participative events locally, it is important that there should be a national overview. With an all-island approach, it becomes clear through the range of projects and the diversity of participants and audiences that there is widespread interest in sharing in community archaeology initiatives. This publication encompasses geophysical surveys, 3D projects, landscape surveys, heritage-based tourism, public art and community excavations and gives voice to a wide range of perspectives, from the community itself to institutional overviews. Participation in community archaeology has been facilitated though the licensing process by the National Monuments Service, Department of Culture, Heritage and the Gaeltacht, and the National Museum of Ireland, and it is clear that this support and the partnership between professionals and communities have been integral factors in the high standards and outcomes of these projects which have added substantially to our knowledge and understanding of our archaeological heritage.

The emergence of community archaeology across the island has connected communities, helped to create and reclaim identities, fostered civic engagement, generated knowledge and contributed to the recording and protection of our archaeological resource. It has been a privilege to work with the authors who have contributed to this publication and I would like to take this opportunity to thank them not only for sharing their results and experiences but also for their patience over the lengthy process of bringing this publication to fruition.

This volume was published with the financial sponsorship of Fingal County Council; the National Monuments Service, Department of Culture, Heritage and the Gaeltacht; and the Heritage Council. For their generous support I am grateful to Chief Archaeologist Michael McDonagh and CEO of the Heritage Council Virginia Teehan. I am also grateful to the Wordwell Group team, especially Nick Maxwell. Special thanks are due to Ian Doyle, Head of Conservation of the Heritage Council, whose support and input into this project have been invaluable.

Christine Baker

Contributors

Christine Baker, Community Archaeologist, Fingal County Council

Dr Conor Brady, Lecturer in Archaeology, Dundalk Institute of Technology

Isabel Bennett, Archaeologist and Curator, Músaem Chorca Dhuibhne, Baile an Fheirtéaraigh

Patrick Benson, Founder and Chairperson, Sailortown Regeneration Group

Dr James Bonsall, Lecturer, Institute of Technology, Sligo

Eddie Cantwell, Waterford County Museum

Naomi Carver, postgraduate research student, Queen's University Belfast

Malachy Conway, Regional Archaeologist, National Trust

Laura Corrway, Senior Excavation Supervisor, Co-founder and Director of the Blackfriary Archaeology Field School

Caroline Cowley, Public Art Co-ordinator, Fingal County Council

Dr Christy Cunniffe, Field Monument Adviser/Community Archaeologist, Galway County Council

Daniel Curley, Manager, Rathcroghan Visitor Centre

Gary Dempsey, co-founder and creative director at Digital Heritage Age; Assistant Lecturer in Game & Animation and Heritage Studies at Galway Mayo Institute of Technology.

Ian W. Doyle, Head of Conservation, Heritage Council

Paul Duffy, Archaeologist

Aidan Giblin, Resurrecting Monuments Community Archaeology Group

Fiona Hallinan, artist and researcher

Neil Jackman, Abarta Heritage

Ian Kinch, Senior Excavation Supervisor, Co-founder and Director of the Blackfriary Archaeology Field School

Christina Knight O'Connor, Waterford County Museum

Dr James Lyttleton, AECOM

Grace McAlister, Centre for Archaeological Fieldwork, Queen's University Belfast

Dr Meriel McClatchie, Assistant Professor in Archaeology, University College Dublin

David McIlreavy, Project Director, the Medieval Bray Project

Sabina MacMahon, visual artist

Neil Macnab, AECOM

Michael Mongey, Resurrecting Monuments Community Archaeology Group

Anne Mullee, curator, researcher and art writer

Professor Eileen Murphy, School of Natural and Built Environment, Queen's University Belfast

Finola O'Carroll, Principal Investigator, Co-Founder and Director of the Blackfriary Archaeology Field School

Orla-Peach Power, co-founder and lead digital editor at Digital Heritage Age; research assistant at MaREI Centre for Marine and Renewable Energy, University College Cork.

Ciara Reynolds, Kilberry Amenity & Heritage Group

Dr Rachel E. Scott, Associate Professor in Anthropology, DePaul University

Dr Liz Thomas, Research Fellow, University of Manchester

Dr Harry Welsh, Centre for Archaeological Fieldwork, Queen's University Belfast

Dr Nora White, Ogham in 3D Principal Investigator, Dublin Institute for Advanced Studies

1. What lies beneath: geophysical surveying and community archaeology in Kilberry, Co. Meath

CIARA REYNOLDS

ABSTRACT

The Kilberry Amenity and Heritage Group (KAHG) are one of a small number of community and voluntary groups who are actively engaged in 'bottom-up' archaeological research and remote sensing. The Group have conducted a series of geophysical surveys of the archaeological monuments within their community. Working with experts and community volunteers, they have explored a souterrain, a barrow, a ringfort, a standing stone and a moated site. Recent projects have included the mapping and recording of headstones in a medieval graveyard, and 3D imaging of the church and selected headstones. Significant results include the discovery of a previously unknown ditch and series of pits around a standing stone, possible evidence for a cairn or barrow within a mound, and the exact location of a souterrain which was previously unverified.

INTRODUCTION

> 'The Meathians are a dull people with very bad memories, big heads and regular Gothic faces, the natural consequence of the stupid rich flat on which they live' (Herity 2001, 30).

John O'Donovan's commentary on the people of Meath, as quoted by Herity, seems unnecessarily harsh at this distance. It was written during his pre-Famine journey around Ireland to record the archaeological monuments and the myths they inspired as part of the Ordnance Survey's mapping exercise, and we can only wonder what had upset him so much during this visit to County Meath that he felt compelled to utter such caustic remarks. The 'stupid rich flat' of Meath hosts some of the most famous and significant archaeological complexes in Ireland, including the Boyne Valley, the Hill of Tara and Loughcrew. Nevertheless, while these landscapes have been systematically researched by archaeologists, the areas in their hinterland remain largely unexplored.

The Kilberry Amenity and Heritage Group (KAHG) are one of a small number of community and voluntary groups who are actively engaged in archaeological research and remote sensing. Kilberry village, Co. Meath, lies to the west of the Brú na Bóinne World Heritage Site, 14km west-north-west of Newgrange, 15km north-west of the Hill of Tara and 10km west-north-west of the Hill of Slane (Fig. 1.1). The ancient site of Teltown lies 3km to the west of the village.

Today, Kilberry is a small rural community with a population of less than 300, many of whom are daily commuters to Navan and Dublin. It was founded as a manorial village, head of the manor of Castletown Kilberry, and strategically located on major north–south (Navan to Nobber) and east–west (Slane to Kells) routeways. There are seven visible recorded monuments within 1km of Kilberry village, ranging in age from the prehistoric (standing stone, barrow) to the early medieval (ringfort, souterrain, mound) and medieval periods (church, moated site).

The Kilberry Amenity Group was founded in 2012 (the 'Heritage' descriptor was added in 2014) to develop and enhance the village. Typical activities undertaken in the last six years include picking up litter, planting flowerbeds, constructing and developing a village garden, and restoring and maintaining an old village water-pump and postbox. In 2013 a flint flake was discovered while members of the community were digging a grave in the local burial ground (surrounding the medieval church). The National Museum of Ireland confirmed that the flake dated from the Mesolithic period (*c.* 7000–4000 BC). This chance discovery sparked an interest in discovering more about local history and the retelling of many old folk-tales about the local monuments. The Group contacted an archaeological geophysicist, Kevin Barton, who specialised in training community groups to survey their local archaeological monuments, and between 2014 and 2017 five archaeological monuments were surveyed using geophysical techniques. In 2017–18 the Group carried out a graveyard recording project with *historicgraves.ie* and worked with the Western Aerial

Fig. 1.1—Location of Kilberry and the monuments discussed in this article (Google Earth).

Survey to map the graveyard using a drone. Projects were funded through a combination of local fund-raising events, donations and grants from Meath County Council and the Heritage Council.

The KAHG had a number of objectives in undertaking the initial research. The first was a wish to learn more about known monuments and the local landscape, together with the tantalising possibility of finding new monuments. We also wanted to encourage the community to have a sense of ownership of their heritage and thereby to help preserve it and explore its tourist potential. Finally, we wished to contribute to national and international archaeological research, both in terms of what a small community group could achieve using innovative geophysical techniques and in terms of augmenting the existing store of knowledge of the site types surveyed.

Each of the five archaeological surveying projects completed was designed to answer a specific research question—for example, to ascertain the exact location

of a feature (the souterrain), to discover the morphology of a monument (the barrow) or to examine whether the geophysical techniques would confirm evidence visible on LiDAR images of the site (the standing stone).

KILBERRY SOUTERRAIN

The first project undertaken by the KAHG was to locate the site of a souterrain (ME018-021). Folk memory in Kilberry had long spoken of a 'tunnel' in the field behind the medieval graveyard that was believed to connect with a ringfort (Rathcoon) on an adjacent hill. To investigate this folklore, the KAHG undertook two training weekends and used a series of remote sensing surveys to pinpoint the site's location. It was marked as 'cave' on the 1837 Ordnance Survey (OS) 6in. map but no visible trace exists today (Moore 1991). A statement from a member of the community

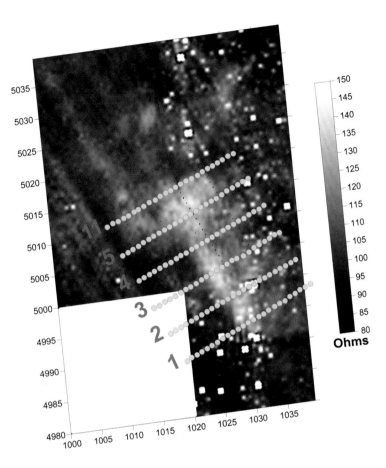

Fig. 1.2—Earth resistance image of Kilberry souterrain with overlaid ERT lines (Kevin Barton).

who remembers exploring the souterrain in the 1960s was used to establish a trial bearing along the expected route of the souterrain to determine its exact location.

A 40m x 40m square was laid out, with the estimated location of the souterrain at its centre. An earth resistance survey found a linear higher-resistance feature, *c.* 25m long, extending south-east/north-west, perhaps representing a passageway (Fig. 1.2). At the north-western end, perpendicular to the linear feature, was a zone of higher resistance about 15m in length which may be a chamber. Its width was difficult to determine, as there are no well-defined 'edges' to the earth resistance data. This area was then investigated with six electrical resistivity tomography (ERT) transects. These showed a higher-resistivity feature in the centre, perhaps relating to a chamber and passage, either open or collapsed (Barton 2013). The white speckled readings on Fig. 1.2 may be the result either of a missed reading or of zones of high resistance that may be stones. This supports a hypothesis that the souterrain may have collapsed and that ploughing activity over the intervening years has scattered its stones.

RATHCOON BARROW

LiDAR data purchased by the KAHG did not extend to the area of the barrow, so a topographic survey was carried out using a total station. Rathcoon mound (ME018-028), 18m in diameter and 2.7m high (Fig. 1.3), was described by the Archaeological Survey of Ireland in 1968 as 'Earthen mound … revetted by a stone wall which has largely collapsed' (Moore 1991). In the Sites and Monuments Record (SMR) (*www.archaeology.ie*, accessed 2018) it is classified as a 'mound barrow'. It is situated just south-west of the summit of a high, broad ridge commanding magnificent views over the plains of Meath. To the north, on a higher ridge, is Rathcoon ringfort.

The barrow is a small, circular earthen mound, the base of which was faced with drystone masonry. There is no clear indication in the earth resistance data that the masonry completely encircled the mound in the past. This facing survives well in the north-eastern quadrant but elsewhere has mostly disappeared. A ring of trees was planted on the mound (one beech survives), probably at the same time as the wall was

Fig. 1.3—Rathcoon barrow: topographic surveying (Justin Kenny).

constructed, as a possible landscaping enhancement.

The barrow was investigated using earth resistance, magnetic susceptibility and ERT. Both ERT transects showed a well-defined high-resistivity zone within the mound (Fig. 1.4). This could represent a barrow with a central cairn or a small passage tomb. There was no strong evidence for an entrance or a surrounding ditch. Further ERT transects are needed to resolve this. An area of higher resistance at the southern edge of the mound may relate to a collapsed entrance or the stone revetting, which might be blocking a possible entrance.

The earth resistance image shows that the mound has a higher resistance than the surrounding land, while the magnetic susceptibility survey shows low enhancement over the mound, which contrasts with higher enhancement in the surrounding area. This may be a consequence of farming activity that respected the monument, resulting in the mound's not being fertilised (Barton 2014a).

RATHCOON RINGFORT

The third site surveyed was Rathcoon ringfort, with its commanding views of Kilberry and the surrounding areas. It gives its name, *Rath Chomhghain* (Cowan's Fort), to the townland. Described as an enclosure (ME018-023) in the SMR (*www.archaeology.ie*, accessed 2018), it has always been known locally as a ringfort. It is *c.* 60m in diameter and was originally planted with beech trees, though only those on the perimeter have survived. Kite aerial photography was used to get a bird's-eye view of the monument (Fig. 1.5). The interior is open to cattle, which access the enclosure via a gap in the south-east which may mark the original entrance or may be modern disturbance. It is a large, approximately circular area, surrounded by a high, steep scarp with a low, broad bank on its top edge. A wide, shallow depression outside the scarp from north-east to east probably represents an original ditch.

As at Rathcoon barrow, there is evidence of stone facing on the north side of the enclosure, and the remains of a shale quarry lie *c.* 35m to the north-east of

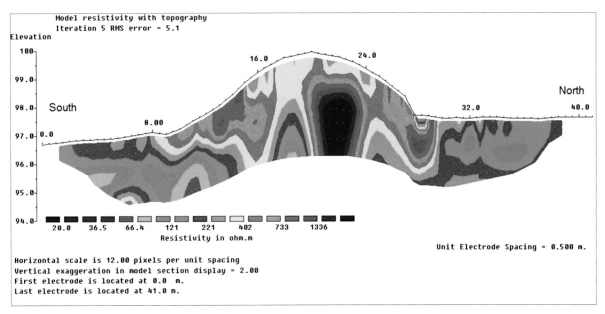

Fig. 1.4—Modelled ERT transect of Rathcoon barrow (x2 vertical exaggeration) (Kevin Barton).

Fig. 1.5—Kite aerial photograph of Rathcoon ringfort, looking north (Justin Kenny).

Fig. 1.6—Earth resistance survey at Rathcoon ringfort (Ciara Reynolds).

the site. Unfortunately, the wet and very cold weather during the surveying week affected the quality of the results (Fig. 1.6). Evidence was uncovered for a possible outer ditch and for a high-resistance zone on the northern edge of the site, which may be constructed of stone and could be a souterrain (Barton 2014b).

BALSAW STANDING STONE

The Hill of Balsaw, at an altitude of 116m, has beautiful views over the surrounding counties. The Hill of Tara and the Loughcrew Hills are clearly visible from the summit, along with local sites such as Rathcoon ringfort and Mullagha Hill (Fig. 1.7). The Record of Monuments and Places (RMP) entry (ME018-018) for the standing stone on this hilltop is brief: 'Oval in cross-section (H 1.6m, 1.15m by 0.7m) and tapering to a blunt point at top' (Moore 1991). The stone is aligned north-east/south-west and a preliminary examination by a geologist, Dr Robert Meehan, has identified the material as greywacke, a common stone across north Meath, but a full petrographical analysis would be needed for a positive confirmation.

Standing stones are an enigmatic site type; it is difficult to date them or to identify their function, particularly when they occur in isolation. Although individual standing stones are commonly dated to the Bronze Age, they are known from the Neolithic to the early medieval period. They can occur in isolation or in pairs or rows. They appear to have served a variety of uses, such as burial-markers, boundary-markers and

Fig. 1.7—Balsaw standing stone, looking south-west (Justin Kenny).

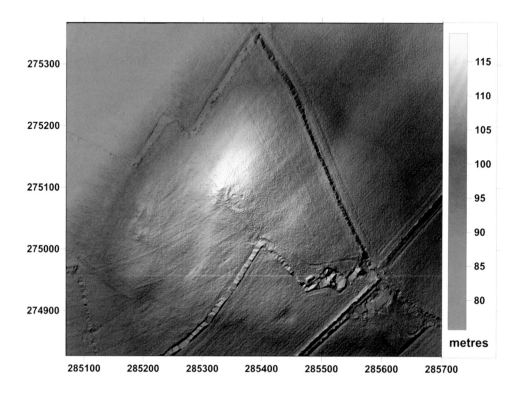

Fig. 1.8—LiDAR shaded relief image, illuminated from the north-west at 40° above the horizon, of Balsaw standing stone, showing enclosure (LiDAR data source: Ordnance Survey Ireland).

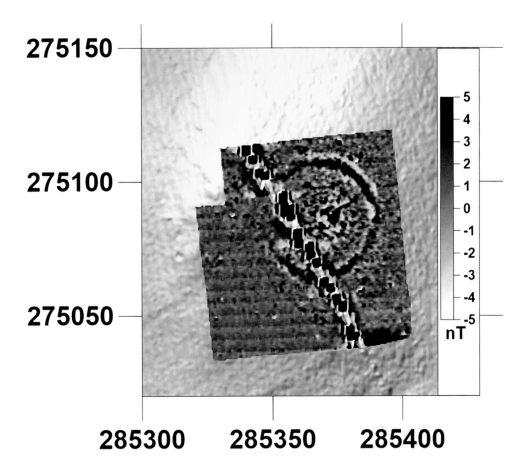

Fig. 1.9—Magnetic gradiometry of the area of Balsaw standing stone overlaid on the LiDAR image (LiDAR data source: Ordnance Survey Ireland).

memorials. When they do appear with other sites, these are usually of a funerary nature, such as ring-ditches, barrows or cremation pits (Ó Ríordáin 2015, 143–6). While there are thousands of standing stones throughout Ireland, there are only 51 recorded examples in County Meath, mainly isolated examples scattered around the county but with distinct clusters around the Loughcrew complex near Oldcastle and in the Boyne Valley (Archaeological Survey of Ireland).

Using multiple geophysical surveying techniques, the objective of the survey was to investigate a LiDAR image of the Hill of Balsaw that had shown an enclosing element around the standing stone (Fig. 1.8). The low topographic profile of this 'bank' was not clear at the north and north-east, which may be due to rock outcrops in that area. There was no visible trace of this feature on the ground and no documentary or cartographic evidence of its existence.

The magnetic gradiometry survey area covered the entire enclosing element of the standing stone as shown in the LiDAR data. Owing, however, to the presence of a modern wire fence running north-

west/south-east to the west of the stone, the magnetic response was severely disturbed in these areas. The enclosing element as seen on the LiDAR is represented as a band of positive magnetic gradient, which is interpreted as a ditch. The ditch appears to be broadest in the north-east and narrowest in the vicinity of the standing stone in the west. There may also be a gap or entrance in the east-south-eastern sector (Fig. 1.9). This magnetic gradiometry indication of a ditch is supported by a south–north ERT transect which was carried out across the northern sector of the enclosing element (Fig. 1.10). The data suggest that the ditch is inside the bank but further targeted surveying is needed to confirm this (Barton 2015).

Within the enclosure there are a number of apparently isolated features of positive gradient, which appear to be pits. In some cases they seem to be clustered around the standing stone, forming a circle around it. A linear feature also identified in the magnetic gradiometry survey extends west-north-west from the standing stone and terminates close to the edge of the enclosure.

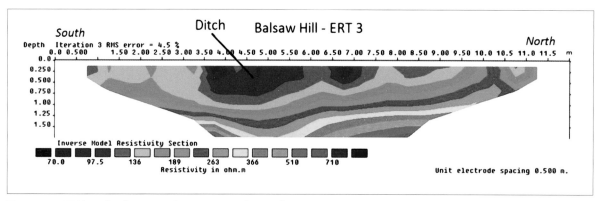

Fig. 1.10—ERT 3 of Balsaw standing stone enclosure (Kevin Barton).

Fig. 1.11—Surveying Balsaw standing stone (Ciara Reynolds).

The earth resistance survey was carried out in very variable weather conditions, with blustery wind and heavy rain showers (Fig. 1.11). There was some evidence for higher resistance surrounding the standing stone. This could be due to subsurface packing stones supporting the stone or to an area of compaction caused by livestock, or a combination of both. A localised area of higher resistance was detected immediately to the east of the modern fence. This may relate to the former site of a nineteenth-century trigonometric pillar located nearby. It might also relate to shallow bedrock, which is prevalent in this area.

Overall, the earth resistance results showed a large number of isolated areas of slightly lower resistance. These could be due to pits similar to those recognised in the magnetic gradiometry data or to poaching of the ground by cattle. A group of larger pits

appeared to correlate in places with the enclosing element seen in the LiDAR and magnetic gradiometry data. If this is the case, it may be tentative evidence that the eastern part of the ditch was formed of post-pits that may have contained wooden posts or stone orthostats. Further ERT transects through the ditch may clarify these results.

The combined geophysical survey results have confirmed the presence of the enclosing element first recognised in the LiDAR data. Within the enclosure, evidence for pits was seen in both the magnetic gradiometry and earth resistance data. The distribution of the pits is not clear but they may encircle the standing stone. There is also a suggestion that the eastern part of the ditch is constructed of post-pits. Obviously the geophysical data do not allow us to date these features or even to determine whether they are contemporaneous. There may have been several phases of activity on the Hill of Balsaw, with a multitude of features being reused and repurposed over time. It may also be a fortuitous coincidence that the standing stone was erected in the centre of an older enclosure, though this seems very unlikely and the accuracy of its location at the centre appears deliberate.

With that caveat in mind, there are a number of excavated examples of standing stones that can be examined for parallels to the site on the Hill of Balsaw. Historically most of these excavations were carried out to re-erect stones that had fallen or been damaged, but in the last two decades, primarily as a result of increased infrastructural development, a number of excavations have encompassed the wider landscape around the standing stone.

Excavations at Kiltullagh Hill in Roscommon over a number of seasons by the University of Manchester and Queen's University Belfast uncovered a small ring-barrow in conjunction with a standing stone. An excavation in 1993 in the area around the standing stone produced a shallow cremation and a male inhumation, which were dated to the late Iron Age or the early medieval period. In 1996 the ring-barrow was partially excavated. It consisted of a circular ditch and an internal bank, similar to the arrangements at Balsaw. A central pit had been disturbed and produced the disarticulated bones of several individuals (Coombs and Maude 1996).

Other sites that might offer us parallels for Balsaw include Ask, Co. Wexford, which was excavated as part of the N11 Arklow to Gorey link road. This multiperiod site, dating from the late Neolithic to the Viking period, included a ring-ditch cemetery, burial enclosures, cremation pits and a standing stone (site 44). The standing stone was dressed *in situ*, with waste pieces used as packing and support. Stake-holes found near the stone indicated that tethers held down by stakes kept the stone temporarily in place while wedges were set (Stevens 2007, 42). The small circle of pits/post-holes directly around the Balsaw standing stone may also be part of the construction phase.

No other archaeological features were located close to the Ask stone, however. The main complexes were 50m away and it has been suggested that this stone and its counterpart outside the excavation area could have been markers for the boundaries of the burial complex (*ibid.*).

One of the most interesting parallels was excavated as part of the N25 Waterford road scheme in 2005: three standing stones at Kilmurry, Co. Kilkenny. There was a possible cist burial at the foot of one but no surviving bones or artefacts. Stone A was 1.45m high and aligned north-west/south-east. Excavation revealed twelve post-holes surrounding the stone, echoing the arrangement at Balsaw (Wren 2003).

Further geophysical investigation will be necessary on the Hill of Balsaw, along with additional research to consider how the site relates to the wider landscape of Teltown, the Loughcrew and Boyne Valley complexes and the Hill of Tara to the south. The unusual name Balsaw can be translated as *Baile Shadhbha*. *Sadhbha* can mean 'sweet' or 'good', and in Irish mythology Sadhbha was the consort of Fionn MacCumhaill and the mother of Oisín (Pádraig O'Riain, pers. comm.). It is interesting to note that the standing stone has long been the subject of local folklore associated with Fionn MacCumhaill. On its south-west face there are three ridges running parallel, with the longest measuring 1m. There is also a small hole *c.* 0.8m from the base on the same face (Fig. 1.12). Locally this was referred to as the Giant's Stone. The three ridges and the hole were presumed to be marks left by Fionn MacCumhaill's fingers and thumb when

he threw this stone from the Hill of Tara, ten miles away, to land on the Hill of Balsaw.

DEMAILISTOWN MOATED SITE

The final monument surveyed by the KAHG, in a week-long project in 2016, was Demailistown moated site (ME018-019). Located *c.* 0.75km from the Pale ditch, which runs through the area, is a large, broadly square monument with an internal diameter of 42m and an external diameter of 60m. It sits on the uppermost slopes of a ridge at an altitude of 100m. O'Donovan described it as 'nearly square and has on the outside a large ditch provided with a raised bank' (Herity 2001, 648).

Moated sites are associated with the Anglo-Norman occupation of Ireland and are traditionally seen as the homesteads of Anglo-Norman farmers as part of the settlement phase of the thirteenth century. They are typically rectangular in shape, with defensive ditches and banks and a central habitation area. They are common in the south-east of Ireland but less so in County Meath (Barry 1987).

The objective of the survey was to determine whether the site had any features in the central habitation area. The moated site is now overgrown, with ash and elder trees planted on the banks, and there was evidence of cattle in the interior.

Earth resistance, magnetic gradiometry and ERT techniques were used during the week (Barton 2016). The earth resistance survey area of 40m x 30m identified a central area of undifferentiated lower resistance. This is likely due to a clay or saturated soil. A 'rim' of higher resistance extending around the south-west, west and north-west of the platform is likely to be composed of compacted and/or stony soils and may be related to the construction of the site.

Magnetic gradiometry survey data were collected on two 20m x 20m grid squares at the south of the platform and one 20m x 10m grid square at the north-east. The north-west of the survey area could not be surveyed owing to the steep topography and overhanging branches.

Three main features can be seen in the magnetic gradiometry data (Fig. 1.13). First, the overall background response in the survey area is 'noisy', indicating that the soils are magnetically variable owing to loose stones and cobbles and modern ferrous debris. Second, there is a distinctive magnetic anomaly, which does not have a coherent shape, in the approximate centre of the site. The source may be geological in the

Fig. 1.12—Balsaw standing stone, showing ridges (Ciara Reynolds).

form of stones or gravels, or it may represent the site of a fire with burnt residues. Third, there is a linear-like feature of positive gradient running east–west in the south of the platform. In most circumstances positive gradient responses are due to 'cut' features such as silted ditches and pits. There is no visible evidence of a ditch in the area of the anomaly (Barton 2016).

KILBERRY CHURCH AND GRAVEYARD

Since 2017 the KAHG have been working with *historicgraves.ie* to catalogue and record the inscriptions on all headstones in Kilberry graveyard (ME018-022001). A road traffic accident in 2016 damaged the outer boundary wall of the site and Meath County Council used the opportunity to repair the old wall and improve safety of access to the graveyard,

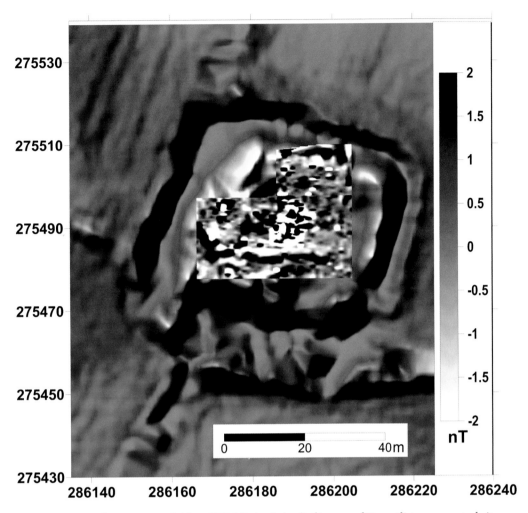

Fig. 1.13—Magnetic gradiometry overlaid on LiDAR shaded relief image of Demailistown moated site, illuminated from the north-west at 40° degrees above the horizon (LiDAR data source: Ordnance Survey Ireland).

which is located on a narrow road with substantial volumes of traffic. The excavation of the wall uncovered significant quantities of building materials and fragments of the roof and windows from the medieval church, now in ruins (see *excavations.ie*, 2017:651). After a training weekend for the community and a Heritage Week event, all 182 memorials in the graveyard have now been recorded and photographed and are available to view online on the *historicgraves.ie* website. The second phase of this project, which concluded in spring 2018, used drone technology to map the graveyard and individual graves and to cross-reference them with the previously recorded inscriptions. The oldest grave identified dated from 1709, and a wide range of carvings and decorations are visible and now recorded for posterity. A number of the more important features—including the church ruin, a chest tomb, graveslab and medieval font—were also 3D-imaged using photogrammetry.

FUTURE PROJECTS

In future plans the KAHG intend to focus on the rediscovery of a tower-house that overlooked the junction in the village, known only through the Down Survey map. To date, no other documentary sources that mention this tower-house have been discovered, though research is ongoing. There are no visible remains of this monument and it does not appear on the RMP or the historic OS maps.

COMMUNITY ARCHAEOLOGY

The archaeological licensing system in Ireland protects and upholds our archaeological heritage and has extremely high standards of reporting and best practice. In contrast to the situation in Britain, which is not as highly regulated, it is not feasible for

Fig. 1.14—Rathcoon barrow: topographic surveying (Justin Kenny).

community groups or non-professionals to engage in excavation of archaeological sites without partnering with archaeological professionals (Cody 2009). The avenues of independent field exploration open to community groups interested in their local archaeological monuments are more closely monitored and regulated than in the United Kingdom and elsewhere. The impact and origins of community archaeology in Ireland have been well documented (Kador 2014; Doyle 2018), and community archaeological remote sensing was discussed by Barton and Curley (2018). Doyle (2018), in considering community archaeology in Ireland, focused on six community-based projects and mapped them onto Kador's (2014) framework, which represents the degrees of public involvement in archaeology. The four thresholds of this framework can be used to situate community involvement in archaeology projects. Only one, Sliabh Coillte in Wexford, achieved threshold four, which describes a community who design, run and have significant control over the project, with copyright and authority to disseminate results remaining with the community group. This highest level of involvement allows a community group to fully own the process of engaging with their local archaeology. While professional expertise is almost always present (indeed, in the case of Ireland's archaeological licensing system, necessarily so), it is the community themselves who have full ownership of the project.

Having considered the projects undertaken in Kilberry, this paper proposes that the KAHG should also be recognised as having attained the fourth threshold of community archaeology on Kador's framework. The five geophysical surveys completed to date were all designed with the full involvement of the community group. Following the discovery of the graveyard flint, the KAHG identified an appropriate research area centred on the village and purchased the relevant LiDAR data from Ordnance Survey Ireland. A research programme was developed by the KAHG, focusing on one archaeological monument a season (to maximise Heritage Council and Meath County Council Heritage funding opportunities). With the assistance of a professional archaeological geophysicist (incidentally the same professional who worked with Sliabh Coillte), the Group were introduced to LiDAR and trained in several non-invasive surveying techniques, including earth resistance, magnetic susceptibility, magnetic gradiometry, ERT and ground-penetrating radar (Fig. 1.14). Preliminary data were downloaded and processed on site, which allowed the KAHG to further investigate particular sections of the monuments as guided by the new results.

The KAHG undertook a training weekend in field-walking with Dr Conor Brady on the site of a souterrain. Flint flakes and prehistoric and medieval pottery sherds were collected during this exercise. Several KAHG members have assisted other community groups with magnetic gradiometry, topography and earth resistance in the Leinster area.

In fully realising the potential of the surveys undertaken, the KAHG have also benefited from the expertise of many of their members and of the wider community, including a former archaeologist who conducted research on each monument, accessing the National Topographic Files in the National Museum of Ireland and SMR files in the National Monuments Service; a geologist who interpreted the natural and non-natural features on LiDAR data and gave advice on the morphology of any stone features on site; and a pilot who took aerial photographs of many of the sites in the research area. Both of these latter activities allowed the KAHG to place their local monuments within the broader landscape. Other members of the community assisted by cutting back grass and undergrowth to allow for better surveying results or by volunteering on training weekends. Without exception, landowners were welcoming and interested in the projects and readily gave permission to access their land, perhaps because they were personally acquainted with the members of the KAHG who would be undertaking the research.

During the research period the KAHG held a number of open days, showcasing their work to the wider public, as part of Heritage Week events. Site tours, demonstrations of the geophysical techniques used and presentation of our results allowed the community and schoolchildren to engage with their local heritage. The KAHG also presented their research at a series of conferences and events, including the Boyne Valley Research Seminars, the Rathcroghan Community Archaeology conference and the Aerial Archaeology Research Group international conference, as well as submitting a poster for the ArchaeoLandscapes Europe conference in Frankfurt. In 2015 the Group were awarded first prize for Heritage in the Meath County Council Pride of Place awards for their work on the Balsaw standing stone.

CONCLUSION

The KAHG have taken a leading role in the new arena of community archaeology. Working with experts, they are empowering the local community to undertake original and significant research into the archaeological monuments amongst which they live every day. This ensures that the community has a real sense of ownership, of pride and of responsibility for preserving their cultural and historical heritage.

ACKNOWLEDGEMENTS

The KAHG wish to thank all the volunteers and members of the community who have assisted in our surveys. Special thanks to those professionals who have worked with us: Kevin Barton, Landscape and Geophysical Services; John Tierney, Historic Graves; Dr Conor Brady, Dundalk Institute of Technology; Paul Naessens, Western Aerial Survey and Photography Services; Dr Robert Meehan, geologist, Talamh Ireland; Niall Roycroft, Meath County Council Project Archaeologist; and Dr Loreto Guinan, Meath Heritage Officer. This paper is dedicated to the memory of Seán Clarke, KAHG member, who was passionate about Kilberry and its history.

REFERENCES

Archaeological Survey of Ireland 2018 *Archaeology.ie* (accessed 25 April 2018).

Barry, T.B. 1987 *The archaeology of medieval Ireland.* Routledge, London.

Barton, K. 2013 Topographical and geophysical survey of Kilberry souterrain. Unpublished report.

Barton, K. 2014a Topographical and geophysical survey of Rathcoon barrow. Unpublished report.

Barton, K. 2014b Topographical and geophysical survey of Rathcoon ringfort. Unpublished report.

Barton, K. 2015 Topographical and geophysical survey of Balsaw standing stone. Unpublished report.

Barton, K. 2016 Topographical and geophysical survey of Demailistown moated site. Unpublished report.

Barton, K. and Curley, D. 2018 Archaeological remote sensing: some community engagement in Ireland. In L. Ciolfi, A. Damala, E. Hornecker, M. Lechner and L. Maye (eds), *Cultural heritage communities: technologies and challenges*, 20–37. Routledge, London.

Cody, E. 2009 Listing archaeological sites, protecting the historical landscape. The situation in the Republic of Ireland. In P.A.C. Schut (ed.), *Listing archaeological sites, protecting the historical landscape*, 63–9. EAC Occasional Paper 3. Archaeolingua.

Coombs, D.G. and Maude, K. 1996 Kiltullagh Hill. *Excavations.ie* (accessed 25 April 2018).

Doyle, I. 2018 Community archaeology in Ireland: less mitigator, more mediator? In V. Apaydin (ed.), *Shared knowledge, shared power: engaging local and indigenous heritage*, 45–61. Springer, New

York and London.

Herity, M. (ed.) 2001 *Ordnance Survey Letters Meath*. Four Masters Press, Dublin.

Kador, T. 2014 Public and community archaeology—an Irish perspective. In J. Lea and S. Thomas (eds), *Public participation in archaeology*, 35–47. Boydell Press, Woodbridge.

Moore, M. 1991 *Archaeological inventory of County Meath*. Office of Public Works, Dublin.

Ó Ríordáin, S.P. 2015 *Antiquities of the Irish countryside*. Routledge, London.

Stevens, P. 2007 Burial and ritual in late prehistory in north Wexford: excavation of a ring-ditch cemetery in Ask townland. In J. O'Sullivan and M. Stanley (eds), *New routes to the past*, 35–46. National Roads Authority, Dublin.

Wren, J. 2003 Kilmurry. *Excavations.ie* (accessed 25 April 2018).

2. Digital counties—building a framework for community-focused 3D digital heritage projects

GARY DEMPSEY AND ORLA-PEACH POWER

ABSTRACT

Over the last few years digital heritage recording has emerged as a practical and affordable method of recording cultural heritage objects. This paper will outline some of the new recording methods, such as photogrammetry and laser scanning, made popular through digital projects. An examination of a number of such projects in Ireland will follow the work of Digital Heritage Age, a research group founded to encourage community groups to engage with new digital recording skills. The paper will outline the benefits to local community groups of adopting these new skills, which have aided in the discovery of new archaeological features, while increased awareness of local heritage collections fosters a sense of pride in local heritage. The paper will conclude with a look towards the future of digital heritage projects and how a wider adoption of digital recording can enrich our knowledge of Irish heritage and preserve records of heritage objects for future generations.

INTRODUCTION

'Digital heritage' is a broad term that covers both digitally created and digitally recorded content. In the context of this paper, digital heritage refers to tangible heritage objects that are recorded using digital images to produce 3D models, providing an accurate geometric record of the surface of an object. Thus 3D models can be used to inform conservation plans and agendas, to promote awareness and as teaching and learning tools. The use of 3D models to promote heritage is increasing. Museums and cultural institutions are engaging with this new digital technology to encourage people to virtually interact with collections in new and exciting ways (Smith Bautista 2013). The Smithsonian launched their X3D project in 2013, noting that, while only 1% of their collection was on display, 'digitisation affords the opportunity to bring the remaining 99% of the collection' to the public forum (Mack 2013). Community groups can use digital models of cultural heritage objects in similar ways, providing access to local heritage through an online platform. This form of cultural heritage promotion encourages communities to engage with and manage their own heritage, while providing a lasting record of heritage objects for future generations.

Digital Heritage Age, an Irish research group who promote the use of digital recording methods among community groups, aim to demonstrate the benefits of digital heritage through flagship projects and to offer workshops and training courses to encourage the development of locally curated digital heritage museums and collections. It was formed in 2015 by Gary Dempsey and Orla-Peach Power, who met during the Roscommon Cross-Slab Project (RCSP) and, through a shared interest in digital heritage and community engagement, saw a need to develop a set of guidelines for community-focused digital heritage practices. The work of Digital Heritage Age has played an important role in promoting digital recording methods in Ireland, as it has developed both CPD (Continuing Professional Development) and community training programmes, while demonstrating the benefits of digital heritage through projects such as Sheela-na-Gig3D and the Rathcroghan Legacy Project.

DIGITAL HERITAGE METHODS

Digital Heritage Age utilise a number of digital capture methods when recording heritage objects. These include photogrammetry and laser scanning, which are both popular ways of creating 3D digital models. When engaging with community groups, however, photogrammetry is the preferred method, owing to its low cost and the ease with which it can be taught.

Laser scanning
Laser scanning is the process of recording the 3D topology of an object in real time, using specialised equipment and software. Minute surface details of an object are recorded by passing a light or laser over the surface of the object within the scanner's field of view. This light generates a point cloud, which in essence is a collection of individual measurements that represent

the distance between the scanner and the surface of the object being scanned.

Digital Heritage Age use an Artec Eva hand-held structured light laser scanner to record archaeological objects and features. The Artec Eva 'can capture and simultaneously process up to [...] two million points per second with up to 0.1mm accuracy' (ARTEC 2019), providing precise measurements at high resolution. This scanner is also equipped with a mounted camera, which allows for the accurate recording of an object's surface colour.

Laser scanning is a method that is used in small to large-scale survey works (both aerial and terrestrial), but its application in the field of archaeology is dependent both on the project requirements and on funding. As such, it is not always viable or necessary for community-based initiatives to apply this method of digital recording. In those instances where a laser scanner may not be required or may not fit one's research agenda, photogrammetry is a suitable alternative.

Photogrammetry

Photogrammetry is the process of creating a 3D model from a sequence of overlapping photographs. It has been seen as a valuable heritage tool since the late 1980s, but it has become more popular in the last decade owing to advancements in home computing (Remondino 2011; Bedford 2017). The cost of implementing this methodology will vary depending on the scale of the project and the intended outcomes of the 3D data and models. Typically, photogrammetry can be undertaken using a 'point-and-click' compact digital camera or a smart phone capable of taking photographs greater than 8 megapixels. The use of photogrammetry for large-scale projects (aerial surveys or larger monuments) will, however, require a small upfront cost to groups in order to get started. Costs will include the purchase of a mid-range digital camera and a computer capable of running specialist software such as Agisoft Photoscan or 3DZeypher, both of which offer free trials with the option to purchase an upgrade. A basic understanding of photography and computers is important for achieving good 3D models using this method.

Data capture/recording your object

Photogrammetry is commonly referred to as structure from motion, and requires a 60–80% overlap in your photographic sequence in order to produce an accurate 3D model. To ensure that a sufficient sequence has been captured, photographs should be taken at set intervals around the circumference of an object and at different elevations (top to bottom). This will also facilitate pair-matching during the post-processing phase.

Photographs must be clear and sharp, and avoid noise. It is also important that shadows, if present, do not change drastically between shots or throughout the sequence. The best way to achieve this is to take photographs on an overcast day, avoiding those times when sunlight is too bright. This method of recording can complement a mixed survey approach, where traditional methods that rely on good lighting can be carried out during the times when direct sunlight might hinder a photogrammetric survey. Photogrammetry can be applied to smaller portable heritage objects using the above methods. In order to record an object on all sides, the camera is placed on a tripod and set in a stationary position. The object can be placed on a 'lazy Susan' and rotated between photos. This process is repeated at multiple heights to ensure full coverage. The base of the object can be revealed and the process repeated to create a 'watertight' 3D model. The images are 'masked' using software, which isolates the object from the background, allowing the software to see the object from all sides and match the images. Careful consideration of these guidelines when taking photographs of an object will ensure that you produce a true replica of the subject being recorded. Once you have captured your photographic sequence, the software will do the rest.

The digital workflow

The overlapping photographs are aligned using a custom computer algorithm, known as a Scale Invariant Feature Transform or SIFT algorithm (Lowe 1999), which looks at the light and dark areas of each photograph and determines common features between the photographic sequences. This results in the creation of a point cloud, which represents the number of pixels from each matched photograph. This point cloud, after some editing to remove unwanted points, will undergo a number of processes in your photogrammetry software to become a complete, textured 3D model (Fig. 2.1). The completed 3D models can be shared online using digital publishing tools like Sketchfab, which allows users and institutions to disseminate and promote their 3D collections across a range of digital platforms and devices. Sketchfab offers free professional accounts to cultural heritage organisations and has worked with Digital Heritage Age to provide a number of free accounts as part of the Digital Counties Initiative, which was launched with the Roscommon3D project in 2016.

Fig. 2.1—Workflow for creating a 3D model in Agisoft Photoscan (@DH_Age, 2018).

ROSCOMMON3D—LEARNING TO EXPAND A PROJECT FOR LOCAL NEEDS

The Roscommon3D project was a natural outgrowth from the RCSP. When Nollaig Feeney (County Roscommon Heritage Officer) was first approached in early 2015 about the possibility of undertaking a digital heritage project focusing on cross-slabs in County Roscommon, she immediately enquired whether this could be turned into a community training project. Nothing like this had been attempted in Ireland. A number of digital recording projects had been established at an institutional level by the Discovery Programme (3D Icons) and the Dublin Institute for

Fig. 2.2—Gary Dempsey speaking with community groups during the RCSP (Orla-Peach Power, 2015).

Advanced Studies (Ogham in 3D), but these had not incorporated community participation at that stage and there was no call for digital recording projects at a community level. The Digital Design Studio of Glasgow School of Art had field-tested the concept through the Archaeology Community Co-Production of Research Data (ACCORD) project in 2014, successfully demonstrating not only that there was a clear value in encouraging community groups to record local heritage using 3D digital methods but also that there was a great interest in utilising such methods in the recording of cultural heritage sites (Jeffrey *et al.* 2014). Focusing the Roscommon project on cross-slabs attracted the interest of community groups and individuals, and it quickly became evident that there was a wider interest in the alternative uses for 3D digital recording methods.

The training course was delivered over five days, spread out at weekly intervals. Workshops were book-ended by an introductory session in week 1 and a presentation of work completed in week 5. Weeks 2–4 were split between indoor workshops at Roscommon County Library and fieldwork at various locations where participants gained hands-on recording experience (Fig. 2.2). It was during fieldwork that the true benefits of the community-led focus of the project revealed themselves. Participants were interested in learning the new digital recording skills offered but they were also interested in the history and oral tradition associated with the sites visited. Among the participants were a number of heritage experts, including Mary and Martin Timoney and Dr Christy Cunniffe, who have an in-depth knowledge of graveyard iconography. The combined participation of community groups (who have a detailed local knowledge) and heritage professionals fostered a dual focus which encouraged groups to incorporate both traditional recording methods and new digital methods into individual projects outside of the initial scope of the RCSP. During fieldwork at the sites of Roscommon Abbey (week 2) and Clontuskert graveyard (week 3), the groups used an amalgamation of traditional survey techniques and their newly acquired knowledge of 3D digital recording methods to reveal carved features, not visible to the naked eye, on commemorative stones. This also led to the discovery of a number of previously unrecorded heritage objects.

Frank Scott (Roscommon Heritage Forum) identified a number of carved stones at Roscommon

Fig. 2.3—Detail of carving on graveslab (RO039-055010) revealed during the RCSP (@DH_Age, 2015).

Abbey, which were included in the RCSP project survey. These were revealed to be examples of medieval carved stones that had previously been mentioned by Bradley and Dunne (1998) during the Urban Archaeological Survey but had been believed to have gone missing. A further collection of reused stones from Roscommon Abbey were rediscovered in the grounds of an adjacent building and later incorporated into the Sites and Monuments Record (SMR) (RO039-099). The most important discovery that Frank made at Roscommon Abbey was a graveslab (RO039-055010) not recorded on the SMR. It was initially identified by Brian Shanahan during survey work carried out for the Discovery Programme's Medieval Rural Settlement Project, and Gary Dempsey's survey revealed carvings of a large cat with a smaller animal in its mouth, overlaid on a cross stem with fleur-de-lis decoration at the head (Fig. 2.3).

A collection of cross-slabs, inscribed stones and architectural fragments which were previously discovered by the local graveyard committee and reset in the north wall of Clontuskert graveyard were identified by Dr Christy Cunniffe (Galway Community Archaeologist) and Peter Naughton (Moore History Group) during the RCSP survey. These stones appeared to have crosses inscribed on them, with one also

bearing a portion of Irish script. A total of nine stones (RO037-001022–RO037-001031) were subsequently reported to the National Monuments Service and digitally recorded for posterity.

At the conclusion of the RCSP, the Moore History Group requested that the digital survey be extended to three graveyards in south Roscommon. It was at this stage that the project evolved into the Roscommon3D project, a dedicated 3D archive of heritage objects for County Roscommon, driven by local community groups. The Moore History Group were interested in enhancing their existing *historicgraves.ie* recording project by including 3D models of headstones. As the scope of their project was quite large (three historic graveyards with hundreds of headstones), the group decided to include only headstones that were difficult to read using traditional methods, or stones that demonstrated skilled craftsmanship in their accompanying iconography. The project recorded 25 headstones across the three graveyards, revealing partial or full inscriptions for all. The 3D models were made available through Sketchfab via the Roscommon3D collections page, and a link was added to the relevant *historicgraves.ie* record page. The project also recorded two cross fragments at the request of the Moore History Group. These had been noted during

Fig. 2.4—Detail of carving on cross RO056-007004, showing the robed figure (@DH_Age, 2016).

initial RCSP surveys but were never recorded, as the SMR did not highlight any features of interest. Local information provided by the Moore History Group indicated, however, that carvings could be seen on the crosses under low lighting conditions on a winter morning. Digital recording methods were therefore applied to the two fragments, revealing a carving of a robed figure and a decorative leaf design on one of them (RO056-007004) (Fig. 2.4).

Engaging with the local community and using digital recording techniques have yielded many benefits. The known heritage collection for the county has been enriched and the local community group have gained the skills and knowledge to carry out their own heritage surveys incorporating digital heritage. Roscommon3D has expanded to include a digital survey of stone Crucifixion plaques, funded by the Roscommon Heritage Research Bursary 2017, and a digital survey of Sheela-na-gig carvings as part of a larger national survey funded by the Heritage Council. The 3D models of the Roscommon3D project have been viewed a total of 7,652 times in three years, with a total of 143 objects recorded in the same time (2015–18).

GALWAY3D—A NEED FOR CONTINUED SUPPORT

The Galway3D project was developed with the support of Galway City Museum, Marie Mannion (Galway County Heritage Officer) and the National Museum of Ireland–Country Life in 2015. Following the success of Roscommon3D, Dr Christy Cunniffe had enquired about introducing a similar project to County Galway, and after a meeting with Brendan McGowan of the Galway City Museum joint funding for the project was secured between Galway City Museum and the National Museum of Ireland through the Irish Community Archive Network (iCAN). This innovative project helps communities to care for their own local heritage and 'encourages collaborative engagement with local collections of photographs, documents, material and oral histories' (Elms 2018). The Galway3D project invited members of the Galway and Mayo iCAN groups to learn photogrammetry at the Galway City Museum. Three days of training were delivered over a period of a month, with an introductory class, practical demonstration and fieldwork at St Nicholas Collegiate Church in Galway City. The project was not as successful as the Roscommon3D endeavour and a planned extension did not proceed, as funding was not

Fig. 2.5—Clonfert Madonna and Child and wooden statues in Loughrea Parish Museum (@DH_Age, 2018).

secured. This has provided Digital Heritage Age with a suitable opportunity to review the format of Galway3D and to see how it might be better implemented in the future. With hindsight we observed that, unlike Roscommon3D, Galway3D did not have a primary dataset to promote the project and encourage the involvement of local community groups. Whereas Roscommon3D began as a project to record a collection of medieval cross-slabs, Galway3D had no such focus. The lack of a follow-up project directly after the training also meant that groups received no encouragement to develop their own projects that could be completed within their own time-frames. The Galway3D project expanded in 2018 with the assistance of funding from Marie Mannion and the Heritage Council. Two projects helped to revive it and give it a new lease of life: the Galway Ecclesiastical Heritage Project commissioned the digital recording of four medieval wooden carvings, including the thirteenth-century Clonfert Madonna and Child and two wooden statues in Loughrea Parish Museum (Fig. 2.5), while the Slieve Aughty Uplands Project pushed the project further with the challenge to record low-lying post-medieval hut sites in the uplands of east Galway. The features included a sweathouse, prayer stone and several booley huts. This project was further expanded in 2019 and 2020 with funding from Galway City and County Heritage officers (https:// sketchfab.com/ galway3d/collections).

Success was observed in the similiar Corca Dhuibhne 3D project, whose initial focus was on recording ogham stone collections in County Kerry but which was later extended to include other archaeological features (Corca Dhuibhne 3D, 2018.). This clearly demonstrates that projects with an initial directed focus can inspire community groups to take stewardship of projects and develop them further.

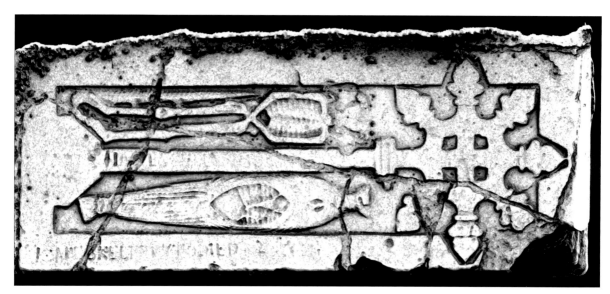

Fig. 2.6—Detail of cadaver tomb KD040-002033, revealing a pillow supporting the head of James Tallon and features of the lizard that extends along his right leg (@DH_Age, 2018).

COMMUNITY-INITIATED PROJECTS— ENGAGING WITH NEW TECHNOLOGIES

The Roscommon3D project saw the first community groups engage with digital heritage recording for graveyard surveys. As outlined above, the Moore History Group incorporated digital surveys into their Historic Graves mapping in south Roscommon. Shortly after that, two graveyard committees in County Longford (St Paul's Historic Graveyard, Newtownforbes, and Templemichael St John's, Longford Town) reached out to Digital Heritage Age to develop a photogrammetry course. They were interested in revealing details on a number of stones within their respective graveyards. Two training days were organised in County Longford at the Longford Westmeath Education Training Board, who provided access to computers and classroom facilities. Classroom-based work in the morning was followed by fieldwork in the graveyards in the afternoon. During the fieldwork at Templemichael St John's, a portion of a quern-stone was discovered while recording the detail on a recently uncovered gravestone. This came as a surprise to the local graveyard committee, who had not observed it during their clean-up of the graveyard, when they had lifted fallen table tombs and headstones. This again shows the importance of developing such projects with heritage experts who can inform participants of best-practice guidelines and advise them on how to identify archaeological features. During fieldwork at St Paul's in Newtownforbes, the community group were shown traditional recording methods, including headstone rubbing and the use of various lighting techniques to read some of the less-worn stones. The group found that photogrammetry was useful for reading the older headstones and also for revealing finer detailed carvings on the top of the headstones. In 2017 Digital Heritage Age were commissioned to carry out a further survey in St Paul's to assist in reading headstones ahead of the publication of burial records for the graveyard. A total of 25 headstones were recorded, many of which revealed dates in the 1700s and some of which were included in the publication (McHugh and Mooney 2017).

Castledermot Local History Society

The Castledermot Local History Society commissioned Digital Heritage Age to carry out a survey of several carved stones in St James's Church and graveyard, Castledermot, and a further tomb in Castledermot Friary. The project was funded by the Kildare County Community Heritage Grant. Working closely with Dr Sharon Douglas, a local archaeologist, we recorded several medieval stone fragments, using both photogrammetry and laser scanning techniques. As the latter method requires low lighting, it was primarily used on carvings indoors and under covered conditions. It was used to record the double effigy tomb in the Franciscan friary. This cadaver stone, or *transi* tomb (KD040-002033), was dedicated to James Tallon and Joanna Skelton. Like a number of examples in the broader Irish catalogue (Roe 1969), it is exposed to the elements and has been the subject of ongoing concerns as a result of weathering and general structural damage.

Fig. 2.7—Gary Dempsey demonstrating the 3D workflow to community groups in County Meath (Dennis Finegan, 2017).

Laser scanning proved successful in revealing long-worn features on the stone, including evidence of a pillow supporting the head of James Tallon, rope detail and diagonal stitching on the shroud of Joanna Skelton and details of the lizard that extends along the right leg of James Tallon (Fig. 2.6). A number of additional medieval stones were identified at the friary, where it is hoped that a further survey may reveal more carved features.

The survey at St James's Church included the Castledermot 'hogback' stone. This is an ornamental stone from the tenth or eleventh century associated with Viking culture and is the only identified example of this type in Ireland (Lang 1971). The Castledermot Local History Society was the first group to work with Digital Heritage Age who formed their own digital archive of 3D models using Sketchfab. In the past, Digital Heritage Age have hosted 3D models on accounts managed primarily by themselves. Since 2017 there has been a move away from this remotely curated version to a locally curated account that can be managed by the local community, with the intention that the collection will be added to over time (see https://sketchfab.com/CastledermotHistory).

Cruicetown Cemetery

In June 2017 the Cruicetown Cemetery Conservation Committee and St John's Old Cemetery Restoration Group undertook a three-week workshop in photogrammetry. The workshops took place in the George Eogan Cultural and Heritage Centre, Nobber, Co. Meath, and were organised by Henry Cruise with funding from the Heritage Council. Initial training took place over two days, with an introductory lecture followed by practical demonstration and software workflow (Fig. 2.7). A number of tombs were recorded at both Cruicetown and St John's during the training, highlighting the wealth of carved funerary monuments within the local area. Heather King (2005; 2007) carried out a survey of St John's and recorded many of the early medieval features of the site. The survey that accompanied the community training in Nobber focused on the sixteenth- and seventeenth-century effigy tombs in the area. The survey revealed a number of common carving styles among the effigy tombs within the wider region, suggesting that they were carved by an individual or by craftsmen following a school of carving. A detailed survey of the late 1600/early 1700 effigy tombs for County Meath would prove useful in developing this hypothesis. John Corbally was helpful in identifying another tomb at Kilmainhamwood, which was recorded as part of a Heritage Week event, along with a cross-slab/holed stone and an early eighteenth-century grave-marker in Kilmainhamwood.

A graveyard cross (ME005-071021) was also discovered at St John's in Nobber during workshops. The stone had been previously recorded by King (2007) as a possible window mullion, perhaps a secondary use of the stone. Upon physical inspection Gary Dempsey identified the crossed feet of Christ on the stone, and recorded it using photogrammetry to determine whether his identification was correct. The survey revealed the stone to be the lower portion of a cross showing the Crucifixion. The right side and back of the stone revealed lettering, but the inscription was only partial. Building on the suggestion that effigy tombs within the local area had a similar carving style, this stone was examined alongside the cemetery cross at Cruicetown cemetery. The style of lettering and the inclusion of similarly styled nail heads in the feet of Christ in both carvings suggest that they may have been carved by the same person.

The work carried out during the Cruicetown and Nobber surveys is available to view through the 'collections' page of the Digital Heritage Age Sketchfab account (https://sketchfab.com/DH_Age). Images captured from the digital models have also been added to the SMR, as well as links through the National Monuments Service historical viewer (http://webgis.archaeology.ie/HistoricEnvironment). Digital Heritage Age made the decision to link the 3D models hosted on Sketchfab with the SMR numbers. This provides a direct link to the official archaeological record and allows the National Monuments Service to link back to the 3D models through the use of a common naming system.

DIGITAL COUNTIES INITIATIVE

The digital projects undertaken in counties Roscommon, Galway, Meath, Longford and Kildare prove that there are communities who see the benefits of incorporating digital heritage methods in promoting local heritage. Digital Heritage Age have seen a need for wider national support for digital heritage projects and for continued support for community groups after initial training. The Digital Counties Initiative seeks to meet this need, aiming to encourage local community groups, heritage centres and museums to develop digital heritage projects and to use 3D models to raise awareness of local heritage both nationally and internationally.

The Digital Counties Initiative is currently in its early stages of development and Digital Heritage Age have been refining guidelines for future participants. Building on feedback from the projects outlined above, it is clear that communities will need access to training and equipment to aid in the development of future projects. This could be achieved through a national programme supported by the Heritage Council and delivered through local heritage officers. Local county museums may also have a role to play in ensuring a continuation of engagement by encouraging new groups to participate in the project through education and outreach programmes. Funding for such projects could be supported through partnerships with local enterprises, as seen in the Kerry Groups support for the Corca Dhuibhne 3D project (2016). Digital Heritage Age have confirmed agreement from Sketchfab that cultural heritage organisations will be provided with free professional accounts, which will aid in reducing the long-term financial worries of such projects.

The basic requirements for developing a digital counties project include:

- guidelines for both traditional and digital survey methods;
- eagerness to promote local heritage through skills-based training;
- cross-generational engagement and involvement;
- manageable and finite collections (achievable goals/deliverables).

The digital skills should not deter people from engaging with the project, as they can be learnt by virtually all members of the community. The Digital Counties Initiative facilitates a cross-generational involvement between community groups. Heritage groups working with younger demographics will allow for both groups to learn something about local heritage while developing new skills. Local projects tend to work best when centred on a manageable collection, like the Roscommon cross-slabs. This focus allows groups to learn the traditional and digital survey skills with a project goal in mind.

In 2018 Digital Heritage Age expanded the number of active Digital County Projects with the addition of counties Cavan, Down, Donegal, Kerry, Tipperary, Meath and Laois. The Hunt Museum in Limerick City was the first Irish museum to present digital models of its collection with the Limerick3D project, which invited members of the public to learn digital recording skills firsthand. This project proved a great success and it is hoped to further develop the Digital Counties Initiative with a number of projects through interactive workshops and community projects. These projects can be found on *sketchfab.com* by searching the county name followed by the '3D', where many of the models can be downloaded and reused under a Creative Commons Public Domain Licence for free. Digital Heritage Age are happy to engage with community groups, heritage centres and museums, and offer a free consultation with those who want advice on developing their own projects.

BIBLIOGRAPHY

ARTEC 2019 *Artec Scanners booklet* (https://www.artec3d.com/files/pdf/ArtecScanners-Booklet-EURO.pdf).

Bedford, J. 2017 *Photogrammetric application for cultural heritage: guides to good practice.* Historic England, Swindon.

Bradley, J. and Dunne, N. 1988 Urban Archaeological Survey—County Roscommon. Unpublished report commissioned by the Office of Public Works, Dublin.

Castledermot Local History Society (n.d.) Revealing hidden heritage in Castledermot (http://kildarelocalhistory.ie/news/revealing-hidden-heritage-in-castledermot/; accessed 1 March 2018).

Corca Dhuibhne 3D (2018) Welcome to Corca Dhuibhne 3D (http://www.corcadhuibhne3d.ie/home.php; accessed 25 February 2018).

Elms, L. 2018 About the Irish Community Archive Network (http://www.ouririshheritage.org/content/about/irish-community-archive-network-2; accessed 25 February 2018).

Jeffrey, S., Hale, A., Jones, C., Jones, S. and Maxwell, M. 2014 The ACCORD Project: Archaeological Community Co-Production of Research Resources. In F. Giligny, F. Djindjian, L. Costa, P. Moscati and S. Robert (eds), *CAA2014—21st Century Archaeology. Concepts, methods and tools. Proceedings of the 42nd Annual Conference on Computer Applications and Quantitative Methods in Archaeology*, 289–98. Archaeopress, Oxford.

King, H.A. 2005 Nobber's early medieval treasures revealed. *Archaeology Ireland* **19** (3), 21–4.

King, H.A. 2007 Nobber: an important early medieval ecclesiastical site. *Ríocht na Midhe* **18**, 39–66.

Lang, J.T. 1971 The Castledermot hogback. *Journal of the Royal Society of Antiquaries of Ireland* **101** (2), 154–8.

Lowe, D.G. 1999 Object recognition from local scale-invariant features (PDF). *Proceedings of the International Conference on Computer Vision* **2**, 1150–7.

McHugh, D. and Mooney, D. 2017 *St Paul's Historic Graveyard, Newtownforbes, Co. Longford. Clongish memorial and burial records 1698–2016.* Turners, Longford.

Mack, E. 2013 Smithsonian now allows anyone to 3D print (some) historic artefacts (https://www.forbes.com/sites/ericmack/2013/11/13/smithsonian-now-allows-anyone-to-3d-print-some-historic-artifacts/#22c53a0523b2; accessed 9 February 2018).

Remondino, F. 2011 Heritage recording and 3D modelling with photogrammetry and 3D scanning. *Remote Sensing* **3** (6), 1104–38.

Roe, H.M. 1969 Cadaver effigial monuments in Ireland. *Journal of the Royal Society of Antiquaries of Ireland* **99**, 1–19.

Smith Bautista, S. 2013 *Museums in the digital age: changing meaning of place, community and culture.* Altamira Press, Lanham, MD.

3. Engaging the community: the Kilcashel Landscape Project

JAMES BONSALL

ABSTRACT

This paper assesses the notion of 'community participation' in the Kilcashel Landscape Project, describing how the local community of Kilmovee, Co. Mayo, were recruited to join in the research, which examined the archaeology of Kilcashel townland over a five-year period. The challenges faced by the archaeologist seeking to involve a community are examined—from over-ambitious aims and objectives to the recruitment of volunteers and contacting landowners. A pivotal aspect of community involvement was the collection of previously unrecorded folklore that forms the Kilcashel Folklore Database. The research raised awareness of often-overlooked sites and helped to strengthen a positive relationship between the public and archaeology. The notion of 'giving back' to the community was implemented in a variety of ways, such as increasing computer skills and online learning, assisting in national and regional tourism initiatives and providing links with the National Monuments Service. The community were taught to use various online resources to study their landscape, which in turn increased their own curiosity about historical family names and landscape change. Non-destructive investigations were carried out by a combination of professional geophysicists and community volunteers. Some techniques required specialist and experienced (professional) practitioners only, whereas other techniques were easily used by non-specialists in a socially engaging atmosphere. The community involvement at Kilcashel continues long after the initial five-year project, greatly expanding the potential for future research avenues.

INTRODUCTION

The Kilcashel Landscape Project (KLP) is an investigation, coordinated by the author with assistance from Earthsound Archaeological Geophysics, the Centre for Environmental Research Innovation and Sustainability at IT Sligo and the community of Kilmovee, into the archaeology, history, folklore and topography of Kilcashel, a townland in north-west County Mayo, located to the south of Kilmovee village (Fig. 3.1). The KLP examines settlement patterns from cashel to cottage and from bog to field by mapping extant, destroyed and abandoned structures, from protohistoric enclosures to nineteenth-century homes and field walls. As an archaeological geophysicist, my typical approach is to scientifically investigate landscapes via remote sensing and analysis without the need to carry out excavation. A key aspect of the KLP was to attract and mobilise the local Kilmovee community into participating in various aspects of the project. This paper will look at the KLP experience of community archaeology, how we reached out to people (both locally and globally), how they responded and how the project benefited from community involvement.

Kilcashel is an average Irish townland (107 hectares in size, occupying 0.019% of County Mayo), which is precisely why it was selected for study.

Without any *a priori* bias or agenda, the KLP asked 'What cultural, historical and archaeological information can be derived from an in-depth analysis of a typical Irish townland'? The objectives of the KLP were (1) to carry out a desk-based assessment of the townland, (2) to study the architecture and ecology of the townland, (3) to establish a folklore database to record stories of the local community and Irish emigrants, and (4) to use the above elements to identify suitable targets for non-intrusive fieldwork (principally geophysical survey, unmanned aerial vehicle survey and photogrammetry).

Kilcashel: the townland and archaeology

Kilcashel townland is located immediately south of Kilmovee village. Its name, the Anglicised version of *Coill an Chaisil*, 'the wood of the stone fort', probably referring to the extant remains of Esker Wood in the south-west of the townland, is first recorded in the seventeenth century (Logainm 2018). Kilcashel has ten monuments listed in the Sites and Monuments Record (SMR): a *fulacht fiadh*, an undated enclosure, a bullaun stone (once located in the latter enclosure but currently on a field wall at the edge of Esker Wood) and three early medieval cashels, two of which contain a souterrain and one of which contains two house sites. The largest and most imposing of the three (MA073-030001-), 37m in diameter, is presumably the origin of

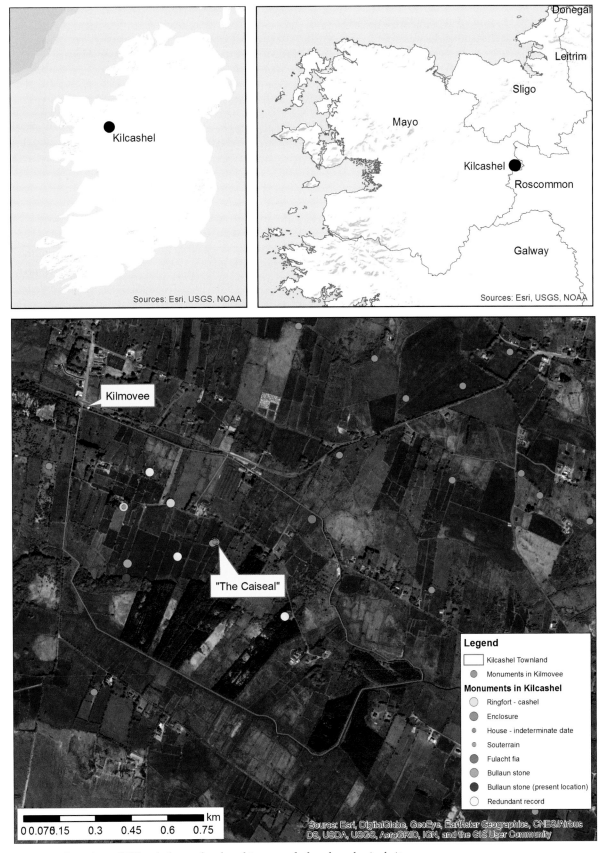

Fig. 3.1—Location of Kilcashel townland and its recorded archaeological sites.

Fig. 3.2—The Caiseal (MA073-030001-) is the dominant archaeological site in Kilcashel and Kilmovee.

the -cashel suffix in the townland name and features most prominently in local knowledge. Much of the KLP research focused on this cashel, as it is locally regarded as the most dominant landmark in the townland. Known by the community as 'the Caiseal', 'the Stone Fort', 'Culcastle', 'the castle' and 'Cashel Mhór', it is the only major surviving archaeological monument in Kilcashel (Fig. 3.2). It was recorded by antiquarian Thomas J. Westropp and is the only monument in Kilmovee to have undergone a modern archaeological excavation (Fitzpatrick 1999). The site is in the care of the Office of Public Works (OPW), which has carried out significant restoration works. Further, a wealth of documentary research is available on the cashel that other monuments in Kilcashel lack. Henceforth this cashel (MA073-030001-) is referred to by its local name, the Caiseal.

COMMUNITY PARTICIPATION

The Caiseal has engendered a lot of local pride but has been largely overlooked in academic research and has no tourism plan or support beyond Kilmovee village.

You could drive from Ireland West International Airport at Knock, just a few miles from Kilmovee, continue straight through the village and remain completely unaware that one of the best-preserved stone forts in Ireland is located here. I had the archaeological knowledge and enthusiasm to begin a project but, as a blow-in, I had no local knowledge and wanted to recruit local volunteers. To let the community know about the research, I used a method that had served me well during my undergraduate studies in England: I contacted the Three P's—the Postman, the Publican and the Priest. This triumvirate allowed me to reach out to the community. Via the postman I discovered local names and landowners rather than wandering aimlessly, asking random strangers. Via the publican I advertised the project by leaving leaflets at Duffy's Bar and chatting with locals. Via the priest at the Church of the Immaculate Conception, I wrote a short piece for the parish newsletter. Before long, various volunteers began to contact me. A website, funded initially by a grant from the Heritage Council, was launched in 2010 (*www.kilcashel.com*). The leaflets, parish newsletter and website all advertised the broad aims of the KLP in an

What is the Kilcashel Landscape Project?

Kilmovee, County Mayo, Ireland

The aim of the project is to apply the methods and techniques of landscape archaeology to comprehensively assess the townland of Kilcashel and disseminate that information to the public. A 5 year plan (2009-2014) has been established to collate historical & archaeological data of Kilcashel and combine this with new data gathered non-intrusively by field-walking, topographic mapping, geophysics and standing building recording. The data will be examined and compared with the settlement history and the natural resources of the area. This data will examine how resources have been exploited throughout history by the local community, what influences the community has had on land beyond the immediate study area and how Kilcashel itself has been influenced by external forces and events.

We have several more exciting areas of research over the next few years. In order to achieve all this, we've broken down the work into a number of research areas:

Dusty Old Maps!

By carrying out a Desk-top analysis we can bring together all the known history and archaeology of Kilcashel and the surrounding area. This is an important first step upon which future work can be based.

Lumps, Bumps and Wellie Boots!

A Walkover survey through Kilcashel's fields and woodlands will help us to map and record any potential archaeology that is not already known about. This may suggest new areas of interest for further work.

Sit down and have a Gossip!

We'll be talking to local residents and landowners to record some local oral history. Discussions of field and place-name evidence is very important as they may contain clues to historical and archaeological events that don't appear in the written record. We'll also collect local folklore from Kilcashel and Kilmovee and record it all in a database.

X-Ray Vision!

We'll be carrying out Geophysical surveys using equipment that can see beneath the soil and make a map of the buried archaeology. We'll be using this technology inside the Kilcashel Stone Fort to map any internal features. We'll also use it over archaeology that has been buried or destroyed above ground including a lime kiln, Father Hugh Henry's Fort, two more cashels and a bullaun stone.

Drawing with Lasers!

Laser-scanning of the Kilcashel Stone Fort will create a detailed drawing of the fort, souterrain, house sites and wall chambers, from which we can create a 3D model.

Build me a Wall!

How much effort does it take to build a wall? The size of the Kilcashel Stone Fort is very impressive - surely it must have taken a huge effort to construct it in the Early Medieval period? But that's just the beginning - in the 19th century, Kilcashel was transformed from open areas of uncultivated bog and scrubland to perfectly planned ladder-shaped field systems built of local stone. We're going to work out how much stone was used in the various construction projects and how many people may have contributed to the legacy of Kilcashel's stone walls.

Fig. 3.3—Part of an advertisement to recruit community volunteers to the KLP, as featured on the project website and leaflets distributed throughout the community.

accessible manner that presented the research as both informative and appealing to a wider community who had no knowledge of archaeological techniques (Fig. 3.3). Slowly but surely the various elements started to coalesce, thanks to the support and engagement of Kilcashel landowners and Kilmovee residents.

Using freely available online resources

Community volunteers from a range of backgrounds and age profiles became involved in the KLP. Not all were physically able to carry out archaeological fieldwork, but there were a variety of ways in which people could participate. The Kilmovee community actively promote their local history, archaeology and environment through the Cois Tine Heritage Centre in Kilmovee village, which is used for a variety of social gatherings and talks. One of our research themes, a desk-based analysis of the townland, was advertised to the community as 'Dusty Old Maps!', inviting the community to gather data from early Ordnance Survey (OS) maps and a wealth of online resources. Gathering in Cois Tine, we established quite quickly how many of the community volunteers had access to a computer and the internet. A small number of those were given a mini-workshop on how to use freely available online resources to research historical and cartographic data about the townland. Volunteers were taught how to carry out a simple regression analysis of historical 1842 and 1888 OS maps, comparing these with a modern OS map (Fig. 3.4). A significant consequence was that community volunteers identified 27 sites of archaeological and historical importance. These included vernacular houses, barns, limekilns, mill buildings, a quarry, wells and canalised water features, all of which were compiled into a gazetteer and GIS of recorded historic features older than 50 years. Realising that new and significant discoveries about their own community could be made quite easily using online resources, the volunteers were eager to progress to other sources of historical data.

Participants were introduced to online versions of the Down Survey of Ireland (1641), the Tithe Applotment Books (1827) and Griffith's Valuation (1847–64), which all recorded forms of taxation, landownership and landholdings. Recently compiled databases, such as the Irish Famine Eviction Project (2016), the National Folklore Collection (2013), the Connacht and Munster Landed Estates Project (2011) and the Placenames Database of Ireland (2008), were also introduced. Each of these resources contains important information on various townlands and estates throughout the country. KLP volunteers were taught how to search these resources and how to obtain screen shots and PDFs of the relevant sources, which I was later able to collate into a usable dataset. Importantly for the archaeological research, I could also see the areas, pages or resources that had not been examined and that I could subsequently investigate to ensure a rigorous, coherent and consistent approach. An in-depth exploration of these resources led to the creation of a detailed history of the Kilcashel landscape, which, combined with local community knowledge, produced a rich dataset for the townland.

The KLP volunteers discovered that Kilcashel was one of more than 900 townlands owned by Viscount Dillon and his descendants since the late seventeenth century, having been granted to him after the Ulster Rebellion. The Tithe Applotment Books recorded the head of household for agricultural holdings larger than one acre (0.404ha). For the first time, the volunteers

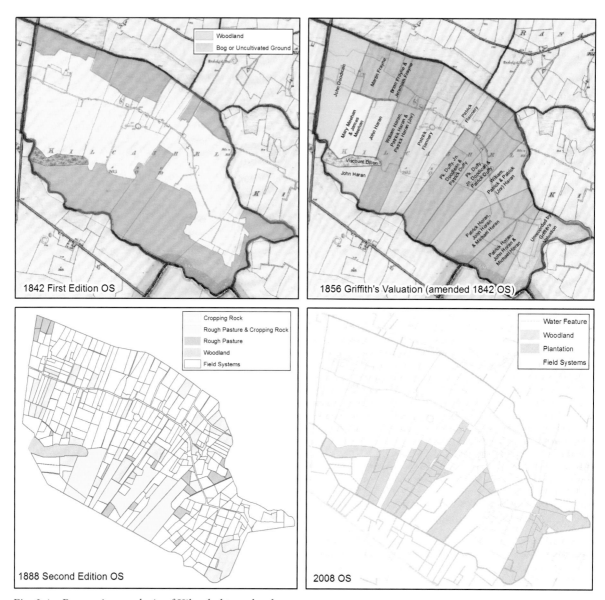

Fig. 3.4—Regression analysis of Kilcashel townland.

were able to ascribe personal names to places and fields within their own community as known almost 200 years ago. They could trace their ancestors (or geographical antecedents) and identify familial (and familiar) names, such as 'Bryan Flanary' and 'Mr Duffy'. In the mid-nineteenth century the Dillon family reorganised the field systems of Kilcashel, transforming bog and rock outcrops (seen on the first-edition OS map) into the regular striped 'ladder-style' stone-wall field systems identified in Griffith's Valuation that are still visible today. The Great Famine (1845–49/50) occurred three years after completion of the first-edition OS map and six or seven years before Griffith's Valuation. Community volunteers used online mapping to reveal the pre- and post-Famine landscape.

The KLP community volunteers found that the 1856 Griffith's Valuation assessed eighteen different people in Kilcashel for property tax; they noted seven different surnames, which they could add to the local history record and mapping. For instance, John Doodican rented one of the largest parcels of land and a house; the Meehans, the Fraynes, the Harans, the Flannerys and the Duffys all held lands, houses and offices in Kilcashel; while the Horan family had land and a house. It is interesting to note that 29 years after the Tithe Applotment Books both the Duffy and Flannery [Flanary] families were still resident and farming in Kilcashel. For our community volunteers, recognising these names was important, particularly the Duffy name, which appears prominently in

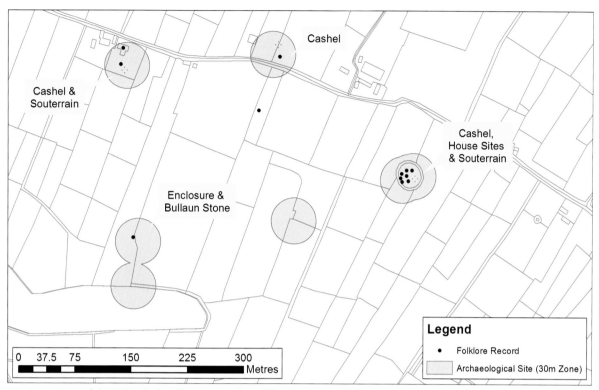

Fig. 3.5—Part of the Kilcashel Folkscape. Each Folklore Record represents a unique story, many of which centre on known archaeological monuments.

Kilmovee today in Duffy's Bar. It is equally important that the Doodican, Meehan, Frayne and Haran families have disappeared from Kilmovee. These family names from relatively recent times often surprised the local community; some names stirred distant memories while others had been lost to the collective memory, causing the volunteers to contemplate the fate of all those who went unrecorded long before taxation records existed. We know of a Bronze Age *fulacht fiadh*, three early medieval cashels and a landscape populated by nineteenth-century structures, yet history records only seven surnames for the townland and a total of just twenty individuals who lived or worked in Kilcashel less than 200 years ago. The community were engaged and hungry to learn more about their landscape.

Creating a 'Folkscape': the Kilcashel Folklore Database

Our most successful research theme was advertised to the community as 'Sit down and have a Gossip!'. This worked remarkably well. I simply visited people's homes and chatted with them in an informal setting about their landscape, history and the folklore they knew. I collated the cultural and historical knowledge, traditions and folklore of Kilcashel townland, as told

to me by the people of Kilmovee (and further afield), into a folklore database (Fig. 3.5). This contains much previously unrecorded information. The 'Dusty Old Maps!' research theme demonstrated that the local community had already forgotten the names of families who lived in the area in the nineteenth century. What stories did those families take with them when they left Kilmovee? What other folklore had already been lost? It was important to record what had survived before it too was lost.

The folklore research theme encouraged the local community to begin to share their oral history. The word 'begin' is important. I found that multiple visits to the same family home over many years yielded multiple stories rather than a single version that might be captured in a 'one-off' meeting. Current events, new people arriving in the village, subsequent chats with their own families and friends—each prompted memories of stories that had not previously been shared. I found that visiting someone's house and chatting over a cup of tea was much more likely to yield stories and information than the formality of lectures or mini-workshops. For instance, I know that every time I sit down in the kitchen of Culcastle House I will get a new story from Tess Regan, or her son, or her husband, or further detail on a story that had

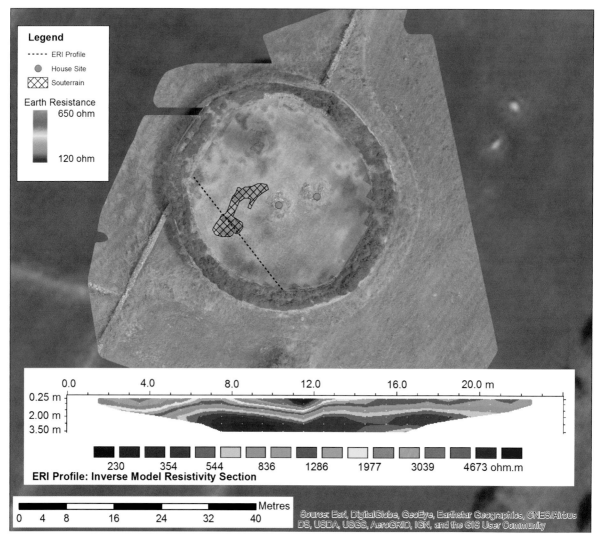

Fig. 3.6—Geophysical surveys in the Caiseal. The souterrain was mapped using an earth resistance survey to identify its extent (plot transparency at 75%, over an orthophoto of the monument) and an electrical resistivity imaging (ERI) profile to record its depth.

previously been told. The same is true of our global emigrants (discussed below): one email will yield important information, but multiple emails and an ongoing online conversation will yield large quantities of data.

All folklore data were recorded, regardless of how they compared to known empirical data: the database records the *perception* and *interpretation* of archaeology and history from a personal viewpoint regardless of scientific veracity. This is important because it shows how sites are reinterpreted and reimagined in modern times. The sites may not be actively used in a utilitarian sense, or even visited, but the stories illustrate that some ancient places are 'active' in the modern landscape; it is not a passive place devoid of detail. While the KLP's study area is confined to Kilcashel townland, strict geographical boundaries were not

possible for the Kilcashel Folklore Database; stories extended to the wider Kilmovee area to create a 'folkscape' of often-interlinked stories, many of which featured the souterrain located in the Caiseal.

Archaeological geophysical survey
Archaeological geophysics is used to map small magnetic, electrical and/or electromagnetic contrasts in the subsoil, to identify the presence of archaeological features beneath the ground. This was advertised in our leaflets to the community as 'X-Ray Vision!'. For this element of the KLP, geophysical surveys were carried out in the Caiseal, looking for evidence of settlement activity and mapping the depth and extent of the (now-blocked-up) souterrain within the Caiseal. The geophysical survey was carried out by Earthsound Archaeological Geophysics and four community

Fig. 3.7—Cois Tine Heritage Centre in Kilmovee (James Bonsall and Deirdre King).

volunteers. The volunteers carried out an earth resistance survey across the interior of the cashel. Earth resistance is an excellent technique for engaging volunteers; it is slow and uses equipment that looks like a Zimmer frame (and requires a similar walking pace), allowing the operator to move slowly, inserting probes into the ground every 0.5m. It thus allows people to converse freely. It is simple and repetitive and I've found that people of all ages, from students to retirees, can use the equipment easily. Earthsound staff carried out magnetometry and electrical resistivity imaging (ERI) surveys, which require specialist knowledge—and, in the case of magnetometry, a faster pace and non-magnetic clothing. These features make it a more complex operation for non-specialists than the earth resistance technique, as well as less sociable.

The souterrain passage was mapped by the volunteers and its depth was identified via the ERI survey. It continues both north-east and south-west from its entrance, measures 10.5m by 2.8m and lies 1m beneath the surface. It terminates within the Caiseal, about 1.7m from an early medieval house site (MA073-03005--) (Fig. 3.6).

GIVING BACK TO THE COMMUNITY

Embedded within Kilmovee is a vibrant community spirit that engages the local population. The KLP found many ways to feed its project outcomes and ongoing research back into this community. It built on the local pride of residents in their heritage and culture, supporting a pride of place and local identity. The Caiseal is without doubt a local icon. Visible on the skyline and only 100m from Canon Henry Park (home of the Kilmovee Shamrocks GAA club), the Caiseal is featured most prominently in a mural inside the Cois Tine Heritage Centre, reflecting the highly visual significance of archaeology within the community (Fig. 3.7). Our folklore records show that the Caiseal was central to community identity and history, with ceilidhs and pattern dances held there up to the 1950s. The Caiseal was also recently replicated as a bench in Kilmovee by Dominic Keogh, a stonemason of the Drystone Wall Association and a native of Kilmovee. The structure was built using drystone wall techniques as part of a Mayo, Sligo and Leitrim Education and Training Board Adult Educational Guidance Service course (Fig. 3.8).

Fig. 3.8—Stonemason Dominic Keogh and volunteers building a stone bench at St Michael's Estate, Kilmovee. The design of the bench was inspired by the Caiseal, even mimicking the vegetation planted by the OPW during their consolidation works in the 1990s (Dominic Keogh).

The annual Seosamh Mac Gabhann Summer School is a music school for children, held at the Cois Tine Heritage Centre every summer. In 2015 the school's Heritage Tour was officially opened by Seamus Caulfield, Emeritus Professor of Archaeology at UCD, and included, as always, a trip to the Caiseal. The Heritage Tours encourage discussion and appreciation of Kilmovee's historical and archaeological sites, and are followed by tea, home baking, music, singing and recitations in Cois Tine. The summer school brings new and young people to the village each year and exposes them to the local archaeology and culture.

The Winter Lecture Series, held in Cois Tine, is a forum for the community to hear experts from a variety of disciplines present their findings on topics of interest in the local area and regionally. The outcomes of the KLP were presented to the community at Cois Tine in 2015 and at a conference held the same year at IT Sligo (Bonsall 2015a; 2015b), and this has given the community a chance to respond with questions and to direct new areas of interest. Our lectures, for example, led to invitations from landowners for further walk-over surveys to explain the significance of stone walls and ruined limekilns on their land.

Funding from the Heritage Council in 2010 allowed for the construction and initial hosting costs of the KLP website, *www.kilcashel.com*. Launched in August 2010 to coincide with Heritage Week, it is updated with the latest results and announcements of future fieldwork opportunities for volunteers. Ongoing sponsorship through advertising has meant that the website has continued to be self-funded without incurring annual fees. The Kilcashel Folklore Database was transferred to a Geographical Information System (GIS) that can be viewed online as a Google Map or downloaded as a .kmz file. These outlets allow users to browse and identify locations associated with folklore and to see those entries via a clickable map. Not only is our folklore shared widely but it also illustrates the wealth of information available. The KLP website has been the first port of call for emigrants living abroad who searched the internet for their ancestral 'Kilcashel' townland name. In finding the KLP, they have shared their stories, passed down from parents or grandparents. In 2017 we received an inquiry from the prospective purchasers of a house in the townland that had been partially built into another cashel (MA073-028----) in the twentieth century. They were concerned about their potential responsibilities to the archaeological site if they bought the property. We put them in contact with the National Monuments Service, who advised accordingly and, as a by-product of the query, carried out a site visit, which gave them the opportunity to update their own records.

The KLP had a wider impact in County Mayo when it was featured prominently in *The Lie of the Land*, a five-part radio series broadcast on Claremorris Community Radio, produced, written and presented by Darren Regan of Earthsound Archaeological Geophysics. The show featured contributions from the KLP and segments were recorded in the Caiseal as part of an audio walking tour.

In 2016 the KLP wrote a letter of support for Kilmovee's application to the Heritage Council's Adopt a Monument Ireland scheme, as the local community wanted to adopt the Caiseal and develop it as a tourist destination. The application committee was provided with our research outputs, as well as copies of lectures and photographs. The application was unsuccessful but the community still plans to develop the site for tourism, which requires consensus between the OPW (in whose care the Caiseal is) and the owners of private land surrounding it; there is goodwill between all stakeholders, but funding is needed to provide a safe and publicly accessible path.

The KLP also contributed to the trail report for the proposed Kilmovee Loop Walk. Comprising four separate routes across areas of 'rich cultural significance' (McDermott 2016, 3), the walks included ringforts, the Caiseal, an ogham stone, bullaun stones, an early medieval church site and 'a flourishing variety of place-names and local stories'. Importantly for us, three of the four proposed loop walks featured archaeological sites in Kilcashel, demonstrating the continuing interest in archaeological aspects of the townland. Pride of place, as discussed above, is very important, and by raising awareness of local heritage the KLP has helped strengthen a positive relationship between the public and archaeology.

THE BENEFIT OF 'COMMUNITY ARCHAEOLOGY' TO ARCHAEOLOGY

The KLP has, since 2009, helped to develop community pride in archaeology, but there has also been a valuable payback. Archaeological sites in Kilcashel have benefited greatly from community involvement, something that was not instigated by the KLP—the local community have always been mindful of their cultural resources. For instance, the Regan family own land adjacent to the walls of the Caiseal. The site itself, a National Monument (No. 619), is in the guardianship of the OPW. It was the local community, headed by Tess Regan, who wrote to the OPW to request that Dúchas carry out repairs to the National Monument in the late 1990s, when the Caiseal was crumbling. As a consequence, the walls and architectural features were rebuilt and the top course of stones was consolidated and stabilised by the planting of peat and heather. Here the local community was instrumental in the long-term preservation and conservation of a National Monument.

A further—very tangible—benefit from the community has been the folklore database associated with the KLP. As *the* local landmark, the Caiseal features in the majority of stories in our folklore database. Four stories revolve around 'the tunnel in the Caiseal', centred on the souterrain (MA073-030003-) within the cashel walls. No two stories agree on a single end destination for the tunnel (Fig. 3.9). In one story it is linked to another hilltop fort, a cashel known as Cashelgal (MA073-018----), located some 600m away beyond a stream and a valley. In a second story the tunnel is linked to another of the three Kilcashel cashels (MA073-028----), 390m away. The third story relates that 'local youngsters used to go through the tunnels as a dare' (Kieran McGee, pers. comm.), crossing beneath the River Lung and surfacing in Clooncarha townland, 4km to the east. In the fourth story the tunnel emerged near Moran's Bar and Kilmovee National School, 1.57km to the north-east. The validity of these stories was tested via the earth resistance survey carried out by the community volunteers, which (unsurprisingly) identified the terminus of the souterrain within the Caiseal. Nevertheless, despite the scientific evidence, the folk belief provides a connection between the landscape, archaeology and the people (and future descendants) of Kilmovee. The folklore and oral history are a vital, unseen—and, until now, unrecorded—part of the cultural landscape. The Folklore Database is a unique dataset for Kilcashel and Kilmovee, a collated 'folkscape' that does not exist

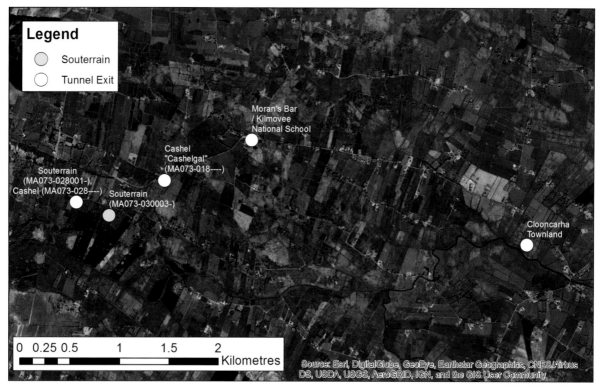

Fig. 3.9—The souterrain and its four exits, according to local folklore. Each of the four tunnel exits represents a unique story, as told by four different people—none agree on a single 'common' exit for the tunnel.

elsewhere. None of our folklore appears in the National Folklore Collection UCD Digitization Project (available at *https://www.duchas.ie/en*). This is significant because it demonstrates that there is a rich resource of local information yet to be formally collected, not just at Kilmovee but throughout Ireland. To prevent folklore from being 'lost', it simply needs an active and willing community to record it.

This research has also shone a spotlight on lesser-known archaeological sites within Kilcashel townland. An enclosure (MA073-039- - - -) was destroyed in the twentieth century to the extent that not even a faint earthwork survives, but the local people remember this monument as the site of 'Father Henry's Fort'. A bullaun stone (MA073-043- - - -) currently sits on a stone wall at the edge of Esker Wood, but it was previously located within the now-destroyed enclosure. Father Hugh Henry reputedly used the bullaun stone as a Mass rock during Penal times. The approach of taking landowners across their fields and asking them to explain the lumps and bumps on their land has proved to be a valuable exercise.

Some folklore can increase a monument's chances of physical preservation. One cashel (MA073-028- - - -) was substantially affected by the construction of a bungalow in the twentieth century. Local knowledge claimed that 'the stone from the fort had been taken to build the house' (Tess Regan, pers. comm.). This reuse did not contravene the planning laws of the time, but folklore has remembered the event darkly. One informant remembered that a previous owner of the bungalow used to suffer mentally from 'the small people that do be coming around'; evidently the fairies were distressed at the disturbance and caused distress in turn. This story is not just recalled by older generations in the community; a young woman who lived in the bungalow in the last decade reported that the house 'had a creepy feel to it'. Such preventative folklore serves as a warning to those who might consider interfering with an ancient site. Again, from an archaeological perspective, this aids in the long-term preservation of monuments.

The wider community, a global emigrant community, used the KLP website to contact us and share stories. One folktale—of an escape route from the Caiseal, crossing beneath the River Lung and surfacing 4km away—was reported to us by Kieran McGee of Bromsgrove, UK, via email. The story had been passed on to him from his grandparents, Philip and Mamie Hunt, who were both born and raised in Kilmovee. Their story dated from the 1920s–30s. This folktale and the archaeological site connect Kieran not only to the landscape, to Kilmovee and to Ireland but also to his grandparents. Today, women in Kilmovee are retelling similar stories to their young children. For instance, Paula Ryder, a lecturer at IT Sligo, recalls the folktale of the Caiseal tunnel exiting near Moran's Bar and Kilmovee National School, 1.57km away. The stories continue to be passed on to the next generation.

LESSONS LEARNED FROM THE KILCASHEL LANDSCAPE PROJECT

A key aspect of the success of the KLP was the establishment and maintenance of links with landowners. In some cases, however, landowners could not be reached; the research coincided with the economic crash and some had emigrated or were absent from the townland for many years. Without contact details or permission, we could not access all of the landholdings of interest. In one happy case, this was recently overturned when the absentee owner of a bungalow (and cashel MA073-028- - - -) sold it to Mr Fred Marden in 2017. Within a few months, not only had Fred moved in but he had also welcomed us to carry out further research on his property, which began in 2018 with UAV photography and photogrammetry of the cashel. Thus a 'five-year' project that began in 2009 continues to reap new rewards.

In 2009 we intended to use terrestrial lidar (laser scanning) on the Caiseal. Unfortunately we did not secure funding for this, but in 2010 a series of photographs taken by the community were stitched together to form a rudimentary model of the Caiseal interior. By 2018 we had captured new photographs and imported these along with the earlier ones into Free Open Source Software (FOSS) to digitally recreate the fort using photogrammetry, which produced a high-resolution model. Such software was unavailable in 2009. Today any local community can create an archive of high-quality photographs using a smart phone and, with some tuition, can use FOSS to build meaningful and spatially accurate digital models of archaeological sites and monuments.

Mini-workshops were used to teach community volunteers how to use and search for relevant online resources. Initially the work required a small level of supervision, but after a few sessions of directed learning the community continued the work themselves. Peer-to-peer learning allowed participants to assist one another and ultimately led to the discovery of new online resources as they became available, such as newspaper archives and links via genealogy websites in which some of the volunteers were specifically interested. A little direction from us led to an interest in online learning,

and some users anecdotally reported an increase in their general online skill set. This was an unexpected and gratifying result of the KLP, as some of the volunteers, although willing and able, had not previously ventured far in the online world beyond basic search engines and news websites.

The folklore database relied solely on data gathered from local sources, with time spent by the author to collate and map them using a GIS. Our focused local study at Kilcashel gathered in-depth information on local folklore and previously unrecorded oral history. It also utilised the established and focused community spirit to share those stories and keep them relevant and alive within the 'folkscape'. Open days and invitations to events were a key benefit to us. When we carried out the geophysical surveys at the Caiseal, we were visited by many people, not only raising awareness of archaeology but also creating another opportunity to collect stories and folklore from people who had not previously had the chance to share their knowledge. The folklore demonstrates that some archaeological sites in Kilcashel are still relevant to the modern community (for instance, the Caiseal and its souterrain; Father Hugh Henry's Fort and the bullaun stone; or the bungalow in the cashel), while others have faded into obscurity and are unknown (such as the third—completely destroyed—cashel in the townland, the *fulacht fiadh* or the numerous nineteenth-century limekilns identified from OS maps).

Looking back at the objectives identified in 2009, the KLP was overly ambitious for a five-year project. Many of the research areas discussed in our initial advertisements and briefing documents were trimmed back, principally owing to lack of funding. In fact, nearly a decade later, the research continues in an unfunded and piecemeal way, driven by community interest and new, often freely available, digital technology and online resources. The age of the 'armchair archaeologist', once the preserve of those enjoying innumerable archaeology programmes on TV, now provides a realistic opportunity for willing communities to engage with their heritage using computers, smart phones, a clipboard and a cup of tea. Specialisms and specialist equipment (geophysics, UAV, photogrammetry, GIS) will often add detail, but an eager community base can collect and record large quantities of primary data that are useful to the archaeological researcher and reveal unique aspects about a site, a townland or a landscape. As we discovered with the available historical records, linking lost family names to places in a townland can stir local emotions and prompt us to reflect on the lives and hardships of those who lived and farmed the landscape long before us, connecting the past to the present.

ACKNOWLEDGEMENTS

The Kilcashel Landscape Project would not have been possible without the involvement of the Kilmovee community, who helped to make this project possible. Particular thanks to Tess Regan, Martin Regan, Thomas Regan, Deirdre King, Dominic Keogh, Kieran McGee, Fred Marden and Paula Ryder. Sincere thanks to Dr Marion Dowd of IT Sligo for very valuable comments on an early draft of this paper. The Kilcashel Landscape Project would also like to thank the Heritage Council; the National Monuments Service; the Office of Public Works; the Institute of Technology Sligo; Heather Gimson, Pauline Gimson, David Gimson, Darren Regan, Cian Hogan, Ursula Garner and Ciarán Davis of Earthsound Archaeological Geophysics; Claremorris Community Radio; Michael Hambly, Mary Esler, Antonio Pogliani and Cristina Plazio of Mayo Ireland Ltd; and Martin Fitzpatrick of Archaeological Consultancy Ltd.

REFERENCES

Bonsall, J. 2015a Archaeology of Kilcashel. Lecture delivered in the Kilmovee Winter Lecture Series, Kilmovee, Co. Mayo, 15 December 2015.

Bonsall, J. 2015b There's always a secret tunnel: folklore, fact and fiction in the Kilcashel Landscape Project. Lecture delivered at the Stones and Bones Academic Research Conference, Institute of Technology Sligo, 17 April 2015.

Fitzpatrick, M. 1999 Archaeological excavations at Kilcashel Stone Fort, Kilcashel, Co. Mayo. Unpublished report for Archaeological Consultancy Ltd.

Logainm: *The Placenames Database of Ireland*. Available at https://www.logainm.ie/en/36684 (accessed 16 January 2018).

McDermott, J. 2016 Kilmovee, County Mayo. Unpublished trail report for Mayo County Council.

Tithe Applotment Books: Mayo: Kilmovee: Kilcashill. Available at http://titheapplotmentbooks.nationalarchives.ie/search/tab/home.jsp (accessed 4 July 2018).

4. Ogham in 3D and community participation

NORA WHITE AND ISABEL BENNETT

ABSTRACT

This article outlines the work of three quite different community projects associated with the Ogham in 3D project, which was set up to record ogham stones in 3D and to make the 3D models and information about each ogham stone available online. Initially, 3D scanning of ogham stones was undertaken by surveyors from project partners the Discovery Programme, but in recent years an alternative method of 3D capture (Structure from Motion/Photogrammetry) has become viable. This method facilitated participation by a community group in west Kerry in the 3D recording of their local ogham stones and other monuments. Thanks to support from the Heritage Council and Adopt a Monument Ireland, more community groups are now getting involved in the interpretation and preservation of their local archaeological and cultural heritage sites. A second community project, at a multiple ogham site in County Waterford, stemmed from this development. Finally, a third community participation project in County Cork focused on various ogham sites around the county and involved individuals and groups from the local communities in a 3D survey. These community projects have hugely benefited the Ogham in 3D project, the communities who participated and the ogham stones and sites involved.

OGHAM STONES

Ogham stones are stones onto which inscriptions in the ogham script were carved, predominantly in the centuries leading up to the eighth century AD. The script was developed for an early form of the Irish language and ogham stones bear the earliest known writing in Ireland. The inscriptions consist of personal and kin-group names, suggesting a memorial function for the stones. Another possible function of ogham stones may have been to mark territorial boundaries, as some are found at or near townland and parish boundaries. While it is generally accepted that most of our surviving ogham inscriptions date from the fifth and sixth centuries, it appears that ogham was already well established as a script with a consistent alphabet and orthography by the time it was carved on stone (McManus 1991, 40). Although found in most counties in Ireland, the highest concentrations of ogham stones occur in counties Kerry, Cork and Waterford (Fig. 4.1).

THE OGHAM IN 3D PROJECT

The Ogham in 3D project was set up in 2010 in the School of Celtic Studies at the Dublin Institute for Advanced Studies (DIAS). The main aim of the project is to record in 3D as many as possible of the surviving ogham stones and to make the 3D data (along with the associated metadata) available to both specialist researchers and the general public. In the first couple of years, scanning was focused on the National

Museum of Ireland ogham collection and on-site ogham stones in the Leinster area. In 2012 funding was made available for a period of three years by the then Department of Arts, Heritage and the Gaeltacht to focus on ogham stones in State care or with a Preservation Order throughout the country. Collaborating with the National Monuments Service and the Discovery Programme, 74 ogham stones in State care were scanned (Fig. 4.2), along with others not in State care but which were included in the project as they were located close to the targeted sites. In 2013 the Ogham in 3D website (*https://ogham.celt.dias.ie*) was launched to allow the 3D models to be made freely available online, along with descriptions of the sites, stones and ogham inscriptions. By 2015 all of the ogham stones in State care had been recorded, digitised and added to the website, bringing the total available to over 100, approximately a quarter of all known ogham stones.

By this time, advances had been made in the capabilities of 3D software to more quickly and accurately produce 3D models from photographs (Photogrammetry/Structure from Motion), so that this was now a viable (and cheaper) alternative to laser or structured light scanning. Also around this time, community archaeology was becoming more popular in Ireland. Inspired by the well-established Historic Graves project, the ACCORD project in Scotland and the then recently developed Roscommon 3D Project, we started our first community cooperation initiative in west Kerry.

Fig. 4.1—Distribution map of Irish ogham stones (Gary Devlin, Discovery Programme).

Fig. 4.2—3D-scanning ogham stones with an Artec Eva structured light scanner at Coolmagort (Dunloe), Co. Kerry.

THE CORCA DHUIBHNE 3D PROJECT

Introduction

Work began in earnest on the Corca Dhuibhne 3D project in the spring of 2016 and has being going from strength to strength ever since. This initiative was originally conceived as a way to assist in the progress of the work of the Ogham in 3D project of the Dublin Institute for Advanced Studies, which was carried out in conjunction with the Discovery Programme. The west Kerry area (i.e. the barony of Corca Dhuibhne) has the greatest density of ogham stones in the country, and this project was set up to assist in creating 3D models of stones not already surveyed by the Ogham in 3D project. The work is project-managed on the ground by the curator of Músaem Chorca Dhuibhne, Baile an Fheirtéaraigh (Isabel Bennett), with the museum acting as a base for the project, where the project computer is situated and where participants can come to work on their models (Fig. 4.3). The participants were quick to take ownership of the work and have spread their wings in various directions, surveying a wide variety of monument types as well as most of the ogham stones that were the primary aim of the project.

Successes

The introductory talk to the community, held in the autumn of 2015, was very well attended. During this session the technique of creating models using Structure from Motion was explained, along with the history and context of ogham stones and the work of the Ogham in 3D project that had already taken place in the area. This was followed in early 2016 by training sessions/workshops where the technique was put into practical use, using the excavated monastic site at an Riasc, where several cross-inscribed stones can be seen, as the 'classroom' (Fig. 4.4). Since that time, a core group of ten–twelve participants have photographed and created (with assistance from Gary Devlin, formerly of the Discovery Programme) a large and ever-growing selection of models, and not just ogham stones. A further participant volunteered as webmaster, setting up and managing the website *www.corcadhuibhne3d.ie*, although he has not got involved in the actual photographing and recording of monuments.

The introductory talk was held in Baile an Fheirtéaraigh, which is situated 13km west of Dingle, in a rural, sparsely populated area. The fact that so many people attended the talk and then participated in the workshops shows the interest of the local

Fig. 4.3—Nora White of the Ogham in 3D project (second from left) offering mentoring to members of the Corca Dhuibhne 3D project at Músaem Chorca Dhuibhne.

Fig. 4.4—Community training in the use of Structure from Motion 3D recording at an Riasc, Co. Kerry (Gary Devlin, Discovery Programme).

population in their archaeological heritage, and their eagerness to learn about new and exciting survey methods. Members of the final core group of participants come from all walks of life, and some of them are retired; there are also participants who are originally from outside Ireland (France and the Netherlands) but who have made their homes in this area.

The main successes of the project to date can be summarised as follows.

- The vast majority of ogham stones on the Dingle Peninsula have now been recorded in 3D (Fig. 4.5), and the models are shared on the Ogham in 3D website (*https://ogham.celt.dias.ie/menu.php? lang=en&menuitem=30*). This was the original aim of the project.
- There have been a couple of new discoveries of inscriptions and of other carvings on stones.
- Two articles have been published to date (Bennett *et al.* 2016; 2017), and papers have been delivered by project participants in past years at an Institute of Archaeologists of Ireland conference and at a Virtual Heritage Network conference.
- The website, *www.corcadhuibhne3d.ie*, has been set up to show the work of the project, and is

constantly being added to, edited and improved.
- Some participants are becoming more deeply involved in researching the monuments that they are recording, leading to new discoveries.
- Participants have improved their computer skills and are now very comfortable with reading maps and researching sites online and elsewhere.
- A larger cohort of people than those actively involved in the project have been introduced to the idea of recording images in 3D and have learned that this type of technology, though previously fairly complicated and requiring specialist equipment, can now be carried out with a basic digital camera or with the camera on a mobile phone, and so is now available to everyone.
- There is an active Facebook page, with 239 followers at the time of writing and numbers growing steadily each week (*https://www.facebook. com/search/top/?q=corcadhuibhne3d*).
- A larger audience has been introduced to Músaem Chorca Dhuibhne (*www.westkerrymuseum.com*) and, from the museum's perspective, this is an exciting educational outreach project, successfully targeting an adult group.
- Participants are actively researching favourite sites in archives that they might not have known existed

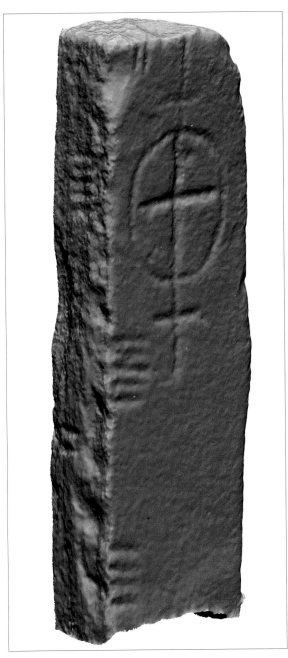

Fig. 4.5—3D model of Rathduff II ogham stone by Corca Dhuibhne 3D participant Kathleen Reen.

prior to getting involved in the project and, indeed, have travelled as far afield as Dublin to look at original sources in academic institutions; some have also obtained further training in 3D recording techniques.

Challenges

After the initial enthusiasm, some of the participants have not, for a variety of reasons, been in a position to actively continue with the work. Some have found

aspects of the computer work challenging and/or tedious. Each person has a different level of skill in using computers and this can lead to some difficulties, though help is generally at hand either from another participant or at the end of the phone (thanks particularly to Gary Devlin). The members have a wide variety of skills; some excel at photography, while others have the right kind of personality for interacting with landowners. Other skills, such as researching and writing up sites, are still being developed in some cases. Our webmaster is very patient, as he faces the challenge of introducing each monument surveyed to the wider world, sometimes only having been initially provided with very basic information! Some participants now work from home, having acquired the necessary software and installed it on their own computers; others continue to work in the office at Músaem Chorca Dhuibhne, using the computer set aside for the purpose of this work. This can lead to a lack of coordination in the short term, but that is generally quickly overcome.

The future

Although the active core group is small (six–seven people), new sites are continually being surveyed and modelled. It is recognised that more work is needed to make the website a more useful source of information about each individual site recorded. This is being tackled but will require more research and report-writing, which is not as much fun for participants as carrying out the photography and creating the models! When we began this project we could not foresee how it would develop, and facilitating this, and the interests of the participants, is all part of the work ahead.

Conclusion

Lessons have been learned from the project, not least that there is an eager audience in Corca Dhuibhne who are willing to support heritage-related activities such as this. Although many more attended the initial workshops than finally participated in the project, there is still a great interest in heritage in the wider community, with some of the original attendees expressing plans to perhaps participate at a later date. Others who did not attend the initial sessions have also expressed interest in participating, and it is hoped that more people will join the group in the future. At the time of writing, another heritage-related project by a neighbouring community group, Comharchumann Dhún Chaoin, is being planned at and around a site that was also looked at by our project (*http://www.corcadhuibhne3d.ie/bhiocaire.php*, accessed

27/3/2018); they hope to carry out geophysical and other surveys of the site and to delve into the folklore and history associated with it, with participation from volunteers and from the local primary school. Members of our project look forward to also participating in this, and perhaps further utilising the 3D skills that they have learned.

Some participants have begun to look at monuments outside the core study area of the barony of Corca Dhuibhne, and sites in other parts of County Kerry, and even elsewhere in Ireland, have been photographed and models created. This was not originally envisaged when the project was set up but it shows the breadth of interest of the participants and how the project is developing—that it is organic, fluid and flexible, and very adaptable.

All this is good, and the project will continue to grow and hopefully also continue to encourage the growth of other heritage-related projects in the area. The main benefit, of course, is that now there are several 3D models available of many of our vulnerable carved monuments and these can be viewed by interested parties from anywhere in the world, thanks to our website.

THE KNOCKBOY CONSERVATION PROJECT

Background

A multiple ogham site in County Waterford became the focus of another community project in recent years. The site is the parish church of Seskinan at Knockboy in west Waterford, which appears to have been built in the late fourteenth century but was already derelict by 1588. Located in rural farmland between the Comeragh and Knockmealdown Mountains in the ancient territory of *Sliabh gCua*, it is thought to have been an early ecclesiastical site although no direct evidence for an earlier church survives. Traces of a possible circular enclosure (indicating an early ecclesiastical site) were recorded in the late nineteenth century but are no longer evident (Brash 1868–9, 127; Power 1898, 84). There is, however, the site of a holy well (Tobaratemple, 'well of the church') *c.* 250m to the west, which is also suggestive of an early ecclesiastical site. The exceptional thing about this church is that all but one of the lintels over the windows and south door are reused ogham stones. Eight ogham stones in total have been discovered at this site, two of which were free-standing. One of these was moved to Salterbridge House near Cappoquin but hasn't been seen since the 1940s. The site also has a historic graveyard with a number of finely carved eighteenth- and nineteenth-

century headstones. The Knockboy Graveyard Committee, a local voluntary organisation formed in the 1990s, maintain the graveyard and ensure that the pattern day (8 September), which was restored in the 1970s, continues. The committee also erected a detailed information panel at the gate and organised, with help from Waterford County Council, the tarring of the long church boreen in 2009.

Origins of the project

When the Ogham in 3D team first visited the site in 2013, the church was heavily covered with ivy and other vegetation. There was obvious loss of stone from the building and the double bell-cote over the west gable was partially collapsed. We realised that without expert intervention, and despite the efforts of the Graveyard Committee, the church ruin (along with the incorporated ogham stones) was in danger of collapse. The Knockboy Conservation Project was set up to bring together the Graveyard Committee, Waterford County Council, the National Monuments Service and conservation professionals to ensure the survival of this unique structure (Fig. 4.6).

Achievements to date

To start with, an archaeological assessment of the site was funded by the Heritage Council and carried out by Dungarvan-based archaeologist Dave Pollock. His recommendations included cutting back the vegetation on the church to facilitate a conservation assessment. In 2017 we received a further grant from the Heritage Council to begin this process. Also in 2017, the site was chosen to be included in the Adopt a Monument Ireland scheme, which was a great boost for the Graveyard Committee and all involved in the Conservation Project at Knockboy. The conservation assessment has now been completed and preparations are being made for the next phase, which will involve carrying out the necessary repair and stabilising works on the ruin. It is planned to involve the local community as much as possible, with training sessions in traditional building methods and interactive events on site focusing on the archaeology, history and folklore of the site during the summer, particularly during Heritage Week. A 3D survey of the site, church ruin and individual ogham stones has also been carried out and the site and ogham stones have been added to the Ogham in 3D website. The 3D photogrammetric survey was undertaken by Waterford native Simon Dowling; a follow-up 3D survey, once the works have been completed, is also planned. A dedicated Facebook page (*https://www.facebook.com/KnockboyOgham*

Fig. 4.6—Conservation group on-site meeting at Knockboy, Co. Waterford (Abarta Heritage).

Church/) has helped to keep the wider public informed of our progress in terms of interpretation, outreach activities and the conservation of the site.

CORK 3D SURVEY OF OGHAM STONES

About the project

Another county with high numbers of ogham stones is Cork (Macalister 1945). A third community engagement project was initiated in this county in 2017, thanks to a grant from the Cork Historical and Archaeological Society. As the ogham stones in Cork are more widely dispersed, however, it is difficult to find a central location in which to base a community project on the Corca Dhuibhne model. It was therefore decided to try to make contact with various individuals and groups across the county who might be interested in their local ogham stone(s) and in helping to carry out a 3D survey. Those who contributed in various ways were local historian Gerard O'Rourke (author of *Ancient sweet Donoughmore*) in Donoughmore parish, mid-Cork; Seán Radley (Millstreet Museum) in north Cork; Bishop O'Brien National School, Bartlemy, in east Cork; and Margaret Murphy (Skibbereen Heritage) and Coppeen Archaeological Historical Cultural Society in west Cork. The majority of the work was carried out using photogrammetry. On a couple of visits to mid-Cork, however, we were joined by Dr Orla Murphy (Digital Arts and Humanities, UCC), who brought along an Artec Eva structured light 3D scanner and three willing sons to lend a helping hand. Gerard O'Rourke had made contact in 2016 regarding the ogham stones from the parish of Donoughmore. In addition to arranging visits to the stones with local landowners, he was an excellent local guide and provided much information on the archaeology, history and folklore of the parish, as well as helping with the 3D survey. We were also joined on occasion by archaeologists such as John Sheehan and Gillian Boazman (UCC Archaeology Department) and Connie Kelleher (National Monuments Service), who kindly lent their expertise. There was much discussion on individual ogham stones, ogham in general and the broader archaeological landscape. There was also plenty of exchange of information between specialists and locals.

Results

Despite some quite inclement weather conditions, we managed to visit nineteen ogham stones across the county (Fig. 4.7). One of these (Kilmartin Lower)

Fig. 4.7—Braving the elements to visit Lackabane souterrain in mid-Cork to record a lintel stone with an ogham inscription.

Fig. 4.8—3D photogrammetric model of ogham stones at St Abban's Grave, near Ballyvourney, Co. Cork.

proved to be inaccessible (in a souterrain) and we failed to locate another (Aultagh), although a return visit is planned, as the stone was probably just obscured by overgrowth. In total, seventeen ogham stones in the county were recorded in 3D in 2017 with the help of local participation. These are available to view on the 3D platform Sketchfab (*https://sketchfab.com/ oghamin3d/collections/cork-ogham-stones*) (Fig. 4.8) and are in the process of being added to the Ogham in 3D website. There are still a number of ogham stones to be visited and recorded in 3D, particularly in west Cork. It is hoped to extend this project to record the remaining ogham stones, mainly on the Beara Peninsula, and also to revisit and record the Aultagh stone, as soon as further funding can be secured.

CONCLUSION

Community participation has become an integral part of the Ogham in 3D project in the last few years. It has been a difficult time in terms of securing funding to continue the project, but thanks to the help of community projects like Corca Dhuibhne 3D the work has continued and expanded. The best thing about community participation is that it benefits everyone involved, from local communities to heritage professionals—and, of course, our heritage sites. Our hope for the future, funding permitting, is to extend community participation in the Ogham in 3D project to other areas, such as the Iveragh Peninsula in south

Kerry and the Beara Peninsula in west Cork. Participants on the Corca Dhuibhne 3D project are keen to share their experience and skills to assist other communities in similar ventures. It is clear that cooperation with local communities around the country is the way forward in (re-)discovering, recording and protecting our ogham stones and cultural heritage in general.

REFERENCES

Bennett, I., Devlin, G. and Harrington, C. 2016 Corca Dhuibhne 3D. *Archaeology Ireland* **30** (2), 17–20.

Bennett, I., White, N. and Devlin, G. 2017 Helping the stones to speak: the Corca Dhuibhne 3D community project. *Journal of the Kerry Archaeological and Historical Society* (2nd ser.) **17**, 5–22.

Brash, R.R. 1868–9 On the Seskinan ogham inscriptions, County of Waterford. *Journal of the Royal Society of Antiquaries of Ireland* **10**, 118–30.

Macalister, R.A.S. 1945 *Corpus inscriptionum insularum Celticarum*. Stationery Office, Dublin.

McManus, D. 1991 *A guide to ogam*. Maynooth Monographs 4. An Sagart, Maynooth.

O'Rourke, G. 2015 *Ancient sweet Donoughmore*. Redmond Grove Publications, Donoughmore.

Power, Revd P. 1898 Ancient ruined churches of Co. Waterford. *Waterford Archaeological Journal* **4**, 83–95, 195–219.

5. The Medieval Bray Project: investigations at Raheenacluig church, Newcourt, Bray, Co. Wicklow

DAVID McILREAVY

ABSTRACT

In January 2017, members of the Medieval Bray Project arranged a meeting at the ruined medieval church of Raheenacluig on the northern slopes of Bray Head, Co. Wicklow. Examining the heavily conserved remains, it became readily apparent just how little historical and archaeological information was available about the site. The result of this meeting was a year-long investigation, through building and geophysical survey and finally research excavation. The collation of this research is an important landmark for the Medieval Bray Project. This paper is the first major presentation of our work in a collection of similar research projects and has allowed us the opportunity to examine how we define ourselves within the sphere of community archaeology. Furthermore, it offers historical and archaeological evidence for an almost completely undocumented post-medieval history of the church building and its environs from the late fourteenth to the late seventeenth century.

It is hoped that the results presented here will be the springboard for further research into not only this intriguing site but also the remaining medieval heritage of Bray. It is our sincere hope that the example of what can be achieved with a dedicated group of volunteers, some waterproofs and a real hands-on approach will act as a catalyst for future projects throughout Ireland. For further information on the work of the Medieval Bray Project see our website (https://themedievalbrayproject.wicklowheritage.org) or on Facebook (https://www.facebook.com/themedievalbrayproject/).

BACKGROUND

The Medieval Bray Project (TMBP) is a community research initiative founded in 2015 to collate existing research and conduct original research into the medieval manor of Bray. Specifically, the initiative concentrates on the period 1207–1666, tracing the manor of Bray from its origins under Walter de Ridelesford (the younger) after 1207 through to its final dismemberment in 1666.

TMBP AND THE COMMUNITY RESEARCH APPROACH

The research conducted at Raheenacluig has demonstrated that community-driven initiatives such as TMBP can have a dramatic effect both in expanding the knowledge base relating to a particular place and, just as importantly, in empowering the local community to conduct research into their area.

Therese Hicks, Treasurer of TMBP, was already a member of several historical societies when she joined TMBP, and she compares her experience of these organisations to that of TMBP:

'Most historical societies I have been involved in put on monthly talks, conduct outings or arrange trips. You can be as active as you wish, serving on the committee, or you can take in only the lectures that appeal to you. The main difference between a community research initiative and a history society is that it is always local, much more focused, and very much more hands-on …'

The obvious medium for the employment of this hands-on approach is through fieldwork, and a number of TMBP volunteers braved the Irish weather on the northern slopes of Bray in just such a pursuit. As Conor Clancy of TMBP notes,

'With no experience of practical archaeology, and perhaps a little technophobia, it was a daunting prospect to contemplate the level of expertise that those professional archaeologists in the group demonstrated in even setting up such a fieldwork project. But over the seven days that we conducted the geophysical survey surrounding Raheenacluig, the group managed to cover some 12,500 square metres in a variety of weathers. The grim determination in completing a survey square became something of a matter of pride …'

The fieldwork experience, however, is just one avenue of research that TMBP has been keen to promote since its inception. Gerry Morgan and John Harding demonstrated a tenacity in documentary research which sourced correspondence between H.G. Leask and the Bri Chualann Urban District Council in the 1920s, charting the inclusion of Raheenacluig as a National Monument (No. 262). Contained within these papers are important records of the negotiations that took place with regard to the protection of monuments in the first decade of the Irish Free State. In addition, the papers contained a beautiful set of watercolour elevations, compiled by Ada K. Longfield, and photographs of the site prior to restoration works.

The Joint Secretary of TMBP, Mary Hargaden, a stalwart of the Bray Tidy Towns group and a graduate of the MA Archaeology programme at University College Dublin, has proved to be a tireless community promoter. From engagement with local housing associations over the adoption of local historic sites through to the running of TMBP Facebook page, her energy is a testimony to what enthusiasm for an area and its story can achieve. Living in the vicinity of Raheenacluig church gave Mary a very personal perspective on the site:

'Having lived in the shadow of Raheenacluig since the 1980s I was always struck by the fact that, aside from the enigmatic *fógra* sign denoting that the church was under State protection, there was no further information on the history or archaeology of the site. Having watched lines of men walking up to the site as part of the council "make a golf course scheme" in the 1980s, it was with real excitement that members of the TMBP formed our own line to begin investigations in August 2017.'

The present author was fortunate enough to be part of the 2014 Grassroots Archaeology programme of excavations in Baldoyle. What continually struck me was the generosity of spirit demonstrated by the local community, from the donation of patches of urban garden for trenches through to the enthusiasm for post-excavation events throughout the locality. This community engagement in heritage inspired me to launch a similar initiative in Bray. That was in 2015, and since then the work of TMBP has grown in confidence and reach; as we look ahead to future works in the locality, the only limit to what that hands-on attitude can accomplish is set by our imaginations.

RESEARCHING RAHEENACLUIG

Located on the northern slopes of Bray Head, Raheenacluig church (Sites and Monument Record (SMR) No. WWI008-004) is a National Monument (No. 262) (Figs 5.1 and 5.2). While it is of clear medieval origin, little coherent historical or archaeological information is accessible to the public. The description of the church in the SMR concentrates largely on the architectural features of the building:

'Situated on a small level platform overlooking a marked northeast-facing slope with steep ground to uphill to the southwest. A nave and chancel church (L 10.8m; Wth 5.9m) with walls of irregular uncoursed masonry (H 1.5–2.5m; Wth 0.85m). The gables are substantially intact. The door in the north wall, which is slightly west of the centre, splays inwards and parts of the granite jambs survive. There are simple round-headed windows in the east and west gables and a single niche occurs in the south wall towards the west end. The church has been substantially conserved. A rectangular area of rubble and mortar (dims. 4m x 2m) immediately east of the church may represent the foundations of another building. The church is known as Raithín a' Chluig, or *little rath of the bell*.'

Whilst such information is a vital building record, it is no substitute for experiencing a building firsthand. Standing in Raheenacluig church, even with the low reconstructed north and south walls, the first thing that struck the members of TMBP was the small scale of the building. This resonates with O'Keeffe's (2015, 70) statement on medieval buildings:

'The pleasure, even thrill, of exploring a medieval building has a limit: there is a point at which there is no physical space left to explore, and it might only take a few minutes to reach that point. The capacity to make sense of a building brings a longer-lasting pleasure, precisely because it gives a greater purpose to exploration: after all, what exactly, if not knowledge and understanding, are we really looking for when we explore?'

The building itself almost suggests its own questions to

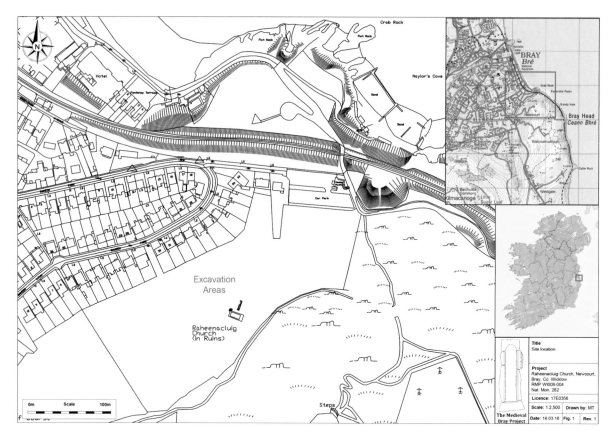

Fig. 5.1—Raheenacluig church: site location.

Fig. 5.2—Raheenacluig church, looking south-west.

Fig. 5.3—Raheenacluig church: reused twelfth-century stonework in east window.

those who explore it, the most frequent being simply when and by whom the church was built.

Professor Tadhg O'Keeffe (pers. comm.) suggests a later medieval date for construction of the church building. The eastern window stonework, however, may be reused and twelfth-century in date (Fig. 5.3), perhaps indicating an earlier ecclesiastical foundation on the site. Providing further support for the suggestion of an earlier church foundation, a battered foundation for the western gable wall (Fig. 5.4) may be part of a construction platform similar to that observable at Kilcroney church (WI007-030) (Fig. 5.5).

The identification of those who constructed the extant church building would have been a significantly longer process without the input of Una Roe, Joint Secretary of TMBP, who highlighted Liam Price's (1983, 332) assertion that the building had been owned by the Friary of the Augustinian Hermits of Dublin; this was confirmed by Duffy and Simpson (2009). Although no contemporary accounts of the friary exist, an eighteenth-century description notes that it was 'a very significant foundation', consisting of a church with

bell-tower, a dormitory, a hall, a cemetery and garden, covering an area of one and a half acres (*ibid.*, 210). The friary was formally suppressed by Henry VIII on 20 April 1540 and an extent dated 31 October of the same year recorded details of its possessions, which included lands, gardens and houses in the parishes of St Andrew's, St Patrick's and St Michael's and in Cloghran, north Dublin.

At Raheenacluig the friary held 51 acres (30 of arable, twenty of pasture and one of meadow), with five attached messuages, valued at 13s. 4d. (Gilbert 1854–9, 170). This comprised a significant estate, amounting to much of the former townland of Raheenacluig. As regards the acquisition of this estate by the friary, Duffy and Simpson (2009, 211) note that a jury in 1542 claimed to be unable to identify the original donors. The *Reportorium Viride*, however, composed under Archbishop Alen in 1533, suggests that the Archibold family may have been the primary donors (Gilbert 1854–9, 170). The date of this donation is not recorded, but a fourteenth-century date may be suggested with some degree of certainty.

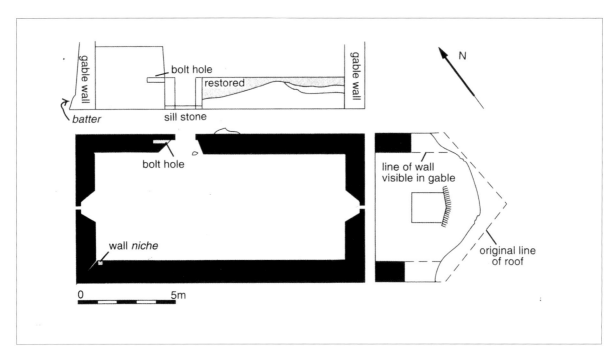

Fig. 5.4—Plan and elevation of Raheenacluig church (Grogan and Hillery 1993, 32) (courtesy of Dr Eoin Grogan, Maynooth University).

Fig. 5.5—Kilcroney church (WI007-030), showing construction platform.

Flynn (1986, 17) notes that the Archibold family was granted the manors of Bray and Kilruddery by Edward III (d. 1377). The family name Archibold is associated with Kilruddery until 1399. Given that Davies (2007, 42) notes that a Geoffrey Crump or Crampe had a lease of the manor of Bray renewed in 1360 and the fact that Edward III died in 1377, the grant to the Archibolds must fall within the period 1360–77. After the dissolution of the Friary of Augustinian Hermits in Dublin, its possessions were leased to lay landlords. In May 1541 a Dublin merchant, Robert Casey, was granted a lease of the lands for an annual rent of £6 0s. 9d. The following year another Dublin merchant, Walter Tyrell, paid the Crown the sum of £114 13s. 4d., and on 10 July 1542 the former possessions of the friary were granted to him for an annual rent of £6 0s. 1d. Interestingly, the former friary lands at Raheenacluig did not form part of the grant to Tyrell; instead, on 15 June 1542 they were granted to 'Robert Eustace and others, to the use of Thomas Lutrell of Luttrelstown' (*ibid.*, 211). By 1641 a James Archibold is recorded as the owner of the Raheenacluig lands, although he had forfeited them by 1670 (TCD Down Survey Historical GIS).

The collation of this information has for the first time allowed a coherent time-line to be presented for Raheenacluig from at least the mid-sixteenth century. Further research will be needed to confirm the Archibold donation and the suggested date in the later fourteenth century. Whilst the original questions formulated by members of TMBP may have been tentatively answered in terms of a construction date and original patrons, the description of Raheenacluig as an estate in 1540 raised further questions relating to the surrounding landscape. In particular, the reference to five messuages means that the monastic estate at Raheenacluig takes on a very different character. This was no isolated ecclesiastical foundation but rather the centre of a relatively large estate with links to a major Dublin landholder.

LOOKING FOR THE 'VILLATE' OF RAHEENACLUIG

The mention of messuages attached to the monastic estate at Raheenacluig prompted further investigation of sources such as the *Reportorium Viride* (Gilbert 1854–9, 170), which noted that Raheenacluig was referred to as a 'villate'. Whilst the term could be translated as 'village', it more than likely refers to a settlement the size of a hamlet. Most importantly, it is likely that such a settlement would be clustered and would make a tempting target for geophysical survey.

The nature of the relationship between the occupants of the messuage plots in Raheenacluig and their monastic landlords is unclear, but it is considered a research avenue which would contribute greatly towards our understanding of the social geography of the estate. In terms of other buildings associated with the church and messuages, it has been suggested (Bermingham 2006) that by the later medieval period a well-run estate would have had structures such as a tithe barn to store agricultural produce awaiting transport to Dublin.

A potential area for just such a grouping of buildings was suggested by an additional SMR number, WI008-00401, assigned to the Raheenacluig site on the basis of an 1838 description by Eugene O'Curry, who identified the enclosure or 'moat feature' in addition to possible building sites next to the church (Davies 2007, 24):

> '… the sites of two smaller buildings, close together, may be traced near it [church] on the east side, with a nearly choked trench running north and south between them and the church. The whole appears to have been enclosed by a "moate", parts of which remain on the east and northwest.'

Unfortunately no above-ground trace of this enclosure could be found on inspection by the Archaeological Survey of Ireland in 1990. O'Curry also mentioned a possible enclosure feature to the south-east of the church building (O'Flanagan 1928, 30):

> 'Twenty eight yards south east of the church is a piece of ground enclosed by a trench and low mound, sixty yards long by twelve broad, two stones at the south east angle would seem to point to the place of a gate or entrance. Probably this was a graveyard …'

Whilst unlikely to have been a graveyard, there is a high possibility that this may represent an enclosure for a tithe barn, as noted above.

GEOPHYSICAL SURVEY

Given the suggestion that there could be previously un-recorded archaeological monuments in the immediate vicinity of the church site, TMBP applied for a licence

Fig. 5.6—Resistivity survey around Raheenacluig church, looking north-west (courtesy of S. Curran).

to conduct a geophysical survey of the surrounding area. In respect of the geophysical survey, TMBP was fortunate to have as a member Susan Curran, a doctoral candidate at the School of Archaeology, University College Dublin, who was specialising in the identification of early medieval settlement using geophysics. Over the course of the work some 12,500m² of the area surrounding Raheenacluig was surveyed in a variety of weathers (Fig. 5.6).

The geophysical survey, Licence No. 17R0017, was conducted over seven days during February and March 2017 and was supervised by Susan Curran, David McIlreavy and Peter Dodd of the TMBP. Some eight members of TMBP assisted with the survey. The survey grid, comprising a series of 20m x 20m grid panels, was located and tied into the Irish National Grid using a Trimble GPS in conjunction with a VRS Now correction service.

Earth resistance survey was undertaken using a Geoscan RM85 Resistance Meter, with data recorded using zigzag traverses at intervals of 1m and a sample interval of 0.5m. A total of 31 grids were surveyed using this technique. Magnetic gradiometry survey was undertaken using a Bartington Grad 01 DL601 dual sensor fluxgate gradiometer, with data recorded using parallel traverses at intervals of 1m and a sample interval of 0.25m (four points per metre along each traverse). A total of nine grids were surveyed using this

technique. All data were processed using Geoscan Research Geoplot version 3 software. A significant amount of magnetic ferrous interference was recorded in the magnetic gradiometer survey. This was considered to be a result of the golf-course development from the 1980s and therefore the magnetic survey was not extended across the entire survey area.

While the geophysical survey results demonstrated that the site had been significantly disturbed by modern intervention, some geophysical anomalies that could be suggestive of potentially unrecorded archaeological features were noted. Without excavation and scientific dating, the exact nature of these anomalies could not be determined with absolute certainty. Of particular interest to the TMBP were some anomalies that were considered targets for further investigation (Fig. 5.7).

An area of high resistance (R17) in direct proximity to the eastern end of the extant church was considered to relate either to collapse from the church building or to the two buildings observed by O'Curry in 1838. A low-resistance anomaly (R23) followed a curvilinear route surrounding the church. This was considered to correspond to a ditch feature, possibly the 'moate' recorded by O'Curry. There is no trace of this potential ditch to the west of the church and the projected south-west return could not be surveyed

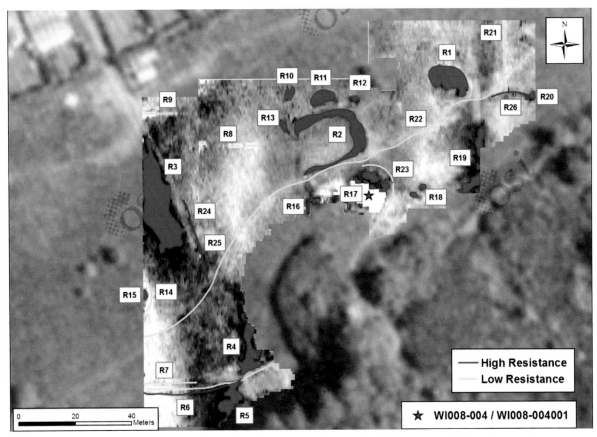

Fig. 5.7—Resistivity plot with R numbers referred to in text (Curran 2017) (courtesy of Susan Curran).

owing to dense undergrowth.

In addition, R19, an area of high resistance approximately 27m to the east/north-east of the church, appears to form a right-angled feature. This may be evidence of a stone-filled bank or stone wall and may be consistent with the 'low mound' referred to by O'Flanagan (1928, 30). Two distinct high-resistance anomalies (R18) to the east of the church may correspond to the two stones that O'Flanagan (1928, 30) mentions as being a possible gate or entrance. They are facing north-west and there is a gap of *c.* 1.5m between them. R19 was not included in the area to be investigated by excavations in 2017 (Curran 2017). The results of the survey were extremely encouraging, and the TMBP is indebted to Susan for providing her time to supervise this area of the project, and for processing and filing her report with the National Monuments Service (NMS) on TMBP's behalf.

EXCAVATIONS

Having identified an area that would seem to correlate to building remains described by O'Curry (geophysical anomaly R17), members of TMBP applied for a licence to conduct test excavations under David McIlreavy. The licence (17E0356) was granted with permission to excavate two trenches, the first to the north of the church to investigate the area of high resistance (R17) and ditch feature (R23), the second to investigate the area of the batter/construction platform noted at the north-west corner of the church.

Excavation commenced on 19 August 2017, during Heritage Week, and TMBP has to thank Deirdre Burns for her continuing support in liaising with Bray Municipal District and for providing funding contributing to public liability insurance. The excavations at Raheenacluig exposed TMBP to a much wider audience than experienced before, the area being a popular recreational area for the local community. There were multiple enquiries every day for opportunities to participate and to examine what the group had unearthed. The excavations ran in tandem with two talks, the first staged in Bray Library on 23 August to present the initial research findings on the church site, the second held in the Taylor Centre, Bray, on 25 August to present the preliminary excavation findings.

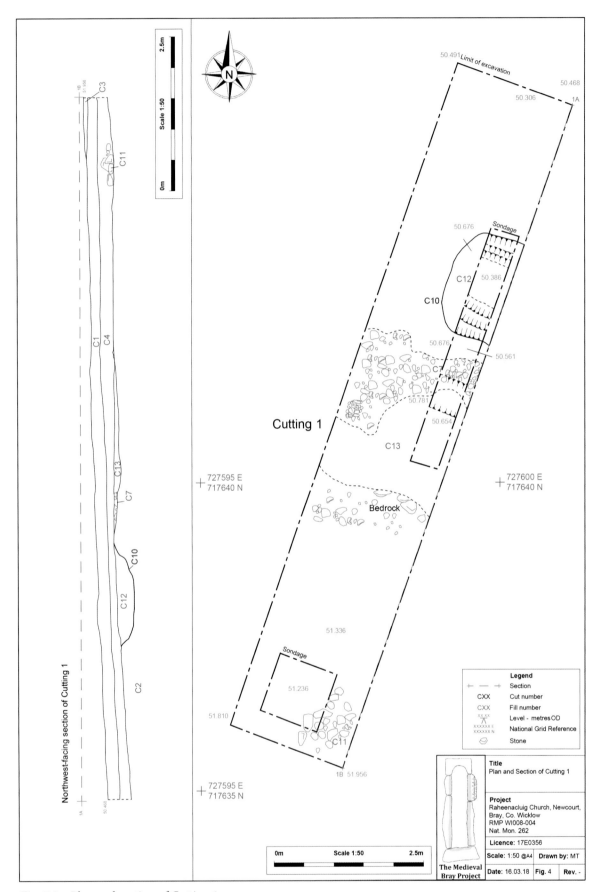

Fig. 5.8—Plan and section of Cutting 1.

Cutting 1 (Fig. 5.8)

The initial results from the excavations suggested that both cuttings had been subjected to significant disturbance. Whilst a ditch feature and probable packed-earth building floor were uncovered in Cutting 1, both were heavily truncated and no artefactual evidence was recovered to suggest a date of construction (Fig. 5.9).

The ditch feature is considered to correspond to the low-resistance geophysical signature identified as R23 and would morphologically fit the profile of an enclosing ditch for an early medieval ecclesiastical enclosure, but accessibility issues in the south-west area of the church did not allow the potential ditch feature to be traced in this area. The high-resistance features denoted as R17 do not relate to the buildings described by O'Curry. Instead, R17 corresponds to a mixed gravel-rich 'levelling deposit' which extended across the cutting (Fig. 5.10).

This levelling deposit did not extend over the area of R23, which is why the ditch feature was visible in the initial geophysical plot. Whilst R17 did not

contain building debris as might have been expected, it did contain a mixed range of artefacts dating from the late sixteenth century to the twentieth century. Examination of the artefactual assemblage within this levelling deposit suggested three distinct clusters of post-medieval activity. Sixteenth-century activity was represented by a small looped handle from a fine glazed red earthenware mug, jug or tyg (17E0356:4:9), produced in Yorkshire/English midlands. Ticknall in south Derbyshire is known to have been an important production centre for these wares. Later seventeenth-century activity was represented by examples of North Devon Gravel-Tempered Ware (17E0356:1:1–2; 17E0356:4:4), North Devon Gravel-Free Ware (17E0356:4:5), Tin-Glazed Earthenware (17E0356:4:6), Manganese (17E0356:4:7) and Staffordshire–Bristol Slipware (17E0356:1:3; 17E0356:4:8). A minimum number of six ceramic vessels were represented within the finds assemblage (Fig. 5.11).

The North Devon Ware sherds represented elements of large hollow vessels, and the

Fig. 5.9—Cutting 1 after excavation, showing truncated ditch (foreground) and building floor, looking south-south-west.

Fig. 5.10—Cutting 1: levelling deposit R17, which contained the majority of the artefactual material, looking south-west.

Fig. 5.11—Examples of late seventeenth-century ceramics from the levelling deposit: (left to right) North Devon Gravel-Free Ware (17E0356:4:5) and North Devon Gravel-Tempered Ware (17E0356:4:3).

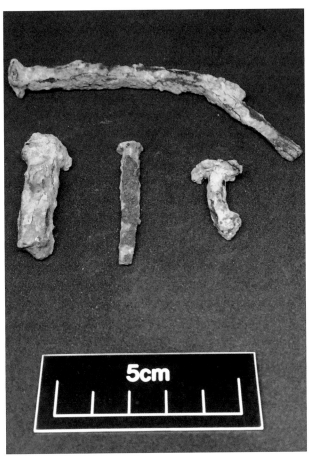

Fig. 5.12—Range of late seventeenth-century ferrous fixings: top, structural nail (17E0356:4:49); bottom (left to right), structural nail (17E0356:4:48), floorboard nail (17E0356:4:57) and furniture tack (17E0356:4:58).

Staffordshire–Bristol Slipware elements of a jug, mug or tyg. The major producers of the North Devon Wares were Barnstable and Bideford, whilst Staffordshire–Bristol Slipware and Manganese Glazed Wares were both produced during the same period around Bristol. It is likely that all these ceramic types came through Dublin port during the later seventeenth century. A minimum number of six represented vessels is considered a significant concentration of ceramics from this period, and the inclusion of items such as chamber-pots, mugs/jugs/tygs and even flatwares would suggest a heavy domestic bias. Three clay pipe bowls with spur heels (17E0356:4:43–45) may also be of later seventeenth-century date, probably manufactured in Dublin. The most obvious date range of ceramic material recovered from the levelling deposit falls in the nineteenth and twentieth centuries. Most of this material consists of Black-Glazed Red Earthenware (27 sherds) and White-Glazed Earthenware (24

sherds). The majority of these pieces could be attributed to outdoor dining at the site, particularly as Bray became a popular tourist destination with the arrival of the railway.

Aside from the ceramic evidence, ferrous nails were recovered from the levelling deposit, including structural examples, potential floorboard fixings and tacks for furniture. Whilst these items cannot be attributed to any particular period, the range of domestic late seventeenth-century items could suggest that the church was being utilised as a domestic dwelling (Fig. 5.12).

The topsoil from Cutting 1 also produced two chert lithic artefacts (17E0356:1:39–40), analysed by Shane Delaney (McIlreavy 2018, Appendix 3). The pieces were identified as a scraper and piece of débitage, evidence of tool production. Whilst the location would be expected to produce some evidence of prehistoric activity, as excavations carried out within 550m of the site produced only flint artefactual evidence (Licence No. 01E0252), the artefacts could not be more closely dated than to the late Neolithic/early Bronze Age (3000–2000 BC).

Cutting 2 (Fig. 5.13)

Cutting 2 also identified significant disturbance—stone packing around the base of the battered wall foundation, which was considered to be consistent with stabilisation works (Figs 5.13 and 5.14). A 1936 George V silver shilling recovered from the surface of the deposit is considered to provide a *terminus ante quem* date for the deposit. This date is actually later than that suggested by the letters from H.G Leask in the late 1920s regarding preservation of the church and may relate to later attempts to reconstruct the side walls of the building.

The artefactual assemblage from Cutting 2 presented an interesting window on the development of the church building. Several pieces of pantile roofing material (Fig. 5.15), alongside slate, were recovered from the stone packing deposit. The pantile was a fashionable roofing material in the late seventeenth and early eighteenth centuries, and its close proximity to the church may suggest that it was roofed in this style during the period.

Whilst the stone packing could not be totally removed from Cutting 2, a section excavated across the material uncovered some large earthfast stones which could be a continuation of the construction platform suggested along the western gable wall of the church.

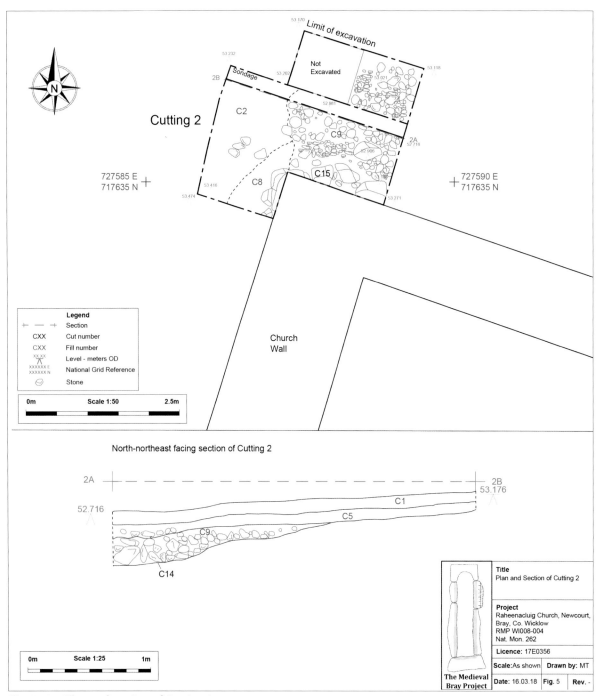

Fig. 5.13—Plan and section of Cutting 2.

CONCLUSIONS

The investigation of the site of Raheenacluig by TMBP has been an instructive and rewarding experience for all who participated in the works. In terms of providing a secure historical time-line for the church building and its environs, TMBP can be said to have delivered answers to at least some of the questions that were regularly posed by those members of the public encountered during our frequent visits to the site.

The building of the church can almost certainly be attributed to the Friary of the Augustinian Hermits in Dublin, a substantial and well-resourced monastic foundation, established in the mid-thirteenth century. Raheenacluig would seem to have been donated to the friary by the Archibold family when they were granted the manors of Bray and Kilruddery in the late fourteenth century.

Examination of the building suggests that the majority of the extant structure could date from the late

Fig. 5.14 (above)—Cutting 2 after excavation, showing 1930s repair work, looking south-east.

Fig. 5.15 (left)—Seventeenth-century pantile from Cutting 2 (17E0356:9:9).

1838 seemed to suggest that the features identified around the church could be the remnants of a later medieval hamlet associated with the monastic estate.

What TMBP volunteers who participated in the excavations did not expect was a window into possible sixteenth- and seventeenth-century habitation at the site. The identification of a significant number of later artefacts, including ceramics, clay pipes and roof furniture, as well as a probable range of structural, floorboard and furnishing nails, suggests that the church site may have been repurposed as a house.

The present thinking in the light of these excavations suggests that the Edwards family, who had replaced the Archibolds as landlords by 1670, introduced new tenants to the landholding at Raheenacluig. These tenants may well have utilised the ruined structure there as a base for their dwelling, reroofed in fashionable pantile. The tacks and floorboard nails recovered from Cutting 1 may suggest furnishings of relative comfort. Certainly, the number of vessels represented by artefacts of this period within Cutting 1 suggests reasonably intensive occupation, but only further research into the later history of

fourteenth century, although the eastern round-headed window could be a twelfth-century feature. The reuse of an earlier feature in such a prime position as the east gable has to be considered a very deliberate choice by its purported fourteenth-century builders.

The geophysical survey of a substantial area produced very exciting results. Documentary references to a 'villate' and even to extant structures in

Raheenacluig will provide further details of the lives of its inhabitants.

ACKNOWLEDGEMENTS

Whilst the Medieval Bray Project would like to extend its thanks to all volunteers and supporters who helped bring the investigations at Raheenacluig to a successful conclusion, several individuals deserve special mention: in particular Paul Duffy for the inspiration of Grassroots Archaeology and Resurrecting Monuments; Deirdre Burns, Heritage Officer, Wicklow County Council, for her unfailing support in the establishment and running of the research initiative; Chris Corlett for visiting the site and providing some much-appreciated pointers during excavation week; Prof. Tadhg O'Keeffe for always having time to answer a tangential email; Susan Curran, UCD Doctoral Scholar specialising in the location of early medieval settlement through geophysics, for all her hard work in pushing the survey at Raheenacluig to conclusion; and Peter Dodd and Niamh Millward for lending their archaeological expertise during Heritage Week excavations. Siobhán Scully conducted the finds analysis, and TMBP is grateful for the significant amount of her time that was donated to the project (McIlreavy 2018, Appendix 2). Special thanks are due to Bray Library staff, who scoured the Library building for extra chairs, and to Delwen Giles of TMBP, who arranged the use of the Taylor Centre in Bray and provided much-needed refreshments for Friday 25 August. Finally, within TMBP, we thank the committee who, month in and month out, keep the initiative functioning and who contributed to this paper: Therese Hicks, Treasurer; Mary Hargaden and Una Roe, Joint Secretaries; and Conor Clancy, Gerry Morgan and John Harding, committee members.

BIBLIOGRAPHY

Bermingham, H. 2006 Priests' residences in later medieval Ireland. In E. Fitzpatrick and R. Gillespie (eds), *The parish in medieval and early modern Ireland*, 168–87. Four Courts Press, Dublin.

Bolger, T. 2017 *Colonising a royal landscape: the history and archaeology of a medieval village at Mullaghmast, Co. Kildare*. Transport Infrastructure Ireland, Dublin.

Bradley, S., Fletcher, A.J. and Simms, A. (eds) 2009 *Dublin in the medieval world: studies in honour of Howard B. Clarke*. Four Courts Press, Dublin.

Curran, S. 2017 Geophysical survey report, Newcourt, Raithín a' Chluig. Licence: 17R0017. Unpublished report for the Medieval Bray Project.

Davies, M. 2007 *That favourite resort: the story of Bray, Co. Wicklow*. Wordwell, Dublin.

Duffy, S. and Simpson. L. 2009 The hermits of St Augustine in medieval Dublin: their history and archaeology. In S. Bradley, A.J. Fletcher and A. Simms (eds), *Dublin in the medieval world: studies in honour of Howard B. Clarke*, 202–49. Four Courts Press, Dublin.

Flynn, A. 1986 *History of Bray*. Mercier Press, Cork.

Gilbert, J.T. 1854–9 *A history of the city of Dublin*, Vol. 2. Dublin.

Grogan, E. and Hillery, T.A. 1993 *A guide to the archaeology of County Wicklow*. Ross Enterprises, Greystones.

McIlreavy, D. 2018 Report on research excavation at Raheenacluig church, Newcourt, Bray, Co. Wicklow (WI008-004, Nat. Mon. 262). Licence Ref.: 17E0356. Unpublished report for the Medieval Bray Project.

Murphy, M. and Potterton, M. (eds) 2010 *The Dublin region in the Middle Ages: settlement, land-use and economy*. Four Courts Press, Dublin.

O'Flanagan, M. (ed.) 1928 *Letters containing information relative to the antiquities of the County of Wicklow: collected during the progress of the Ordnance Survey in 1838*. Bray.

O'Keeffe, T. 2015 *Medieval Irish buildings 1100–1600*. Four Courts Press, Dublin.

Price, L. 1983 *The place-names of County Wicklow, V. The barony of Rathdown*. Dublin Institute for Advanced Studies, Dublin.

Shanahan, B. 2005 The manor in east County Wicklow. In J. Lyttleton and T. O'Keeffe (eds), *The manor in medieval and early modern Ireland*, 132–59. Four Courts Press, Dublin.

Online sources

Duffy, S. 2011 Book review. *History Ireland* **19** (5): https://www.historyireland.com/medieval-history-pre-1500/the-dublin-region-in-the-middle-ages-settlement-land-use-and-economy/ (accessed 13 April 2018).

Sites and Monuments Record WI008-004. WI008-00401: https://webgis.archaeology.ie/historic environment/ (accessed 13 April 2018).

TCD Down Survey Historical GIS: https://downsurvey.tcd.ie/landowners.php#mc=53.198197,-6.111966&z=14 (accessed 13 April 2018).

6. Resurrecting Monuments—St Doulagh's and Tower Hill: philosophy to results

AIDAN GIBLIN AND MICHAEL MONGEY

ABSTRACT

Based in the Baldoyle/Howth area, the Resurrecting Monuments community archaeology group was established in 2015. The initiative developed from an association between the members of Grassroots Archaeology, the Baldoyle Forum and Professor Gabriel Cooney of UCD's School of Archaeology. Resurrecting Monuments was set up with the aim of researching local heritage through an involved and inclusive process of desk-based work, field survey, public outreach and archaeological excavation to develop a greater understanding and awareness of the valuable heritage present in our locality. The group is made up of people with a very wide range of interests, abilities and backgrounds who have a common and enthusiastic interest in local heritage. Members' experiences range from those of professional archaeologists to avid 'Time Team' armchair archaeologists. Since its founding in 2015 the group has undertaken a range of archaeological fieldwork and desk-based research, focusing on local sites and monuments in the Howth/Baldoyle area. Dissemination of research results to a local and wider audience has included presentations at numerous conferences, lectures to local groups and publication of a range of archaeological articles. Resurrecting Monuments has also held an annual Heritage Week event in Howth, attracting both locals and tourists. In this paper we will outline the background to Resurrecting Monuments (including the group's formation and founding ethos) and some research results, with a focus on the results of the group's excavations at two sites, St Doulagh's Church in Balgriffin and Tower Hill in Howth, both in north County Dublin.

INTRODUCTION

Resurrecting Monuments is a community archaeology group based in the north-east Dublin suburb of Baldoyle. It was established in 2015 following the successful community-based Grassroots Archaeology project led by local man Paul Duffy (2013), a professional archaeologist, which was funded by the Royal Irish Academy's excavation grant programme. Building on the success of the Grassroots project, an initiative to set up a new local community archaeology group was supported by Professor Gabriel Cooney of UCD, the local Baldoyle Forum, Dr Gerry Clabby and Christine Baker of Fingal County Council. The project was successful in securing funding from the Irish Research Council's New Foundations grant award scheme for 2014 and thus Resurrecting Monuments was born.

A founding objective of the group was to help local community development through the vehicle of archaeological research and fieldwork. It was hoped that, through local participation and increased awareness, a wider knowledge and appreciation of the archaeology of the area would bring a greater pride in and ownership of the heritage of south-east Fingal, so that local people would become advocates for the protection and promotion of their local heritage. The name 'Resurrecting Monuments' reflects the group's interest in highlighting and researching some of the lesser-known archaeological sites and monuments in the Howth/Baldoyle area in addition to the more iconic local sites, including the late medieval Howth Castle (DU015-027), the megalithic portal tomb known as Aideen's Grave (DU015-032) and St Mary's Abbey and collegiate church (DU015-029).

A continuing aim of the group is to give members the opportunity to participate in the full range of archaeological research and fieldwork, including targeted research excavations with the support of professional archaeologists and specialists. The group also benefits from the wide range of skills that its members bring from a wide range of professions and walks of life. The dissemination of research results through publication and presentations at conferences and to local groups is intrinsic to the group's philosophy. The core group meets every fortnight to discuss projects and current research, and guest speakers often make presentations on aspects of the local history and archaeology. Members consist of a mix of avid enthusiasts, some with archaeological qualifications. Since the group's foundation, a number of its members have expanded their interests in archaeology and have taken the opportunity to engage in further academic study through completion of some undergraduate modules in archaeology through the UCD 'Open Learning' programme. From this base one member has built on her experience with the group and subsequently completed an MSc. degree in Experimental Archaeology and Material Culture in UCD.

Engagement with UCD has provided opportunities for some members to take part in research excavations undertaken by the university's School of Archaeology. Resurrecting Monuments also works closely with Fingal County Council's Community Archaeologist, Christine Baker. Through participation in several of Fingal County Council's community archaeology projects, including excavations at Swords Castle, Bremore Castle and Drumanagh, some members have further developed their archaeological fieldwork skills and experience (http://fingal.ie/planning-and-buildings/heritage-in-fingal/communityarchaeology/).

Links have also been forged with other community archaeology groups at conferences and lectures. In the case of the Ulster Archaeological Society (UAS), survey group reciprocal visits have included the UAS 2018 annual outing to archaeological sites in north County Dublin, which took in some of the sites in Howth where Resurrecting Monuments has carried out research.

Resurrecting Monuments' initial research programme in 2015 focused on four local sites: St Doulagh's Church in Balgriffin (DU015-009), Tower Hill, Howth (DU016-002) (both of which are detailed in this paper), the 'Knock of Howth' burial mound at Burrowfield Road, Baldoyle (DU015-019), and Dungriffin Promontory Fort in Howth (DU016-003). Subsequently, with Heritage Council funding, Resurrecting Monuments has undertaken survey work, including geophysical survey work at Dungriffin Promontory Fort (the site of the iconic Bailey Lighthouse), the preliminary results of which were published in *Archaeology Ireland* in 2018 (Mongey 2018). A survey of St Helen's Motte (DU012-034) in nearby Portmarnock has also been completed. In 2018, with further Heritage Council funding, the group completed a survey of the Aideen's Grave portal tomb.

The group's ongoing outreach work has included presentations at a number of conferences and presentations to local historical and archaeological groups. With the help and support of Fingal County Council, Resurrecting Monuments has hosted archaeology-themed Heritage Week events since 2015 in Howth village. These well-attended events, catering for all ages, have served to further highlight and disseminate the new knowledge gathered about local heritage through its ongoing research programme to both the local community and the many visitors to Howth.

Two research projects undertaken by the group have included targeted research excavations, one at St Doulagh's Church (a site with upstanding medieval structures) and the other at Tower Hill, Howth, a site classified in the Sites and Monuments Record (SMR) as a possible Anglo-Norman motte castle.

ST DOULAGH'S

St Doulagh's Church (also known as St Doolagh's), the focus of the first research excavation undertaken by the Resurrecting Monuments group, is an iconic landmark in north Fingal, located with its associated burial ground on the Malahide Road, 9.6km north of Dublin City (Fig. 6.1). St Doulagh's intriguing architecture (Fig. 6.2) has long attracted the attention of antiquarians and artists such as Gabriel Beranger, particularly in the eighteenth and nineteenth centuries, resulting in a rich illustrated history of the church during this period (Harbison 2009).

Adjoining the nineteenth-century church nave and chancel are surviving medieval buildings consisting of a later medieval tower and two buildings with steeply pitched roofs. Described by Rachel Moss (2002) as an ancient conglomeration of structures, the later medieval St Doulagh's is believed to have originated as an early medieval ecclesiastical site. Another distinctive feature of the site, located to the north-east of the church, is an octagonal baptistery built over a natural well and of probable pre-sixteenth-century date (Swan 1989).

In 2009 the Friends of St Doulagh's commissioned a geophysical survey of the fields adjoining the church site. Using magnetic gradiometry and electrical resistivity, the survey identified a substantial area of archaeological activity around the church site, including a broad, curving anomaly interpreted as representing an early medieval ecclesiastical enclosure ditch (Nicholls 2009).

In early 2015 the newly formed Resurrecting Monuments group, at the invitation of the Friends of St Doulagh's, undertook further desktop research on the site. This formed the basis of an application for an excavation licence to undertake a small, targeted research excavation with funding from the Irish Research Council (Duffy 2015). A single trench was excavated in the field to the north of St Doulagh's Church in order to verify the geophysical results and

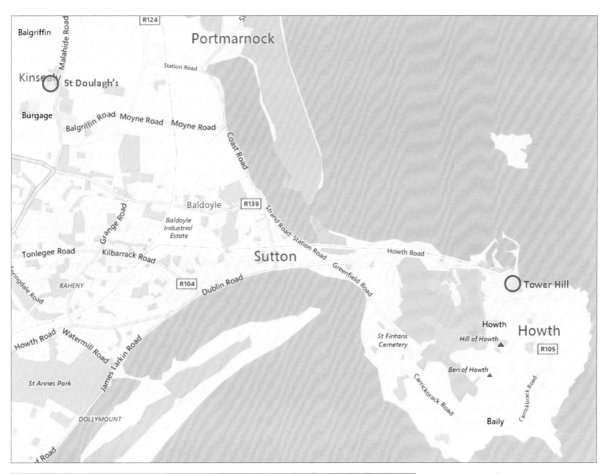

Fig. 6.1—Site location map.

Fig. 6.2—St Doulagh's Church.

to retrieve dating evidence from the anomaly that was interpreted as an enclosure ditch.

Archaeological and historical background

The name of the townland of St Doolagh's is believed to derive from St Doulagh, a seventh-century anchorite, who is reputed to have erected a cell on the site of the church. According to local tradition, he and his successors lived and died within this cell, their remains being buried beneath its floor (Walsh 1888, 31). There are, however, no definitive historical references to St Doulagh's in the early medieval period.

The first clear historical reference to the church of St Doulagh is a 1406 indulgence granted by the archbishop of Armagh to those who visit 'the chapel of the Blessed Virgin and the Holy Apostles Peter and Paul, Seynt Dulagh vulgarly called, in the Diocese of Dublin' and confess their sins to the chaplain, Eustache Roch, anchorite, enclosed in the chapel, and do penance and give alms for 'his support and the repair and ornamentation of the said church which is without means to do so' (Moss 2002, 124).

Peter Harbison (1982) suggests that the eastern end of the surviving medieval church building, known as the oratory, may represent the original single-chambered stone-roofed church dating from the pre-Norman twelfth century. This dating is based on the presence of a steep-pitched stone roof supported by a barrel vault below, described by Moss (2002) as a uniquely Irish roofing system which enjoyed particular popularity in Ireland during this time at buildings such as Cormac's Chapel, Cashel, and St Mochta's 'House' in Louth.

At the current entrance to the site of St Doulagh's Church is a stone cross (DU015-009002), previously located within the cemetery, which may also be early medieval in date.

The fifteenth century saw the addition of the fortified tower to the building. Such towers, which are likely to have been residences for priests, are a feature of many medieval churches in north-east Fingal, such as St Catherine's in Portrane and Baldongan church near Skerries.

In 1989 Leo Swan undertook the first archaeological excavation at St Doulagh's, focusing on three areas affected by conservation work being undertaken at the site. Prior to restoration of the baptistery, then partly collapsed, several test cuttings were excavated. A cutting on the north side of the baptistery uncovered a channel of brick and stone below almost 2m of fill, from which some later medieval and post-medieval pottery was recovered.

Another structure of limestone blocks, interpreted as a bath, was excavated. The fill excavated from this feature contained modern pottery, large quantities of mortar, bone and shell, and a Henry VIII silver penny dated to 1547–51. No early medieval material was recovered from Swan's test cuttings within the baptistery but a significant amount of iron slag (undated) was uncovered outside it (Swan 1989, 3).

Inside the churchyard a 1m-wide test cutting was excavated from the southern boundary wall to the south-facing wall of the church nave prior to the laying of a new electrical connection to the church. This revealed a shallow stratigraphy to the underlying boulder clay, which had shallow depressions cut into it in several places; some of these contained disarticulated bone, hinting at possible disturbed burials. Portions of six human skulls were identified. Swan (1989, 4) did not believe that these burials were early medieval in date.

During the monitoring of the trench for an electricity cable across the field to the north of the church, a 15m-long portion of a V-shaped ditch was uncovered. This feature, 2.5m wide and 1m deep, had steeply sloping sides and curved slightly from the south-west towards the north-east. Swan (1989, 6–7) suggested that, if projected, it would have enclosed the area of the burial ground within its curving line.

In 1990 Swan carried out some further excavations at the site as the tiled floor of the chancel was lifted. The deposits below the floor were disturbed and were a mix of disarticulated bone with rubble and mortar. The location of some of the bone suggested that it could be early medieval in date (Swan 1990). He concluded that St Doulagh's was an Early Christian site of the eighth or ninth century (Swan 1989, 1–2) but no definitive dating evidence was recovered, nor was any radiocarbon dating undertaken on samples from the small excavations.

In 2009 the Friends of St Doulagh's commissioned a geophysical survey (09R165) of the fields to the north and south of the church and graveyard. In his report summary, Nicholls (2009, 3) described the survey as recording the subsurface remains of a substantial archaeological site (Fig. 6.3).

A major feature recorded by the survey was a broad enclosing ditch surrounding the surviving church and burial ground, which Nicholls interpreted as the remains of the early medieval enclosure ditch (DU015-009005), 162m in diameter. It is probable that the section of ditch uncovered by Leo Swan corresponded with this anomaly.

The survey identified several smaller associated

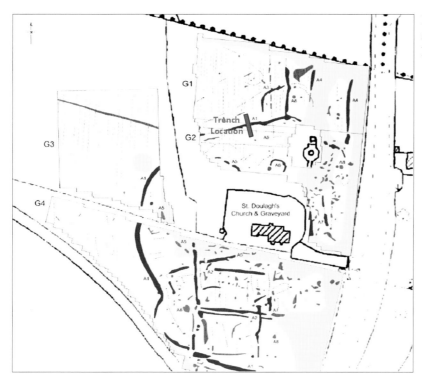

Fig. 6.3—Results of geophysical survey of St Doulagh's (John Nicholls, Licence No. 09R165).

enclosure ditches, multiple pit features and several possible structures. Several subcircular anomalies, 1.5–4m in diameter, demonstrating magnetic enhancement, were interpreted as possible kiln remains, suggesting industrial activity at the site. Swan's 1989 excavation did produce evidence for what he described as substantial ironworking on the site in the form of slag recovered from the test trenches (Swan 1989, 7). The survey also suggested that there are probable further archaeological remains beyond the southern limit of the area surveyed. Nicholls (2009) interpreted his geophysical results at St Doulagh's as archaeological remains similar in format and dimension to the results of geophysical surveys that he had undertaken at Milverton (03R047) and Oldtown (03R095), just to the west of Swords.

Archaeological excavation

The Resurrecting Monuments 2015 excavation (Licence No. 15E0329) aimed to test the geophysical anomaly thought to represent the outer enclosing element of the suspected ecclesiastical enclosure. This had been identified in the 2009 geophysical survey (Fig. 6.3). Under the direction of Christine Baker and Paul Duffy, the excavation team was a mix of volunteers, Resurrecting Monuments members and participants from the Baldoyle Forum back-to-work scheme, many experiencing their first archaeological excavation.

A single test trench, 1.5m by 8m, was hand-excavated over the anomaly during the week-long

excavation (Fig. 6.4). All spoil generated was passed through 30mm sieves. Evidence for three main phases of activity on the site was revealed. The excavation confirmed the geophysical anomaly as a V-shaped ditch, approximately 1.2m deep and 2.7m wide (Fig. 6.5). Its basal fill, a clayey silt with occasional angular stones (C08), was 1.22m deep and 2m wide. Whilst no artefactual material was recovered from this fill, some cockle-shells and molluscs and two small fragments of probable caprovid rib from a sheep-sized animal were extracted from the sieved soil samples. One of these bone fragments was sent for radiocarbon dating and returned a date of BP 1122±42, or cal. AD 853–935 (UBA-30540).

The basal fill (C08) of the ditch was partially overlain on the southern side by a thin layer of silty, gritty clay (C06), 0.23m thick. A charred free-threshing wheat grain from this fill returned a date of BP 204±21 or cal. AD 1790–1831 (UBA-30539), but it is believed that this seed is a contaminant from an upper fill which made its way into the sample.

The ditch was sealed by a layer of compact fine sandy clay (C04), 0.4m deep, with some angular stone inclusions. A sherd of Leinster Cooking Ware and a sherd of Dublin-Type fineware were recovered from this layer, as well as a small perforated bead of soft white stone (Fig. 6.6) and a total of 139 animal bones. The bones were variable in condition but were mostly well preserved or slightly weathered, with occasional fragments being heavily eroded. A few were burnt to a

Fig. 6.4—View south-east across the excavation trench.

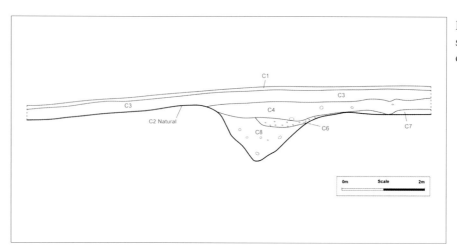

Fig. 6.5—East-facing section of early medieval ditch at St Doulagh's.

white chalky appearance from prolonged contact with fire. Of the twenty identifiable bone fragments, the remains of cattle and sheep are equally well represented, and most of the large/medium-sized mammal fragments may also be of cattle and sheep. Some bone fragments exhibited cut- and chop-marks indicative of butchery and food waste (McCarthy 2015).

A layer of sandy material (C007) 0.16m deep, with some pebble inclusions, was identified extending 1.8m upslope to the south of the ditch cut. It overlay the subsoil and appeared to run parallel to the ditch cut. This feature could represent the remnants of an

internal bank associated with the ditch and may correspond to the traces of a bank which were visible to the north of the graveyard in 1977 (DU015-009005). A total of 26 bones were recovered from this material. Two sheep/goat bones were identified: a scapula of a lamb less than six months old and a molar from a fully adult sheep. Most were small, indeterminate fragments of bone from a medium-sized animal, such as pig (Duffy 2015).

Layer C04, which sealed the main ditch fill deposits, provided evidence of ongoing settlement activity on the site surrounding the church complex

15E0329:3:4

10 mm

Fig. 6.6—Perforated stone bead from the upper levels of the ditch at St Doulagh's.

Fig. 6.7—Early medieval ditch after excavation.

into the later medieval period. Several sherds of medieval pottery, including a sherd of possible Saintonge ware, were also recovered from the topsoil layer during the excavation, in addition to 69 sherds of post-medieval pottery, including glazed red earthenwares, possibly made locally, black-glazed wares and seventeenth-century North Devon mottled wares.

Conclusions

The section of ditch uncovered by the 2015 excavation is similar in depth and width to that uncovered by Leo Swan in 1989. The radiocarbon date from the basal fill confirms the presence of an early medieval enclosure ditch at St Doulagh's, dating from at least the tenth century. It is probable that the enclosure ditch had an associated inner bank (Fig. 6.7). The main ditch fill (C08) contained no artefacts and, apart from the sample obtained through sieving, no animal bone. This suggests deliberate infilling of the enclosure ditch in a single, short-lived action, an occurrence noted at several other early medieval ecclesiastical sites.

This evidence, along with Nicholls's 2009 geophysical survey results, suggests that St Doulagh's was a significant early medieval ecclesiastical site in the kingdom of Brega, despite not being explicitly referenced in early medieval historical sources. The excavation also produced further evidence for continuous settlement activity at the site into the later medieval and post-medieval periods.

St Doulagh's is one of sixteen sites in County Dublin classified as an ecclesiastical enclosure by the Archaeological Survey of Ireland. Many are not recorded in historical sources and have had limited or no archaeological assessment carried out, apart from the major early medieval ecclesiastical sites of Lusk, Swords and Finglas. Apart from St Doulagh's, two other ecclesiastical enclosure sites have been the subject of geophysical survey: St Mobhi's, Milverton, a medieval church site (DU005-024001) just west of Skerries, and Oldtown (DU011-144001), just west of Swords town. The latter, previously unknown, was discovered when construction of a roadway uncovered skeletal material (Baker 2004). A subsequent geophysical survey (Nicholls 2003) identified an inner enclosure surrounding the burials, as well as two outer enclosures. Initially classified as an early medieval ecclesiastical site but with no strong evidence of religious association, Oldtown has now been reinterpreted as a settlement cemetery (Baker 2010b, 19), though possibly on ecclesiastical land farmed by secular *manaig*.

Similar to St Doulagh's, Milverton is a medieval church site associated with St Movee, and the results of a geophysical survey undertaken in the adjacent fields show extensive surrounding enclosures. The site also has an associated holy well (DU005-024002). Stray finds from the site in the nineteenth century include early medieval millstones (MacShamhráin 2004, 59). This evidence suggests that it is the site of an early medieval ecclesiastical enclosure of similar scale to St Doulagh's, but no excavation has yet been undertaken to verify the geophysical results.

While there are still research questions to be answered concerning the extent, nature and evolution of the early medieval ecclesiastical site, the 2015 excavation has confirmed an early medieval date for the major enclosure ditch visible in the 2009 geophysical survey. Together with Leo Swan's earlier monitoring excavations, these results from a small, targeted research excavation undertaken by the Resurrecting Monuments group have added significantly to our understanding of this site. Over the week of mixed weather the group got to experience all aspects of archaeological fieldwork, sieving, washing and sorting finds, recording contexts, and survey and planning—and for many of the volunteers the excitement of making your first find. Members of the group also got to witness and participate in the post-excavation work, including the presentation of the excavation results at several conferences.

TOWER HILL

Tower Hill, which overlooks Howth Harbour and village, is the site of a Martello tower built in 1803, which currently houses the Hurdy Gurdy vintage radio museum. Tower Hill is the northern end of a prominent, naturally formed spur of land which projects northwards from the higher ground to the south. The spur is generally flat-topped and defined by steep sides to the east and west. Its southern portion has been heavily truncated by extensive quarrying in the past.

Historical background

Tower Hill is also classified in the SMR as a motte site (DU016-002001). A Gabriel Beranger drawing from 1775 shows a large, flat-topped mound with an outer ring and a fosse on the top of Tower Hill before the construction of the Martello tower on the site. Locally this motte castle is identified as the site of the first St Lawrence family castle, constructed as part of the initial

Fig. 6.8—La Scalé map showing circular feature at Tower Hill (highlighted in red).

occupation of Howth by Armoricus (Almeric) in the twelfth century. Armoricus Tristram was an Anglo-Norman knight who helped John de Courcey win the Battle of Evora Bridge in 1177 (Ball 1920, 24), when the Hiberno-Norse were defeated and driven out of Howth. He was granted the lands of Howth for his contribution to the victory and he adopted the name St Laurence because the battle was won on 10 August 1177, the feast-day of St Laurence the Spaniard.

The promontory fort at Dungriffin (DU016-003001-), c. 2.5km to the south-east, is a type of fort that is traditionally thought of as Iron Age in date, which indicates that there was probably prehistoric occupation of Howth. Owing to the strategic significance of the Tower Hill site, it is likely that it was inhabited prior to the construction of the motte castle. Beranger's notes on his drawing (RIA Library: Howth, second view) identify the top of Tower Hill as 'The Karne or Ancient burying place of the Pagan Irish Kings & Nobility', suggesting Tower Hill as a possible funerary site from the Iron Age or the early medieval period. The appropriation of a prehistoric burial mound as the foundation for an Anglo-Norman motte is known from a number of locations, most famously at Knowth passage tomb in the Boyne Valley (Fenwick 2012).

Just to the west of Tower Hill is the likely location of the principal medieval settlement of Howth in the thirteenth century, which seems to have been close to the location of the current church, St Mary's Abbey, a

National Monument. The original church on the site was founded by Sitric, king of Dublin, c. 1042. The current building comprises a double-aisled church of largely fourteenth-century date with later alterations. The chantry chapel contains the tomb of Christopher St Lawrence and his wife Anna Plunkett (DU015-029003-). To the south of the graveyard is the College of Howth (DU015-030). This is a T-shaped three-storey building of probable late fifteenth/sixteenth-century date. Evidence for a second structure of probable sixteenth-century date was uncovered during excavations immediately to the east.

In 2015 Resurrecting Monuments undertook a programme of fieldwork at Tower Hill, which consisted of a geophysical survey and a small follow-up targeted excavation to try to find archaeological evidence for the motte site and any earlier settlement. This work was made possible by the award of a grant by the Irish Research Council under the New Foundations Grant Scheme in 2015. The initial Resurrecting Monuments research on Tower Hill involved a desk-based study that included consultation of the Topographical Files in the National Museum of Ireland and examination of the SMR file for the site, along with use of the historic maps section of the Heritage Maps website (*www.heritagemaps.ie*). The discovery of the Bernard la Scalé map from 1773 (Fig. 6.8) showing a circular feature on the summit of Tower Hill prior to the construction of the Martello tower adds to the evidence that there was

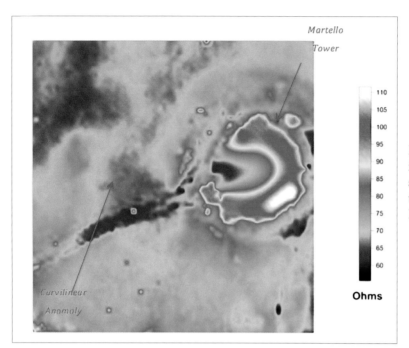

Fig. 6.9—Electrical resistivity imaging, with the Martello tower showing as the red circular feature to the right of the image (Kevin Barton).

an earlier structure on Tower Hill, as depicted in the Beranger drawing.

Geophysical survey

Unlike St Doulagh's, no previous archaeological investigations had been carried out at the site. Resurrecting Monuments therefore sought to establish whether there was any subsurface expression of earlier phases of activity. Kevin Barton of Landscape and Geophysical Services was engaged to undertake a geophysical survey of the site with the participation of group members in May 2015. During the twentieth century the site was the terminus for an early telegraph line to the UK. The remnants of the anchors for the mast had to be considered when assessing any geophysical data.

Two surveys—magnetic susceptibility and electrical resistivity—were carried out over a 40m x 40m grid (Fig. 6.9). Both identified a curvilinear anomaly that partly surrounded the low rise into which the Martello tower was built. The anomaly was targeted using electrical resistivity tomography (ERT) to produce a section through the feature. This revealed a probable cut feature, which we have interpreted as a ditch (Barton 2015). A kite survey of the site was also undertaken, in order to create a 3D model of Tower Hill.

Following this extensive desk-based research and the geophysical work, Resurrecting Monuments applied for Ministerial Consent (Licence No. E004620) to carry out a small-scale excavation targeting this curvilinear geophysical anomaly identified by the survey.

Excavation

In August 2015 the Resurrecting Monuments excavation at Tower Hill was carried out under the direction of Paul Duffy. The excavation team consisted mainly of volunteers from Resurrecting Monuments. A trench (8m x 1.5m), positioned to investigate the curvilinear anomaly, was hand-excavated over a week (Figs 6.10 and 6.11).

Tower Hill was in use as allotments from the early to the mid-twentieth century. Some locals had a memory of the site being used to grow vegetables during the 'Emergency' in the 1940s. The upper layer of cultivated soil (0.7m deep) reflected this. In the eastern portion of the excavation trench, a compact thin layer of redeposited subsoil was observed. This layer (C02) occurred close to the upstanding Martello tower and may represent a working surface dating from the construction of the tower. It overlay a deep deposit of mid-brown silty clay (C04) mixed through with patches of redeposited sandy boulder clay (C05). These layers contained ten sherds of medieval pottery, including Dublin-Type wares, Saintonge ware and Leinster Cooking Ware, as well as post-medieval pottery ranging from North Devon wares to the dipped wares and transfer-printed wares of the last decades of the eighteenth century. Some fragments of clay tobacco pipes were also recovered.

Four metal finds were also recovered from this layer; three were corroded iron nails and the fourth was a metal pin. Analysis by Siobhán Scully (Duffy 2016b) identified this as a copper-alloy dress-pin with a wire-wound ball head, probably of seventeenth/eighteenth-

Fig. 6.10—Excavations at Tower Hill, Howth, August 2015.

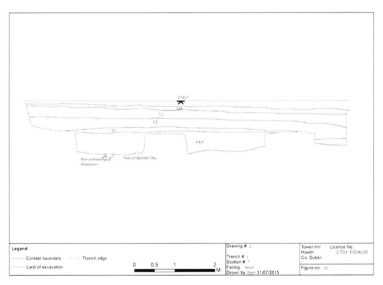

Fig. 6.11—South-facing section of the trench at Tower Hill.

century date (Fig. 6.12). An earlier date for this object is possible, as pin-making essentially remained unchanged from the twelfth to the nineteenth century. Based on the mix of finds, these layers were interpreted as a cultivated plough zone created by the levelling of the suspected motte mound and pre-dating the construction of the Martello tower at the beginning of the nineteenth century.

A total of 212 artefacts were retained during the course of the excavation, which, with the exception of some worked flint, reflect human activity on Tower Hill from the medieval period up to the twentieth century. In the post-excavation process, the finds were catalogued and recorded by the group and the material was prepared to pass on to the specialists for analysis. As a condition of the Ministerial Consent, metal-detection had to be carried out on spoil at all stages of the excavation, This uncovered a live 9mm Webley revolver bullet dating from the early 1900s.

Conclusions

The main research objective of the Resurrecting

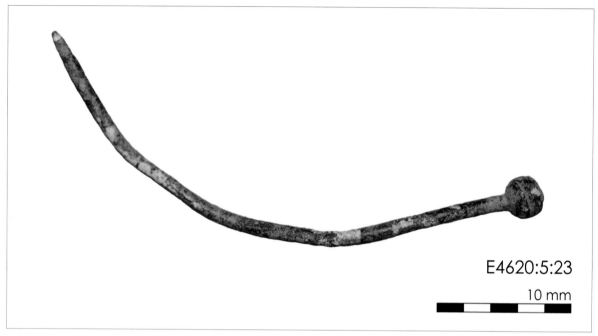

E4620:5:23

10 mm

Fig. 6.12—Copper-alloy pin from C05, Tower Hill.

Monuments Tower Hill project was to find archaeological evidence to support the interpretation of the site as a medieval motte site and to establish whether there was any evidence for earlier settlement. The excavation trench was sited to verify the geophysical curvilinear anomaly interpreted as the position of a subsurface cut feature that could pre-date the construction of the Martello tower (Fig. 6.13). Whilst this week-long excavation failed to reveal a ditch, it did reveal a layer of material which is thought to pre-date the construction of the adjacent Martello tower (DU016-002002) and which we think could represent the levelled motte. While no *in situ* medieval deposits were identified during the excavations, this can be explained by the limited size of the trench and the small areas of subsoil that were actually exposed (Duffy 2016b). The deep deposit of disturbed clays which contained the highest concentration of medieval ceramics uncovered from the excavations suggests that a feature of some kind, potentially a motte, existed here in the medieval period. Test-trenching of the surviving portion of the spur to the south of Tower Hill in 2017 also uncovered evidence of medieval settlement activity (Colfer 2017). Given the disturbed nature of the deposits uncovered by the Resurrecting Monuments excavation trench, any further archaeological investigation should target the area to the west of the Martello tower. This will be required to prove conclusively that Tower Hill was the original site of the initial castle (motte) of Armoricus St Laurence.

In 1235 the St Laurence family moved to the more spacious site of Howth Castle to the west, which remained in the family until recent times.

CONCLUSIONS

Since its foundation in 2015, Resurrecting Monuments has successfully met its founding objectives in consolidating local interest into an ongoing, self-sustaining and self-driven community archaeology group in the Howth/Baldoyle area (Fig. 6.14). The excavations undertaken at St Doulagh's and Tower Hill have added significantly to our interpretation of these sites and form a basis for future follow-up research. In addition to these small research excavations, Resurrecting Monuments has continued with its research, publication and outreach activities.

The group's ongoing research projects include Dungriffin Promontory Fort and the Aideen's Grave portal tomb. Resurrecting Monuments also plans to publish its first book, *An archaeological guide to the Howth Peninsula*.

BIBLIOGRAPHY

Baker, C. 2003 Archaeological assessment, access road, Oldtown, Swords, Co. Dublin. Excavation Licence No. 03E1080. Unpublished report.
Baker, C. 2004 A lost ecclesiastical site in Fingal.

Fig. 6.13—View east across the excavation at Tower Hill, with the Martello tower in the background.

Fig. 6.14—Heritage Week 2015 at Tower Hill.

Archaeology Ireland **18** (3), 14–17.

Baker, C. 2010a *Antiquities of old Fingal.* Wordwell, Bray.

Baker, C. 2010b Occam's duck: three early medieval settlement cemeteries or ecclesiastical sites. In C. Corlett and M. Potterton (eds), *Death and burial in early medieval Ireland*, 1–22. Wordwell, Bray.

Ball, F.E. 1920 *A history of County Dublin*, Vol. 6. Alexander Thom, Dublin.

Barton, K. 2015 Geophysical survey at Tower Hill, Howth. Unpublished geophysical survey report for Resurrecting Monuments.

Branigan, G. 2012 *Ancient and holy wells of Dublin.* The History Press, Dublin.

Colfer, N. 2017 Lands at Balscadden Road, Howth. Excavation Licence No. 17E0533. Unpublished interim report submitted to the National Monuments Service.

Duffy, P. 2015 Preliminary report of archaeological excavation at St Doulagh's Church, Malahide Road, Co. Dublin. Excavation Licence No. 15E0329. Unpublished interim report submitted to the National Monuments Service.

Duffy, P. 2016a The church of Bearach, the grange of Baldoyle and the town of the dark stranger. In S. Duffy (ed.), *Medieval Dublin XV. Proceedings of the Friends of Medieval Dublin Symposium 2013*, 89–118. Four Courts Press, Dublin.

Duffy, P. 2016b Report of archaeological excavation at Tower Hill, Howth, Co. Dublin. Excavation Licence No. E004620. Unpublished report submitted to the National Monuments Service.

Fenwick, J. 2012 Appendix 8. Geophysical survey of Knowth Area 11. In G. Eogan, *Excavations at Knowth in the first and second millennia AD*, 811–30. Royal Irish Academy, Dublin.

Harbison, P. 1982 St Doulagh's Church. *Studies: An Irish Quarterly Review* **71** (281), 27–42.

Harbison, P. (ed.) 1991 *A collection of drawings of the principal buildings of Ireland, designed on the spot and collected by Gabriel Beranger.* Royal Irish Academy, Dublin.

Harbison, P. 2009 Some old illustrations of St Doulagh's Church, Balgriffin, Co. Dublin. In S. Duffy (ed.), *Medieval Dublin IX. Proceedings of the Friends of Medieval Dublin Symposium 2013*, 152–65. Four Courts Press, Dublin.

La Scalé, B. 1757 *A survey of the city, harbour, bay and environs of Dublin on the scale as that of London, Paris and Rome* (http://gallica.bnf.fr/ark:/12148/btv1b53057253b.r=rocquesdublin%20dublin?rk=42918;4; accessed April 2018).

McCarthy, M. 2015 The animal remains from St Doolagh's Church. Excavation Licence No. 15E0329. Unpublished specialist report.

McQuade, M. 2012 Archaeological monitoring of investigative trenches along the R107 Dublin–Malahide road from St Doolagh's to Streamstown. Excavation Licence No. 12E0185. Unpublished report.

MacShamhráin, A. 2004 An ecclesiastical enclosure in the townland of Grange, parish of Holmpatrick. In A. MacShamhráin (ed.), *The Island of St Patrick: church and ruling dynasties in Fingal and Meath, 400–1114*, 52–60. Four Courts Press, Dublin.

Mongey, M. 2018 Dublin's forgotten fort. *Archaeology Ireland* **32** (2), 40–4.

Moss, R. 2002 St Doulagh's Church. *Irish Arts Review* **20** (2), 122–5.

Murphy, M. and Potterton, M. 2010 *The Dublin region in the Middle Ages: settlement, land-use and economy.* Four Courts Press, Dublin.

Nicholls, J. 2003 Geophysical survey: Oldtown, Swords. Detection Licence No. 09R0095. Unpublished report.

Nicholls, J. 2009 Geophysical survey report: St Doulagh's Church and graveyard. Detection Licence No. 09R165. Unpublished report.

O'Keeffe, T. 2000 *Medieval Ireland: an archaeology.* Tempus, Stroud.

O'Sullivan, A., McCormick, F., Kerr, T. and Harney, L. 2014 *Early medieval Ireland AD 400–1100: the evidence from archaeological excavations.* Royal Irish Academy, Dublin.

Reeves, W. 1857 Memoir of the Church of St Duilech. *Proceedings of the Royal Irish Academy* **7** (1857–61), 141–7.

St Doulagh's Heritage Project 1990 *A guide to St Doulagh's Church.*

Scally, G. 2002 Archaeological assessment: north fringe sewer, St Doolagh's Church, Malahide Road, Dublin 13. Excavation Licence No. 99E0470. Unpublished report.

Swan, D.L. 1989 St Doulagh's Church, Balgriffin: Dublin Conservation and Restoration Project interim report on the archaeological excavations, September to December 1989. Excavation Licence No. E000508. Unpublished report.

Swan, D.L. 1990 1990:031 St Doulagh's, Balgriffin: summary report (https://excavations.ie/report/1990/Dublin/0000966/, accessed April 2019).

Walsh, R. 1888 *Fingal and its churches.* William McGee, Dublin.

7. Gallows Hill community archaeology project

CHRISTINA KNIGHT-O'CONNOR AND EDDIE CANTWELL

ABSTRACT

In 2018 human remains were discovered during a community-led excavation at Gallows Hill, Co. Waterford. The excavation was the fourth season of investigations by community volunteers, which included two weekends of geophysical surveys and two seven-day excavations. Community-led archaeology projects like Gallows Hill are often referred to as taking a 'bottom-up approach', where the community initiate and lead projects in a different approach from that of professionals and archaeological contractors holding open days to excavations. The group's long-term aims are to create pride of place in the monument and conservation of a heritage site that can be appreciated by the community and visitors to Dungarvan. This paper will examine the experiences of the volunteers over a four-year period in developing a community-led archaeology project, and the positive benefits for heritage and the local community.

INTRODUCTION

The Gallows Hill project began in 2015, when volunteers with Waterford County Museum commissioned geophysicist Kevin Barton to work with them on a two-day geophysical survey to investigate the origins of a neglected mound on the outskirts of Dungarvan, Co. Waterford. Gallows Hill is enclosed by urban housing estates and until recent years annual Hallowe'en bonfires were lit on its summit. A major obstacle for the group has been challenging the local negative perception of the site, and volunteers have used numerous innovative approaches to promote Gallows Hill in a positive light. Community archaeology is growing in popularity and can include a wide range of activities, from surveys to excavation, led by professional bodies or community groups. The Council for British Archaeology (CBA 2015) has highlighted the benefits of community archaeology in enabling people to become directly involved in the preservation, investigation and enjoyment of their local heritage in constructive and meaningful ways. The project was selected for the Heritage Council's Adopt-a-Monument initiative in 2016, and inclusion in the scheme has had a positive impact on the group's progress.

GALLOWS HILL, CO. WATERFORD

In 2015 Waterford County Museum volunteers began a community investigation of Gallows Hill, an intriguing but neglected landmark in the heart of Dungarvan. Gallows Hill (WA031-006) is a large mound located 1km west of Dungarvan Castle and is recorded as a castle-motte in the Record of Monuments and Places (www.archaeology.ie). The motte-and-bailey-type earthen castles were introduced into Ireland during the Anglo-Norman invasion in the late twelfth century. A wooden tower, or keep, would usually have been placed on top of the motte and surrounded by a wooden palisade, sometimes with a courtyard or bailey at the foot of the mound. The Record of Monuments and Places lists four mottes (Gallows Hill, Pembroketown, Coolbunia and Lismore) and two mottes with baileys (Feddans and Ballyyea West) in County Waterford. The 1175 Treaty of Windsor between Henry II and Rory O'Connor, high-king of Ireland, confirmed Henry's lordship of Dublin, Leinster and Waterford, with its territory from Waterford to Dungarvan (Riley 1853). It may have been at this period that a defensive motte was built at Dungarvan, as a strategically located stronghold for the continued Anglo-Norman invasion and to protect a valuable water source at the neck of the promontory. The mottes at Lismore and Gallows Hill, with heights of 10m and 8m respectively, are significantly larger than the mottes at Pembroketown (3.75m), Feddans (4.3m) and Coolbunia (5m). The number of mottes in Waterford is relatively small compared to the bordering counties of Wexford and Tipperary, and they are concentrated in the areas surrounding Waterford City, Dungarvan, Lismore and the Tipperary border.

Gallows Hill is bordered by the townlands of Fairlane, Spring (*Tobair an Bhile*), Loughmore and Kilrush. A standing stone (WA031-076) is located 100m northwest in the townland of Spring Marquis, and there is

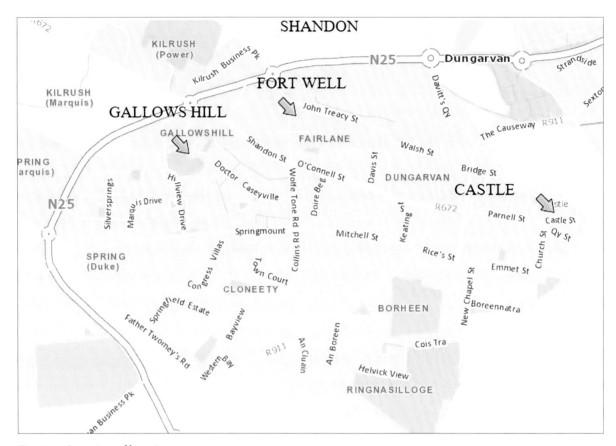

Fig. 7.1—Location of key sites.

an important water source known as Fort Well 350m to the east in the adjoining townland of Fairlane (Fig. 7.1). There are no accounts relating to the historic uses of the hill and the theories of past historians are brief. Smith (1745, 353) described Gallows Hill as a 'Dun or sepulchral monument situated near a highroad on eminence'. The townland of Loughmore aligns neatly to the north with Gallows Hill and its name was suggested by Power (1952) to be a misinterpretation of *Leacht Mór* or 'great grave mound', indicating a monument of prehistoric origins rather than a Norman motte. The spelling *Leacht Mór* was recorded in mid-nineteenth-century baptismal records by the parish priest of Dungarvan, the Revd Jeremiah Hally. Local folklore also describes the hill's creation by a giant, and it has often been associated with stories of the mythical banshee and tales of human burials. The hill today is tightly enclosed by four local authority housing developments, with a small green area to the west, and has developed a negative reputation as a site of anti-social behaviour.

GEOPHYSICAL SURVEYS AT GALLOWS HILL

In 2015 Waterford County Museum was granted funding from Waterford City and County Council to pursue a programme of geophysical surveys to help understand the origins of the mound. Museum members held a public meeting, inviting the local community to get involved with the first geophysical investigation of Gallows Hill. There was considerable interest from the broader community but less enthusiasm among residents living in the estates immediately around the hill. The major challenge for the group was to try to create a new, positive image of Gallows Hill, and this has been the long-term goal of the project. Children's activities were organised on site during the surveys to engage local children in the project and their history. Led by geophysicist Kevin Barton, the group completed earth resistance, magnetic gradiometry and electrical resistivity tomography (ERT) surveys to examine evidence for any features in the green area surrounding the hill or on top of the hill. There was great excitement among volunteers when a curving feature to the west was observed in the data from an earth resistance survey (Barton 2016). The initial community survey led to an

Fig. 7.2—The 2016 ERT survey.

increased local interest in and curiosity about Gallows Hill, and a local craft beer company developed a 'Gallows Hill' brew to mark the initial exploration. In the weeks following the surveys, Kevin Barton delivered a public presentation of the results to a large audience for Heritage Week 2015.

The group was granted additional funding in 2016 by the Heritage Council to continue the programme of geophysical surveys with Kevin Barton (Fig. 7.2). Ground-penetrating radar survey revealed evidence of curving features to the west of the hill that may extend up to 15m from the base of the mound. Also in that year the project was selected to be part of the Heritage Council's Adopt-a-Monument initiative, which aims to empower communities to become involved in the conservation and protection of their heritage for future generations and to raise awareness about the diverse heritage that is in their locality (Burke *et al.* 2017). The group has benefited from being part of this scheme, which has combined the passion and knowledge of the community with the skills and expertise of the professional archaeologists. Volunteers received support, mentoring and training in various aspects of researching and recording local heritage sites as part of the initiative. The group's preparation for a

Heritage Week medieval fair was featured on RTÉ's *Nationwide* as part of a Heritage Week promotion broadcast (Fig. 7.3). In April 2017 the Gallows Hill volunteers were privileged to meet HRH the Prince of Wales at Kilkenny Castle as representatives of the Adopt-a-Monument initiative. This was an unforgettable experience and an opportunity to further promote positive aspects of the Gallows Hill project and monument to the local and wider community. Members of the group also presented their findings from the Gallows Hill investigations at various national events, including the Rathcroghan Community Archaeology conference and the annual conference of the Group for the Study of Historic Settlement in Ireland.

COMMUNITY EXCAVATION, 2017

In June 2017 the group commissioned professional archaeologist Dave Pollock to lead an excavation under licence from the National Monuments Service, to better understand features discovered during the geophysical surveys. The work was funded by the excellent ongoing support of Waterford Council Heritage Section, volunteer fund-raising efforts and

Fig. 7.3—Medieval villagers during Heritage Week 2016.

Fig. 7.4—Archaeologist Dave Pollock with community participants.

generous public donations. This dig was a great way of engaging the community with the story of the hill, as local volunteers gained hands-on experience under the guidance of professional archaeologists (Fig. 7.4). The group published a weekly press release in the lead-up to the excavation, to promote the community dig and to encourage new volunteers to get involved. The School of Irish Archaeology hosted a children's excavation alongside the Gallows Hill trench to allow children to participate in the excavation experience. The children's 'Big Dig', funded by the Heritage Council, was a great opportunity to engage children in the Gallows Hill project.

The community excavation took place over eight days in June and revealed a significant amount of information about the hill's origins. A trench, 22m long x 2m wide, was cut outward and westward from the mound, revealing three concentric ditches. Two of the ditches were deep and we did not reach the bottom, but they are believed to date from the sixteenth/seventeenth century, as one sherd of glazed red earthenware was recovered (Pollock 2017). A cannon-ball and shot that were later found in the spoil heap are also likely to be associated with this period of the mound's use.

A third and earlier ditch close to the mound was quite shallow and flat-bottomed and had mostly been cut away when the later ditches were dug. The trench extended 1m into the western side of the mound and revealed a steep-sided original mound surface that had weathered for several centuries before it was refortified when the two later ditches were cut (Fig. 7.5). The volunteers were pleased that their findings had uncovered a wealth of previously unrecorded information about the history of Gallows Hill. The excavation revealed that the mound was still in use as a defensive fort up to the sixteenth or seventeenth century, when major reconstruction had taken place.

In 1582 an order was made to 'repair the two forts and her majesty's house at Dungarvan' following the Desmond rebellion (Hamilton 1860). There are numerous accounts of battles in Dungarvan between the sixteenth and seventeenth centuries. Gallows Hill was possibly one of the two forts established to protect the town's nearest supply of fresh water at Fort Well (now covered), located close to the present St Brigid's Well (WA031-071). The town's earliest sunken wells were suitable only for culinary purposes and inhabitants had to travel some distance to the springs on the outskirts of the town for fresh drinking water (Parliamentary Gazetteer of Ireland 1846). It was not until 1740 that a sufficient water supply for the town was finally developed, via an aqueduct from the River Finnisk, by aid of a parliamentary grant. The original Fort Well is shown on the first-edition (1841) Ordnance Survey (OS) 6in. map. The later 25in. (1907) OS map depicts only St Brigid's Well, located approximately 5m from the original Fort Well, a central feature of the nine-

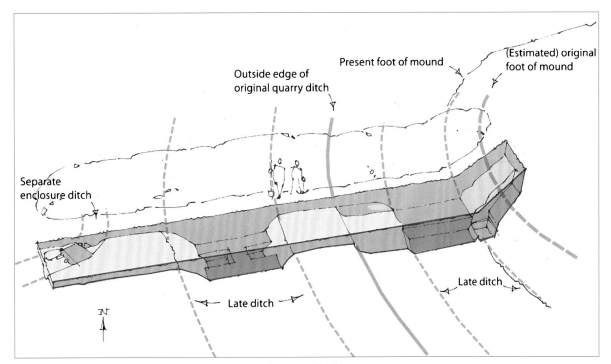

Fig. 7.5—The 2017 excavation results (courtesy of Dave Pollock).

Fig. 7.6—Waterford Community Public Participation, Arts & Culture Award.

teenth-century Power's St Brigid's Well Brewery. The year ended on a high for the group when the Gallows Hill Archaeology Project received the Waterford Community Public Participation, Arts & Culture Award at a gala reception in Waterford City (Fig. 7.6).

EXCAVATION AND MEDIEVAL FAIR, 2018

Heritage Week and the European Year of Cultural Heritage 2018 presented another opportunity to showcase Gallows Hill and to engage with all ages in the community through art and hands-on experiences. The excavation and medieval fair were funded with the support of an award from Waterford City and County Council's Creative Waterford initiative, volunteer fundraising efforts and generous individual donations. The project was also selected in August as County Heritage winner in the National Lottery Good Causes Awards. The group organised a second eight-day community excavation and attracted a considerable number of new volunteers to the project to join existing volunteers. The event was well publicised in weekly press releases leading up to Heritage Week, social media and local radio. During the community excavation a family medieval fair was hosted, allowing visitors to learn about the site's

medieval past; events included battle re-enactments, weaponry demonstrations and a display of dress and customs of the period. Children were immersed in their local history, working with artists to create medieval wall murals; they also had the opportunity to excavate a replica Viking house with the School of Irish Archaeology. Educating and engaging local children is important for the future of Gallows Hill and is essential to the project's long-term success. The children's Big Dig took place alongside the community excavation and gave children the opportunity to understand the role of archaeology at Gallows Hill and to be an active part of the community's explorations.

The Heritage Week excavation yielded a significant amount of new information relating to Gallows Hill. The 2017 excavation had revealed that the mound was an early motte with an associated ditch that was later refortified in the seventeenth century. In 2018 the group opened a trench, 10m x 1.5m, on top of the mound to examine whether any archaeological evidence survived beneath the years of annual bonfires. The volunteers, working with professional archaeologists Dave Pollock and Jo Moran, removed a thin layer of charcoal from the decades of Hallowe'en bonfires and uncovered a layer of fallow soil. A few inches below this soil layer was a gravel surface that had suffered very

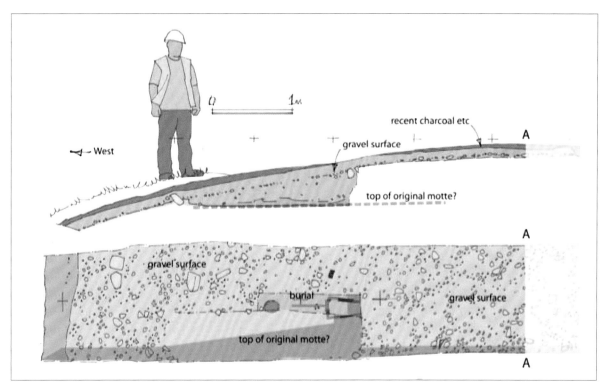

Fig. 7.7—The 2018 excavation results (courtesy of Dave Pollock).

little bonfire damage. Three loose teeth and a partly in-tact human jaw were recovered from the north-east corner of the trench. According to Pollock (2018a, 11), 'The skull fragment with jaw, trampled into the gravel surface of the mound, appears to have been an articu-lated body part, and may have been displayed on a gan-try or a pole; as late as the eighteenth century heads were displayed as a warning to others'.

A fragment of long bone and a damaged human skull were uncovered on the west side of the trench. Further investigation revealed the very fragmentary re-mains of an extended inhumation with the head to the west (Pollock 2018b). The remains were in a poor state of preservation and appeared to have been buried above the originally constructed mound and in a later sixteenth- or seventeenth-century refortified hill. Only two small areas were excavated through the later ma-terial down to a compact clay surface and in both of these areas articulated skeletons were identified (Fig. 7.7). A medieval silver coin recovered from the gravel material on top of the mound has provisionally been identified as a Henry II Tealby penny of 1158–65 (Jerome Waters, pers. comm.) (Fig. 7.8). The coin may be related to the earlier motte although it was found above the burials and later mound material. The initial osteoarchaeological report indicates that the bones be-long to at least two individuals, an adolescent and a

Fig. 7.8—Henry II Tealby penny, 1158–65.

Fig. 7.9—Children's interpretative mural, 2018.

young male adult. It is possible that a third individual is represented among the fragmentary remains, but further analysis will be required to confirm this. Troy (2018, 22) suggested that the articulated burial might be earlier in date than the disarticulated remains. It is also possible that the articulated burial was related to the site's having been used for hangings. The body was orientated in the Christian manner, however, which would perhaps argue against its being a clandestine burial. Further analysis on the remains may reveal whether both individuals are contemporary with one another and allow precise dating of the layers of settlement at Gallows Hill. The recent discoveries have gen-

erated a great deal of interest among residents and the wider community and have brought the human story of Gallows Hill into local consciousness. Once full analysis is completed, there will be a public presentation of results and the future direction of the project will be discussed with the local community.

CONCLUSION

The Gallows Hill community project has uncovered a wealth of previously unknown information about the historic uses of an important local monument. The community investigation is revealing that the mound did not have one static use but was adapted over many centuries as a motte, a sixteenth/seventeenth-century fort and a place of execution. The recent discovery of human remains is highly significant, and the community is keen to learn more about the story of the individuals unearthed.

Consistent promotion has been an important element of the project and this has been achieved through investigations, events, social media, exhibits and regular press releases. The Royal Irish Academy's *Archaeology 2025* publication 'emphasised the importance of archaeology to enrich our quality of life and well-being by characterising landscapes, contributing to place-making, instilling identity, connecting communities, and fostering civic engagement' (RIA 2017, 15). Gallows Hill is a complex site that has suffered decades of neglect, and in the beginning residents were opposed to supporting or engaging with the project. A great deal of work was required to help to foster a sense of pride in the site before a greater level of engagement could be approached. The level of involvement and support increased each year, however, and archaeology has been an effective tool in the process of positively connecting communities with their local monument. This promotion is gradually replacing the negative perceptions that had developed over many decades. Hallowe'en bonfires ceased several years ago; there is no longer fly-tipping or waste left at Gallows Hill, as the local and wider community are developing a new positive understanding of the site.

Community-led archaeology is an opportunity for communities to develop skills and confidence, and to take active ownership of their heritage and culture for the benefit of present and future generations. It is important to engage all elements of the community, however, particularly those with less interest in history or archaeology. Children's events, family days and ongoing art interpretation projects are essential for the momentum achieved through archaeology to continue and develop (Fig. 7.9). The group plans to use the findings of the excavations to develop a heritage walls project in 2019. This will involve local children working with artists to develop murals depicting the phases of the hill's history as revealed through archaeology on the modern walls surrounding the hill. The aim of the arts project is to allow the residents, particularly children, to become empowered in interpreting their own history to a wider audience.

If community-led archaeology is to be effective, it also requires close collaboration with professionals and State bodies to support good practice. Initiatives like the Heritage Council's Adopt-a-Monument scheme are essential for guiding and supporting the work of community groups in conserving, protecting and promoting their local heritage. At the beginning of the project, many of the Gallows Hill project volunteers had no previous engagement with the local museum. Today they are confidently revealing one of the town's most unique historic monuments. The long-term aim of the community project is to develop local pride of place and to finally ensure that Gallows Hill takes its place in the historic narrative of Dungarvan.

ACKNOWLEDGEMENTS

The volunteers would like to thank archaeologists Dave Pollock and Jo Moran, the Heritage Council, Waterford City and County Council, Creative Waterford, geophysicist Kevin Barton, Waterford Heritage Officer Bernadette Guest, Environmental Officer Gabrielle Foley, Roisin Burke and Neil Jackman of Adopt a Monument Ireland, sponsors Ivan Lennon, Michael Ryan, Bobby Breen and Kevin Dalton, photographer John Foley, Print Master, osteoarchaeologist Carmelita Troy of Rubicon Heritage Services, Kayleigh Regan, Tony Hayes, each of our dedicated volunteers, the local community and local businesses for supporting the project since 2015.

BIBLIOGRAPHY

Barton, K. 2016 Preliminary report on ground-penetrating radar survey at Gallows Hill, Dungarvan, Co. Waterford. Unpublished report.

Burke, R., Jackman, N. and Ryan, C. 2017 *Adopt a Monument manual: guidance for community archaeology projects*. The Heritage Council.

CBA 2015 *Workplace learning for community archaeologists: a Skills for the Future project, 2011–2015*. Council for British Archaeology, York.

Hamilton, H.C. (ed.) 1860 *Calendar of the State papers relating to Ireland 1574–85*. HMSO, London.

Parliamentary Gazetteer of Ireland 1846 *The Parliamentary Gazetteer of Ireland: adapted to the new poor-law, franchise, municipal and ecclesiastical arrangements, and compiled with a special reference to the lines of railroad and canal communication, as existing in 1844–45*, Vol. 2. A. Fullarton and Co., Dublin, London and Edinburgh.

Pollock, D. 2017 A research excavation at Gallowshill,

Dungarvan, Co. Waterford in 2017. Unpublished preliminary report by Archaeografix.

Pollock, D. 2017 A research excavation at Gallowshill, Dungarvan, Co. Waterford in 2017. Unpublished preliminary report by Archaeografix.

Pollock, D. 2018 Preliminary report on archaeological research excavations at Gallowshill, Dungarvan, Co. Waterford, in 2018 (17E0245 Extn). Unpublished report by Archaeografix.

Power, Canon P. 1952 *The place names of the Decies* (2nd edn). Blackwell, Oxford.

Riley, H.T. (ed.) 1853 *From the annals of Roger de Hoveden, comprising the history of England and of other countries of Europe from AD 732 to AD 1201, translated from the Latin with notes and illustrations by H.T. Riley Esq.*, Vol. 1. H.G. Bohn, London.

RIA 2017 *Archaeology 2025: strategic pathways for archaeology in Ireland*. Royal Irish Academy, Dublin.

Smith, C.M.D. 1745 *The present and ancient state of the county and city of Waterford* (2nd edn, with additions). Dublin.

Thomas, S. 2010 *Community archaeology in the UK: recent findings*. Council for British Archaeology, York.

Troy, C. 2018 Osteological analysis of human remains from Gallowshill, Dungarvan, Co. Waterford, 17E0245ext. Unpublished report by Rubicon Heritage Services Ltd, Cork.

8. A brief narrative of the first community archaeology project in Sailortown, Belfast

LIZ THOMAS AND PATRICK BENSON

This chapter is dedicated to the memory of Seán Baker, who sadly died suddenly in April 2017. Seán was a founding member of and secretary to the Sailortown Regeneration Group and Sailortown Historical Society and is remembered for being an ardent campaigner for equality for all, especially for the past and future people of Sailortown.

ABSTRACT

In the spring of 2015 the Sailortown Regeneration Group (SRG), in collaboration with Queen's University Belfast (QUB), conducted a community-inclusive research excavation in Sailortown, Belfast, an urban-maritime settlement. The purpose of the archaeological excavation was twofold: to find empirical evidence for living conditions in a nineteenth-century maritime village and to use heritage as a unifying factor between at least two distinct communities—the present and former residents of Sailortown. This project presented many challenges but also made manifest the opportunities, impact and indirect benefits delivered by such heritage projects across local communities.

INTRODUCTION

A single trench in the yard of a public house—an area of 16m² open for just two weeks—caught the imagination of the public, the media, politicians and dignitaries from across the island of Ireland (Fig. 8.1).

From 25 May to 5 June 2015 Belfast's first urban-maritime community-inclusive research excavation featured in broadsheets up and down the country, in TV series and in radio interviews. One example of the support for the project came from Belfast's lord mayor, Nichola Mallon, who in a letter of support to the

Fig. 8.1—The Sailortown trench.

Heritage Lottery Fund wrote that:

'Sailortown is an important historic area of Belfast, linked to the development of Belfast as a world capital in the maritime and manufacturing industries. Through urban redevelopment from the 1970s most of the inhabitants were dispersed across Belfast and much of the historic fabric above ground has been demolished. Most strikingly, the spirit of Sailortown's maritime and industrial heritage persists. Archaeological exploration of what lies beneath the ground is a unique opportunity for interested Belfast citizens from across all traditions to physically connect and engage with Sailortown's rich heritage. In recent years some new inhabitants have returned to the area and, as far as I understand, this project is unique for bringing together current and former residents and people from diverse cultural traditions to engage in a shared learning experience of a part of Belfast's rich past. I wholeheartedly endorse the valuable contribution that this exemplary project will play towards regeneration of an area and towards building a healthier Belfast.'

The public flocked to see this small trench, which opened a window on dockland life in the nineteenth century; whilst the pints flowed inside the Dockers' Club, outside flowed the visitors' talk about the area— an area which has largely 'disappeared'. Few of the original buildings survive; those that do include four houses, St Joseph's Church (deconsecrated and under refurbishment through the SRG's resilient endeavours) and two derelict bars, one of which may be demolished to make way for a hotel complex (Figs 8.2 and 8.3). Sailortown contains a number of Industrial Heritage and Listed buildings, including a demolished bonded warehouse (IHR 10179), St Joseph's Church, known locally as 'the Chapel on the Quays' (HB26/50/095 A), which was constructed between 1860 and 1879 (James Pearse, father of Patrick Pearse, designed the high altar), and the Parochial House (HB26/50/095 B). Yet beyond the archaeological trench was the experience of making this small-scale excavation happen. To begin with, nearly two years of organisation went into making these two weeks: securing support from the local stakeholders (specifically the former and present residents of Sailortown), engaging the wider public, obtaining funding, locating appropriate venues for the dissemination of information and, of course, locating an appropriate site to excavate.

Fig. 8.2—The Chapel on the Quays.

Fig. 8.3—The Rotterdam Bar.

BACKGROUND HISTORY OF SAILORTOWN

At first glance it is difficult to imagine that Sailortown, now in the shadow of the regenerated Titanic Quarter on the opposite side of the harbour, was once a thriving hub of domestic and industrial life. Nevertheless, these near-empty streets are imbued with a rich heritage. Belfast Harbour was first established in 1613, when the town was given its royal charter, and by the twentieth century the port was inextricably linked to Belfast's role as a world maritime and industrial capital. The development of the harbour created welcome job opportunities, particularly in the wake of the 'Great Famine' of the 1840s and 1850s. By the middle of the nineteenth century a thriving community of those working in Belfast's industries had settled in the area unofficially called 'Sailortown'. Throughout the nineteenth century and up to the middle of the twentieth century Sailortown was a diverse community with manufacturing and maritime industries, élite and working classes, and Roman Catholic and Protestant residents. It is estimated that 5,000 people lived in Sailortown at its peak. The name is an unofficial designation for a small enclave of streets in the Docks

Ward, Belfast. The exact location of Sailortown is often disputed but it is generally agreed that it is bordered by Whitla Street, York Street and Dock Street. Its streets include Pilot Street, Pilot Place, Pilot Court, Short Street, Garmoyle Street, New Andrew Street, New Dock Street, Marine Street, Ship Street, Fleet Street, Dock Street, Dock Lane (Thomas Street to Dock Street), North Thomas Street and Earl Street.

Sailortown has always had a strong connection with trade unionism; a visit from James Larkin brought Roman Catholics and Protestants together in the National Union of Dock Labourers in 1907. Sailortown continues to have a very close association with workers' rights and some of the key members of that community were influential in creating our current Health and Safety regulations, which improved and saved many lives in the harsh dockland work environment.

Oral histories from Sailortown describe a life that was tough, sometimes treacherous, and often lonely for the women when the men were away at sea, but the stories also reveal a love for and sense of pride in the Sailortown community (Thomas 2014–17). Although Roman Catholics and Protestants lived side by side in this close-knit community, Belfast's first 'peace line' was

Fig. 8.4—St Joseph's Church today.

built at Sailortown in 1935. During the Second World War the docklands of Belfast were badly damaged in bombing raids in April and May 1941, leading to multiple deaths. The area of the excavation trench was previously occupied by houses that were destroyed in April 1941 (PRONI, War Damage Records, VAL/20/4/44). The site was later cleared for the construction of stables and open green-grassed space, and later for the construction of the new Dockers' Club. In fact, the Dockers' Club celebrated its 40th anniversary in 2018.

The downturn in Belfast's industrial economy, particularly the loss of dock work through the mechanisation of the shipping industry, affected Sailortown. It was simultaneously impacted by the Troubles. It is said locally that every pub except one, the Dockers' Club, was bombed and there were multiple tragedies, including the deaths of two little girls, Paula Strong and Clare Hughes, who were killed by a bomb while playing outside in 1972.

Another major impact on the Sailortown community was the 1960s Urban Slum Clearance scheme. Plans for the redevelopment of the docklands included the demolition of the houses of Sailortown. The residents expected that they would return to new houses in the same area, as was the case in other parts of inner-city Belfast, but the Belfast Motorway Scheme intervened. Instead, to make way for the new motorway, the residents were moved to newly built estates sprawled across Belfast. Although many welcomed the prospect of the luxuries of modern houses, some of the residents left with great reluctance and sadness, knowing that they would probably never return. The relocation of the residents and the loss of employment, which equated to a search for employment elsewhere, hastened the depopulation of

Sailortown. John Campbell, a Sailortown local and a prolific writer of poetry and prose, described the loss of the community as 'its premature death, a bureaucratic disgrace' (Campbell 2009, preface). Eventually, by 2001, the iconic St Joseph's Church had been deconsecrated because of the diminishing population. The SRG now hold a 150-year lease on this church (Fig. 8.4).

Although the residents were relocated to different parts of Belfast, that strong Sailortown community spirit endures, with the former residents still convening at least once a week at St Joseph's Church. The ongoing events and projects conducted by the former residents, including the Dockers' annual cross-sectional commemorative service, boxing matches, charitable events and full participation in the UK's Heritage Open Day, are evidence of how this spirited community value their (now somewhat intangible) heritage and progressively endeavour to use the past to improve the future of the current residents. In 2009, 30 years after the original houses were demolished and the community dispersed, new social houses and apartments were constructed, bringing new residents to the streets of Sailortown. Unfortunately, this area lacked proper infrastructure and was plagued by high unemployment and anti-social incidents, making it an unhealthy environment for families and consequently resulting in a sense of disenfranchisement. Recently, however, a new master plan to reinvigorate Sailortown was launched (https://www.communities-ni.gov.uk/news/givan-launches-masterplan-reinvigorate-belfasts-greater-clarendon-sailortown-area).

COLLABORATION OF ACADEMIC AND COMMUNITY REPRESENTATIVES

Liz Thomas saw an opportunity for an archaeological excavation in this, until then, academically neglected area, and in 2013 she first met with a number of community representatives from the Shared Heritage Interpretative Project (SHIP), the Harbour Lights and the Sailortown Regeneration Group (SRG). The SRG was established to promote urban regeneration, to advance community development and for the relief of poverty, sickness and the aged in Sailortown (http://www.charitycommissionni.org.uk/charity-details/?regid=101870&subid=0, accessed 13 April 2018). Seán Baker, one of the founding members and the secretary of the SRG, was amongst the welcoming group of Sailortown representatives. It would be reasonable to say that up to this point the SRG had lost its faith in the academic

Fig. 8.5—Earl Street School, *c.* 1968/9—Miss O Dwyer with her Primary 1 class.

establishment, especially with regard to its quest to restore St Joseph's Church. Nearly thirteen years of campaigning to find funds for the refurbishment of the church had already passed. It may also be fair to say that Baker was wary of academics; he once told Thomas that 'the academics use' the Sailortown folk for their own benefit and then 'just leave'. Baker, a rough diamond who wore his heart on his sleeve and was an eloquent and colourful orator, was passionate about the people of Sailortown. Ultimately, his ambition, as a founding member of the SRG, was to make Sailortown a positive place for the new residents through endeavouring to provide a playground, a community hub and, fundamentally, its regeneration. Despite having been relocated in the 1960s, he was so dedicated to Sailortown that he returned to one of the new apartments that were built in 2009.

The SRG and Thomas agreed that the past was part of the future. In this case both a 'top-down' and a 'bottom-up' (Baker 2016, 37) approach was applied, whereby the academics and the community group met midway, seeing that an archaeological project would be mutually beneficial for research and impact and that the two parties could effectively apply the necessary

skills to enable this project, with the heritage being the conduit to connect the former and present residents of Sailortown.

THE EXCAVATION

The first and probably the most significant challenge to be met in organising this excavation was to secure funding. In 2014 Thomas was awarded a British Academy Postdoctoral Fellowship to conduct a historical-archaeological study of Sailortown, Belfast, 1800–1975, and this boosted Thomas's and the SRG's confidence to seek funding for the proposed excavation. The significance of a community-inclusive research excavation was not lost on the British Academy, the Leverhulme Trust and the Heritage Lottery, who all generously funded the costs of the excavation and the various aspects of the post-excavation project.

Finding a site to excavate in a heavily developed urban context was the next challenge. Two other excavations took place in 2007 (Licence Nos AE/07/24 and AE/07/51) in which 'nothing of an archaeological

Fig. 8.6—Short Street Compound.

nature was noted during the monitoring' and no further archaeological work was conducted (Heaney 2010; Ó Baoill 2011, 176, 179). Delightfully, Belfast Harbour kindly gave permission for use of their Short Street Compound, the site of former residential houses and the former listed Bonded Store (Fig. 8.6). The excavation commenced under Licence No. AE/15/82. Unfortunately, and unsurprisingly in a historical urban context, asbestos was discovered at the end of the first day. The excavation was immediately terminated for health and safety reasons.

The next challenge was to find another suitable site within this built-up urban environment. The SRG and QUB did not want to lose the interest of the public, which we had already engaged through organising a series of seminars in Sailortown over a period of six months; media coverage was widespread partly because this was a 'good news' story, which positively reduced costs for advertising the then proposed excavation. The first announcement of the excavation had been made in October 2014 (Thomas 2014), and to maintain the momentum and sense of excitement amongst the community a new site had to be found urgently (Figs 8.5 and 8.7).

Luckily, and not surprisingly, our saviour appeared in the form of another Sailortown man,

Kieran Quinn, a member of the SHIP and an 'amateur' historian whose research record would humble any established academic. He selflessly gave his time and effort to arrange for us to dig at the Dockers' Club. Now a yard, the new site formerly contained houses that in 1900 were typically two storeys high, with walls of red brick and roofs of slate. The average number of rooms, excluding the kitchen and basements, was four. These houses were described as 'old' in 1900 and were probably constructed approximately 1859–65 (PRONI, Belfast Re-Valuation Records Fieldbooks 1900, VAL/7/B/4/17; VAL/7/A/31/1 Sheet 23; The Belfast and Province of Ulster Directories).

So the dig was on again! Generally, the archaeological excavation went swimmingly, as (to our relief) no further asbestos was discovered. Members of the public visited the site daily, and contracted archaeologists from the CAF (the Centre for Archaeological Fieldwork, QUB) guided those people interested in excavating. Other visitors just wished to observe and to share their memories. Ultimately, the archaeology itself was not very surprising. The research focus was the exploration of household archaeology and household structures in an urban-maritime settlement. Partial walls and floor surfaces from within one of the former houses were exposed and over 600

Fig. 8.7—Former Sailortown residents.

artefacts, fragments of ceramics, glass, metalwork and slate dating from the nineteenth, twentieth and 21st centuries were recovered.

The most exciting aspect of the excavation was the visitors from across Belfast, Ireland and even from the US who shared their memories of living in Sailortown. Comments included: 'I want to be an archaeologist when I grow up'; 'I lived here till 1968'; 'No connection, except one of us cycles past it often'; 'Glad to see some interest in old Sailortown'; 'Significant development; needs more funding'; 'Very interesting!'; 'Family worked in the Docks'; and 'Pity it can't have been on longer for more people to see!'

The discovery and handling of the many household artefacts sparked great debates amongst the visitors. Old 'Harp' bottle tops triggered memories of authentic beers and the Troubles, while oyster shells got others talking about how they used to fish down at the docks. Some of the metalwork found, in particular

Fig. 8.8—Artefacts from the Sailortown trench.

a piece from an old sash window, reminded people of the old houses. Ultimately, the artefacts yielded unexpected stories of a past life and community, childhood memories of the area, descriptions of various buildings and streets, former schools, eminent characters of the area, social activities and much more. Archaeology, in this case, had successfully reconnected people with Sailortown's past (Fig. 8.8).

Poignantly in view of the comment cited above, 'Pity it can't have been on longer for more people to see!', people continued to visit the site long after the archaeological project had ended. The discovery of asbestos on the first site had made a heavy impact on the budget—hence the short duration of the Dockers' Club excavation. There were further activities, however, which enabled those who missed the excavation to participate in other ways. A 'Celebration Night' was held in the Dockers' Club in April 2016 and many of the former and present residents turned up to learn about and celebrate the excavation, and a public lecture was presented at the Public Records Office with an unprecedented turnout: apparently, for the first time, audience members had to be refused entry because the venue was 'sold out'. Furthermore, the SRG, the SHIP and QUB collaboratively designed two different exhibitions that showcased this Sailortown excavation. One of the exhibitions was placed on the wall of the Old Dockers' Club whilst the other, a portable pop-up, is in continuous use by the SRG at St Joseph's Church and across other venues.

SUMMARY

This small-scale excavation made manifest the challenges, opportunities, impact and indirect benefits delivered by such heritage projects. Ultimately, the objectives of Sailortown's community-inclusive research excavation were achieved: it reconnected people from all across Belfast with Sailortown's past; it connected new and former Sailortown residents through this shared heritage; and it informed new visitors to the area of Sailortown's rich heritage. The two exhibitions are in continuous use and will be incorporated into a planned tourism trail. Finally, it provided a platform for future regeneration of the area. For example, an indirect positive impact has been the new attention given to St Joseph's Church, possibly partly owing to the media coverage of the excavation and the Sailortown area. One current resident commented that 'It is good that Sailortown is getting attention again'. Since then the SRG have successfully secured funding towards the church's restoration and refurbishment. Other heritage projects are ongoing in addition to the regeneration master plan for Sailortown, which was launched in 2016.

Moreover, this collaborative academic/ community project resulted in opportunities to work with and engage wider participation from key local stakeholders, such as Belfast Harbour and Belfast City Council, which contributed to reaching a successful end to the project stretching beyond the archaeological excavation to longer-term positive benefits to the community. None of these objectives, nor the archaeological excavation itself, would have been achieved, however, without the support of the Sailortown community, and in particular the representatives from the SRG and the SHIP.

Whilst it was a successful project, the authors of this paper contend that one of its major challenges was engagement of the present young residents of Sailortown. Just 10% of the visitors were children and none of the children from Sailortown participated on the Dockers' Club site. The finding of asbestos on the first site and its reporting in one of the local newspapers may account for their absence. Another reason may simply have been that the second excavation was held on the site of a public house, which may have been viewed by some parents and guardians as an inappropriate place for children. The Dockers' Club is renowned, however, for its cross-community status and perhaps its reputation may have encouraged the participation of people from different backgrounds, cultures and ages. Another challenge was finding funding to extend the excavation to last beyond two weeks. Disappointingly, this was not achievable at such short notice. With hindsight we agree that such costs should have been incorporated into the budget.

This project provided an opportunity for academics and the community to work productively and cohesively together; this co-authored chapter is testimony to the good working relationship developed over the years, and together we continue to explore various avenues by which heritage can have a positive impact on the former and present residents of Sailortown.

ACKNOWLEDGEMENTS

This archaeological project was made possible through the kind support of many individuals and groups, in particular Kieran Quinn (SHIP), Patrick Benson and Seán Baker (SRG), Brian McCann and Terry Ward (the Dockers' Club), Bernadette Baker (Harbour Lights), Belfast Harbour, Belfast City Council, Queen's University Belfast, the Northern Ireland Environment Agency, the Sailortown Regeneration Group and the Shared History Interpretative Project. The costs of the excavation were generously funded by the British Academy, the Leverhulme Small Research Grants Award and the Heritage Lottery 'Sharing Heritage' grant (QUB in partnership with the SRG).

REFERENCES

Baker, C. 2016 Community archaeology: more questions than answers. *Archaeology Ireland* **30** (3), 37–40.

Campbell, J. 2009 *Once there was a community here: a Sailortown miscellany*. Lagan Press, Belfast.

Heaney, L. 2010 Pilot Street, Belfast. In I. Bennett (ed.), *Excavations 2007: summary accounts of archaeological excavations in Ireland,* 5. Wordwell, Bray.

Ó Baoill, R. 2011 *Hidden history below our feet: the archaeological story of Belfast.* Northern Ireland Environment Agency and Belfast City Council, Belfast.

Thomas, L. 2014 Down at the docks: excavations in Sailortown. *Archaeology Ireland* **28** (4), 31–3.

Thomas, L. 2014–17 Collection of as-yet-unpublished oral histories from former Sailortown residents collected as part of Thomas's British Academy Postdoctoral Fellowship (BAPDF).

Online sources

'Dockers Club in Belfast to mark 40th anniversary with a sing song': https://www.irishnews.com/news/ 2018/02/15/news/dockers-club-in-belfast-to-mark-40th-anniversary-with-sing-song-event-12 55999/, accessed 9 April 2018.

'Givan launches masterplan to reinvigorate Belfast's Greater Clarendon (Sailortown) Area': https://www.communities-ni.gov.uk/news/givan-launches-masterplan-reinvigorate-belfasts-greater-clarendon-sailortown-area, accessed 9 April 2018.

'Sailortown Regeneration Group': http://www.charity commissionni.org.uk/charity-details/?regid= 101870&subid=0, accessed 9 April 2018.

9. Community archaeology and the Hill of Slane

CONOR BRADY

ABSTRACT

This paper gives an overview of the community engagement and involvement with the Hill of Slane, from its ongoing use for religious purposes to recent uses as a venue for unique spectacular events and its role in promoting Slane village as a tourist destination. The central role of the Hill of Slane as one of the key contributors to the character of the village is discussed. The relationship between the local community and the Brú na Bóinne World Heritage Site is also explored, and it is strongly suggested that the significant potential offered by the visitor numbers to the World Heritage Site be investigated in order to generate a creative vision for the tourism and economic development of the region and for the benefit of the local communities. The results of a recent geophysical survey, which was a community archaeological initiative carried out by the Hill of Slane Archaeological Project in collaboration with the Hill of Slane Volunteer Guides' service, are also presented.

INTRODUCTION

The Hill of Slane has long been a focus of interest for people from the Slane community and for visitors from farther afield, perhaps because of its prominent position on the skyline of east Meath but also because of its close traditional association with St Patrick. The silhouette of the ruins on the Hill of Slane is well known to the many travellers on the N2 Dublin–Derry road, which passes close to the site (Figs 9.1 and 9.2). While there is good historical source material relating to activity at the site, it has been established recently that there has also been considerable prehistoric activity there (Brady and Barton 2014; Brady *et al.* 2013; Seaver and Brady 2011; Trench 1995; Westropp 1901). Indeed, it can be argued that the siting of the original monastery at Slane, founded sometime before AD 512 by Erc, was very carefully chosen to capitalise on this prominence and perhaps partly because the site was already a centre for ceremony and ritual (Fig. 9.3). The monastery was active at least until the eleventh century, when the first stone church on the site was

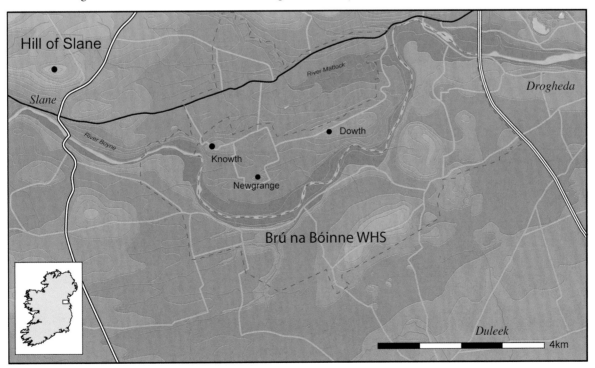

Fig. 9.1—Location map of the Hill of Slane.

constructed, and in the late twelfth century it appears to have been converted to function as the medieval parish church by Richard de Fleming on his arrival as the new lord (Manning 1998).

The construction of Chantry College along with further modifications to the church followed under the patronage of the Fleming family and the church ultimately became the Church of Ireland place of worship for the area, being abandoned in the early eighteenth century when St Patrick's Church of Ireland church was constructed on Main Street in the village. Since this time there appears to have been little activity on the hill, and Beranger's two images of the Hill of Slane, painted in the eighteenth century, depict clearly abandoned and ruined buildings. A third image survives which depicts some architectural details—a font and *in situ* window mouldings (Harbison 1998, 16, 150–3). Beranger appears to have been working at the time with William Burton Conyngham to produce an illustrated record of the principal antiquities of Ireland. William Burton Conyngham lived in Slane Castle and was responsible for designing and overseeing the construction of the village in its present form.

THE COMMUNITY AND THE HILL OF SLANE

The Hill of Slane remains a focus of devotional activity today, with services being held on the hill on St Patrick's Day and, weather permitting, a re-enactment of the

Fig. 9.2—Statue of St Patrick on the Hill of Slane.

Fig. 9.3—Aerial view of the Hill of Slane.

lighting of the paschal fire each Easter Saturday. In 1932, as part of the Eucharistic Congress held in Ireland that year, a Mass was celebrated on the Hill of Slane. It is reported that between 50,000 and 60,000 people attended this event, which was presided over by Cardinal McRory and attended by the taoiseach of the day, Éamon de Valera. In 1961 ceremonies were held on the Hill of Slane to commemorate the 1,500th anniversary of the death of St Patrick, and in the millennium year the principal Holy Year celebration for the Diocese of Meath was conducted on the hill, with 15,000 attending the event. In 2012 the 50th International Eucharistic Congress was celebrated in Dublin and a special Mass was celebrated on the hill by Bishop Smith (Deegan 2012; Wall 2012).

The graveyard, which is now under the management of the local authority, Meath County Council, is still actively used for burials by those families with established plots, and there is a 'blessing of the graves' ceremony held each year in tandem with that at the newer St Erc's cemetery on the main road at the foot of the Hill of Slane.

Today the site is visited regularly by a mix of Irish local people and independent tourists as well as some tour groups. Like most other heritage sites, the bulk of the visits happen during the summer season between May and October, but at other times of the year there is often a steady stream of all types of visitors. Many of the visitors, particularly tourists, also visit the Brú na Bóinne Visitor Centre, which lies c. 8km to the east of Slane. The centre was constructed amid some controversy to provide a mechanism to channel and manage the increasing numbers of visitors to Newgrange in order to reduce the impact on the monument. Prior to the opening of the visitor centre at Staleen on the southern bank of the River Boyne, Slane was one of the main gateways to the World Heritage Site (WHS). Many of the businesses in the village prospered on the basis of the footfall that was created by passing visitors. On the opening of the centre in 1997 the drop in visitor numbers in Slane was dramatic and noticeable and this contributed to the closure of a number of businesses in the village, including the hotel, the Conyngham Arms.

Local experience is that the well-publicised WHS acts as a 'honey-pot' attracting large numbers of visitors, very few of whom spend any further time in the area, thus reducing any potential positive impact for the local community. The potential positive effects of the impressive tourist numbers to the centre are therefore significantly diluted. Looking from a slightly different perspective, however, it can be argued that

this represents an opportunity to increase activity in the region. Although there is a welcome section on sustainable tourism, the current Brú na Bóinne WHS Management Plan contains no statement of vision for using the WHS as an economic driver for the wider region—perhaps this is not the best place for such a vision to be set out—but it is perhaps telling that the responses to such suggestions in the appendices outlining points raised during the consultation process prior to the drafting of the management plan seem to present direct employment of local people as guides and groundspeople by the Office of Public Works (OPW) as sufficient to address this issue. The current management plan recognises the key role of communities and that their involvement is critical to the plan's success.

Although the hotel in Slane has now reopened, there is little focus on developing the opportunities created by the WHS for the benefit of local host communities in line with UNESCO's vision for appropriate economic development in the regions surrounding World Heritage Sites (see discussions in Gómez Arriola 2014; Rofe et al. 2011; Landorf 2009; Li Wu and Ca 2008; Boniface 1995). Significant difficulties are perceived by local people in relation to obtaining planning permission within and in the wider vicinity of the WHS, which, cumulatively, has led to a distinct lack of goodwill towards the idea of the WHS (see, for example, Reilly 2012). The local residents of the WHS, represented by the Boyne Valley Consultative Committee, have had ongoing difficulties with the authorities, particularly in relation to planning. This issue is also having a significant effect on similar applications as far west as the outskirts of Slane village itself, and negative attitudes to the WHS further increased following Bord Pleanála's rejection of Meath County Council's application to build a bypass of Slane village. Local people feel that they are shouldering a significant cost of the WHS in terms of the restrictions and have yet to see any positive return for themselves or their neighbours. Perhaps a second management plan, properly resourced and implemented, is required, similar to the 1996 Brady Shipman Martin *Boyne Valley Integrated Development Plan*, involving all relevant authorities and stakeholders in order to use the WHS as an economic driver for the Boyne Valley region?

In this context the Slane Community Forum has been working to provide a vision for the future development of Slane. The Forum, an umbrella group representing the interests of all social, cultural and sporting groups in the Slane area, held a number of public 'town hall' meetings to generate a list of

Fig. 9.4—'The Flame of Slane', 2013.

priorities to direct their activities in re-establishing Slane as one of the key nodes in the Boyne Valley region. As part of this new strategy, the Forum recognised the strategic position of Slane village at the heart of the Boyne Valley region as well as the value of the village as a heritage destination, on the doorstep of the WHS yet with very distinct heritage of its own. One of the key sites in the area was the Hill of Slane, and it was realised that this would play an important part in any strategy promoting the village as a destination. The strong connections with St Patrick and the Hill of Tara, as well as its close proximity to the Brú na Bóinne WHS, served to firmly integrate the site into the wider Boyne Valley. This has happily been underlined by Fáilte Ireland's inclusion of the site, albeit in small print (probably because of the lack of visitor facilities at the site), on the Boyne Valley Drive map. Furthermore, according to the *Boyne Valley Tourism Strategy 2016– 2020*, the Hill of Slane, along with Newgrange, Knowth, Loughcrew and the Hill of Tara, has been identified in a review of the infrastructure of the Boyne Valley as one of the key 'signature sites' where visitor facilities can be upgraded and a consistent tourism experience can be provided (Boyne Valley Tourism 2016, 19).

In recent times the Slane community has taken a

proactive approach to some of the opportunities offered by the Hill of Slane in generating local pride and interest in the site, as well as the possibility of using it to 'put Slane on the tourist map'. In an attempt to achieve these goals, a number of unusual one-off events have been staged on the hill. In 2012 and 2013 a local group came together to stage a spectacular event titled the 'Flame of Slane'. This took the form of a pageant designed by a specialist landscape spectacle company, LUXe, who took the theme of the lighting of the paschal fire as inspiration for a lavish participative event which was attended by over 2,000 people. In 2013 a similar spectacular show was devised and staged on the hill as part of the Gathering festival. The show was attended by over 4,000 people and comprised music, dance, a homage to the poet Francis Ledwidge (a native of Slane who was killed in World War I), a mini-re-enactment of the Battle of the Boyne, a staging of the story of the Salmon of Knowledge, a pagan wedding and a spectacular fireworks display (Fig. 9.4).

More interest was focused on the story of the Hill of Slane when the site was featured in the RTÉ series *Creedon's Epic East*, produced in 2016 and presented by John Creedon, which covered visits to a selection of sites in the region defined by Fáilte Ireland as 'Ireland's

Fig. 9.5—The bonfire lit for the *Creedon's Epic East* programme.

Epic East'. The programme's producers had the idea of testing the old legend of St Patrick lighting the first paschal fire to see whether a fire lit on the Hill of Slane could be seen from the Hill of Tara, almost 16km to the south-east. They contacted some of the people who had been involved in the 'Flame of Slane' event and asked them to arrange to light a bonfire on the hill. A location for the fire was chosen in consultation with the OPW, owner of the land on which the College stands, and the owner of the adjacent land, and it was agreed to light the fire on the southern slope of the hill about 30m from the gate of the graveyard, on privately owned land in a field that is normally used for grazing cattle. Unfortunately, the area chosen was in a location where geophysical survey had not already taken place, and it is possible that the results of any future magnetic survey there would be compromised by the lighting of this bonfire (Fig. 9.5). John Creedon and a film crew observed from the Hill of Tara as darkness fell, and later joined the large group that had gathered around the bonfire on the Hill of Slane. Creedon dramatically revealed the result of the experiment during the filming: the bonfire had been clearly visible to the observers on the Hill of Tara. As there is a direct line of sight between the Hill of Slane and the Hill of Tara,

this came as little surprise to the locals. For the local community, this event was a further positive reinforcement of the value and importance of the heritage represented by the Hill of Slane.

In tandem with these developments, the Hill of Slane Archaeological Project was initiated in order to bring a new research focus to the Hill of Slane and to produce new material and new knowledge to help tell the story of activity on the hill through the ages. Furthermore, it was hoped that the research activity on the monument complex would provide opportunities to promote the site to the public and generate a new interest in it.

THE HILL OF SLANE ARCHAEOLOGICAL PROJECT

Archaeological research on the Hill of Slane has been under way since 2010 under the banner of the Hill of Slane Archaeological Project. Several areas have been surveyed using a variety of geophysical techniques over a number of separate phases. The initial surveys focused on the motte at the western end of the complex and investigated its structure to see whether it represented a remodelling of an earlier monument like a passage tomb. The bulk of the monument seems to have been constructed in one single phase, with the mound material having been generated from the digging of the surrounding ditch (Seaver and Brady 2011; Brady *et al.* 2013).

Electrical resistivity tomography (ERT) was used to image the interior of the mound. Although there are references in folklore and mythology to the existence of a burial mound on the summit of the Hill of Slane, the ERT survey did not reveal clear indications of any such feature beneath the current mound (Seaver and Brady 2011). It is possible, however, that the mound may have been constructed on a smaller earthen feature or barrow, particularly as there appears to be an extant barrow with a diameter of 30m immediately to the south-east of the motte, with a portion of a second example having been identified by geophysical survey immediately to the north-east of this. An amorphous high-resistance feature was identified on the summit of the motte, possibly representing the remains of a stone feature that once stood there (*ibid.*; Brady *et al.* 2013).

The area of the barrow was surveyed using magnetic gradiometry, earth resistance and magnetic susceptibility. A clear relationship between the barrow and the circular enclosure surrounding the motte had been established from analysis of Ordnance Survey of Ireland LiDAR data, and this was confirmed by the subsequent geophysical surveys.

Magnetic gradiometry, earth resistance and magnetic susceptibility surveys were carried out in the area of the College and identified a range of features, including linear ditch-like features and linear arrangements of pits or post-holes. Bedrock was found to be close to the ground surface, particularly to the west of the College. To the east of the College the magnetic gradiometry survey encountered problems because of the presence of floodlights and an electrical cable from the car park at the eastern end of the site (Brady *et al.* 2012; 2013).

FIELD SCHOOL

In 2012 a remote-sensing field school was held on the Hill of Slane for postgraduate students of archaeology. This course involved introductory tuition and hands-on experience of a variety of survey and other data-capture techniques, including field-walking, surveying, magnetic susceptibility, metal-detecting, earth resistance, magnetic gradiometry, ground-penetrating radar, ERT, terrestrial laser scanning and

kite aerial photography (Fig. 9.6). The main focus for the geophysical survey was a series of 20m x 20m panels set out between the gates of the graveyard and the car park. A series of features were identified which seem to correspond to archaeological deposits recorded during archaeological monitoring of the cable trench for the floodlighting that was dug in 1993 (Brady and Barton 2014).

This event was very successful, and very positive feedback was received from the participating students. A further bonus for the longer-term archaeological project was that new, good-quality survey datasets were generated over the course of the week despite the lack of experience of the student participants.

Another benefit of the field school was that it generated a lot of interest in the local community. The event was well publicised locally and an invitation was issued for people to come and visit the hill during the survey. Many visitors expressed feelings of pride in the site. Coverage of the event by RTÉ News helped to further reinforce the importance of the hill, while also promoting Slane and the archaeology of the Hill of Slane to a national audience.

GUIDED TOURS ON THE HILL OF SLANE

A voluntary tour guide group was set up in 2014 to provide free tours to visitors to the Hill of Slane, and the first tours were given during Heritage Week of that year. Volunteers are members of the local community and the initiative builds on the work started by the Hill of Slane Archaeological Project (Fig. 9.7). The tour was designed to include a variety of published historical and archaeological information, as well as incorporating more local and community-based knowledge. Material generated by the archaeological surveys was also included in the tour.

Since 2015 tours have been available to casual visitors to the hill each weekend and bank holiday between early May and early October. A particular effort is made at the time of Heritage Week each year, when there are tours available on each day of the week. Although most tour group operators seem to prefer to deliver their own information on the site to their patrons despite the tours being offered free, groups are facilitated outside these times by prior arrangement. We have a number of school groups that visit each year, particularly the local national school in Slane. The guides have maintained a record of the numbers catered for on the tours and, although referring only to times when tours are held, these are a strong indication

Fig. 9.6—Students on the Hill of Slane archaeological survey and geophysics field school.

of the popularity of the site (Fig. 9.8). It is hoped to increase the number of volunteer guides in the group over time so that there can be a more continuous presence on the site, at least during the summer season.

2015 GEOPHYSICS

The survey carried out in 2015 had two main aims. The first was the archaeological objective of extending the knowledge created by the earlier surveys. The second was community-orientated and was intended to give the newly formed Hill of Slane volunteer guides group a hands-on stake in the production of archaeological data, as well as an understanding of the process of archaeological survey and the nature of archaeological data. Six guides took part in the programme, which consisted of an introductory evening presentation followed by two days of fieldwork on the site. The introductory presentation outlined the approaches taken on the site prior to 2015, explaining the reasons for the 2015 survey and the approach that would be taken on site. The survey was designed so that the guides themselves would be the ones carrying out the

Fig. 9.7—The volunteer guides on the Hill of Slane.

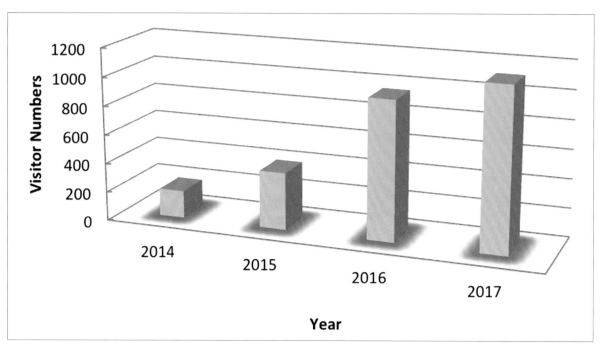

Fig. 9.8—Chart showing visitor numbers to the Hill of Slane, 2014–17.

Fig. 9.9—Some of the guides undertaking geophysical survey.

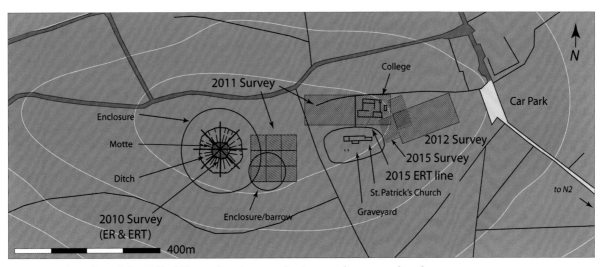

Fig. 9.10—Site plan of the Hill of Slane, showing geophysics panels surveyed to date.

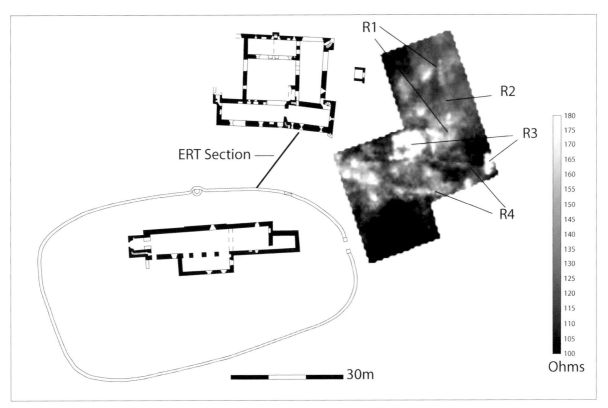

Fig. 9.11—Earth resistance plot with main anomalies indicated. Location of ERT line also indicated.

fieldwork. It was decided to use three geophysical survey techniques: earth resistance, magnetic susceptibility and ERT. These were chosen because of their ease of use for beginners (Fig. 9.9). The geophysical training survey was carried out under licence from the National Monuments Service, Department of Culture, Heritage and the Gaeltacht, and the results presented here are based on the report by Kevin Barton (2015) arising from the survey.

Grid location and set-out

The geophysical survey panels were positioned to add to the geophysical datasets gathered in previous phases of surveying, i.e. in 2011 and 2012 (Fig. 9.10). They were carefully positioned to create a clear connection between the previous survey areas and to help to create a more continuous suite of data. It was considered particularly desirable to survey in the area immediately to the east of the gates into the graveyard, as this was

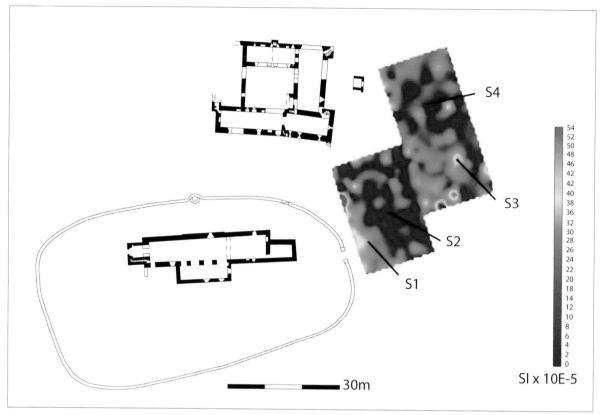

Fig. 9.12—Magnetic susceptibility plot with main anomalies indicated.

considered likely to be a rich area of archaeological potential, certainly more so than the ground further downslope to the east, closer to the car park, which had already been surveyed in 2012. To this end, three 20m x 20m panels were laid out, as well as a further two 10m x 10m panels. Grid points were established using a dGPS system, and the panels themselves were laid out using tapes.

Earth resistance survey

This technique measures the level of difficulty with which an electrical current flows through soil and will identify differences in moisture content in the soil that may be related to the presence of subsurface archaeological features. Earth resistance measurements were taken using a TR/CIA Earth Resistance Meter at 0.5m intervals along each line within each panel. The depth of investigation of the instrument is 0.5–0.75m. The survey results with the principal features identified are indicated in Fig. 9.11.

- R1—indicates two high-resistance linear features, which are interpreted as wall foundations. The features are both aligned north-north-east/south-south-west and may form a boundary wall.

- R2—indicates a significant gap in the features indicated as R1. This may be a break in the walls or an entrance.
- R3—These are two significant high-resistance features, which may be building foundations.
- R4—This indicated two higher-resistance linear features extending in an east-south-east/west-south-west direction, which may relate to an approach route or roadway to the College.

There are other, higher-resistance features not annotated in Fig. 9.11 that may relate to structures or foundations. The area looks to be positive for subsurface archaeology.

Magnetic susceptibility survey

This technique measures the ability of the soil to become magnetised. Where enhancement is identified, it can indicate burning or burnt material or midden material—all associated with settlement and other human activity—incorporated into the soil. The survey was carried out using a Bartington MS2 magnetic susceptibility meter with an MS2D field loop. The loop diameter was 18cm, giving a depth of investigation of about 10cm. The survey was carried out over the same

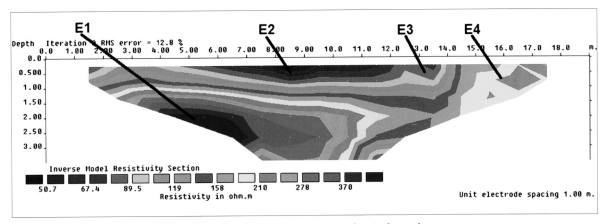

Fig. 9.13—Electrical resistivity tomography plot with main anomalies indicated.

panels as described above on a 2m x 2m grid. The survey results with the principal features identified are indicated in Fig. 9.12.

- S1—A zone of enhancement associated with the graveyard entrance. The enhancement may be due to heavy footfall, soil disturbance and ferrous litter.
- S2—A zone of relatively low enhancement, perhaps reflecting the natural topsoil in the area.
- S3—Three isolated 'spots' of high enhancement. These could be due to modern ferrous items.
- S4—A zone of relatively low enhancement, perhaps reflecting the natural topsoil in the area.

There appears to be datum shift between the adjacent grids, possibly owing to different surveyors exercising different downward pressure of the field loop on the ground surface.

Electrical resistivity tomography

The last technique to be used was ERT. Rather than producing map or plan outputs, this technique generates modelled depth or pseudo-sections looking vertically downwards along a line set out between two end points. A 20m-long line was positioned between the door of the College and the graveyard and an electrode spacing of 1m was used, which gave a depth of investigation of 3m (see Fig. 9.11 for location). This line was positioned to investigate the make-up of the sloping ground between these two features. It is suspected that much of the material in this feature may consist of rubble from the upper courses of the College, and it was considered desirable to establish exactly where original ground level was located. It was not possible to position a 20m line at right angles to the wall of the College, so the line was set out at an angle; 20m was the minimum linear distance that could be used with the equipment available. The topographic profile of the ERT line was recorded manually using a dumpy level. The survey results with the principal features identified are indicated in Fig. 9.13.

- E1—A high-resistance zone likely to be due to shallow or weathered bedrock.
- E2—A significant zone of low resistance, interpreted as soil.
- E3—Possible evidence of a narrow ditch, which is postulated to be associated with the College.
- E4—A higher-resistance zone possibly related to the foundations of the College.

CONCLUSION

There is a widespread realisation on the part of the local community that Slane and its hinterland are particularly richly endowed with features of heritage interest. As the village functions largely as a dormer or commuter settlement, however, the level of knowledge about the local heritage is often low, particularly among those who have moved to the area in recent times. Even among long-standing members of the community, the attitude to the heritage of the area is often one of indifference, and as one approaches the WHS this can, on occasion, develop into outright antipathy. The various initiatives that have been undertaken in Slane over the past number of years have been an attempt to demonstrate to local communities that the heritage of the area is as much theirs as anyone else's; that it is not something negative; that they have options open to them, created by this heritage; and that they should be the drivers or key partners in these initiatives. The challenge is to create sustainable tourism offerings that will allow local communities to take ownership of and benefit from their heritage, with appropriate positive creative supports at local authority and State levels.

The archaeological research project outlined here was successful in its objectives. It has contributed further to archaeological knowledge about the development of the hill while at the same time giving a local stakeholder group an insight into the nature of archaeological remains, their significance and the archaeological research process. Related media coverage was also positive in reinforcing the value of their heritage. The survey has given the guides a degree of confidence in being able to talk about the site to visitors. Such small-scale surveys are relatively cheap to conduct and can have significant impacts. It is possible that a programme of similar small-scale projects might form the basis of a plan to engage and explain key issues to local communities in sensitive areas like the WHS.

ACKNOWLEDGEMENTS

The 2015 training survey was funded by a community grant from the Heritage Council, which is gratefully acknowledged. I am also grateful for the assistance of the Slane Community Forum in administering the grant. The training was provided by Kevin Barton of Landscape and Geophysical Services. We gratefully acknowledge the permission granted to us by the Office of Public Works to carry out the survey on the site, and we thank Ana Dolan in particular for facilitating this.

REFERENCES

Barton, K. 2015 Archaeological and geophysical survey training on the Hill of Slane for the Hill of Slane tour guides. Unpublished report for Slane Community Forum.

Boniface, P. 1995 *Managing quality cultural tourism.* Routledge, London.

Boyne Valley Tourism 2016 *Boyne Valley Tourism Strategy 2016–2020* (http://www.discover boynevalley.ie/sites/default/files/Boyne-Valley-Tourism-Strategy.pdf; accessed 7 April 2018).

Brady, C. and Barton, K. 2014 Lasers, cameras, action! *Archaeology Ireland* **107**, 39–42.

Brady, C., Barton, K. and Seaver, M. 2012 The Hill of Slane Archaeological Project (HoSAP). Unpublished report for the Department of Arts, Heritage and the Gaeltacht Environment Fund.

Brady, C., Barton, K. and Seaver, M. 2013 Recent geophysical investigations and LiDAR analysis at the Hill of Slane, Co. Meath. *Ríocht na Midhe* **24**, 134–55.

Brady Shipman Martin 1996 *Boyne Valley Integrated Development Plan.* Brady Shipman Martin, Dublin.

Deegan, Fr J. 2012 The Hill of Slane celebrates faith, past and future (http://www.dioceseofmeath.ie/news?news_id=83; accessed 7 April 2018).

Gómez Arriola, I. 2014 Sustainable tourism and local communities in the Agave landscape of Tequila. *World Heritage Review* **71**, 2–39.

Harbison, P. (ed.) 1998 *Drawings of the principal antique buildings of Ireland: National Library of Ireland MS 1958 TX / Gabriel Beranger.* Four Courts Press/National Library of Ireland, Dublin.

Landorf, C. 2009 Managing for sustainable tourism: a review of six cultural World Heritage Sites. *Journal of Sustainable Tourism* **17** (1), 53–70 (https://www.tandfonline.com/doi/abs/10.1080/09669580802159719; accessed 7 April 2018).

Li, M., Wu, B. and Cai, L. 2008 Tourism development of World Heritage Sites in China: a geographic perspective. *Tourism Management* **29** (2), 308–19.

Manning, C. 1998 A pre-Romanesque church at Slane. *Peritia* **20**, 346–52.

Reilly, J. 2012 Locals lose out in 'dead zone' of heritage centre: Bru na Boinne visitors bypass Slane—traffic goes straight through (https://www.independent.ie/irish-news/locals-lose-out-in-dead-zone-of-heritage-centre-26833369.html; accessed 7 April 2018).

Rofe, M., Mohamed, D. and Marzuki, A. 2011 The complexities of social sustainability: balancing tradition and change in a UNESCO World Heritage site. In P.E.J. Roetman and C.B. Daniels (eds), *Creating sustainable communities in a changing world*, 95–102. Crawford House Publishing, Adelaide.

Seaver, M. and Brady, C. 2011 *Hill of Slane.* Archaeology Ireland Heritage Guide 55. Wordwell, Dublin.

Trench, C.E.F. 1995 *Slane: Slane Town Trail, Newgrange* (3rd edn). An Taisce, Slane.

Wall, S. 2012 Local notes: Slane (https://www.independent.ie/regionals/droghedaindependent/localnotes/slane-27169147.html; accessed 7 April 2018).

Westropp, T.J. 1901 Slane in Bregia, County Meath: its friary and hermitage. *Journal of the Royal Society of Antiquaries of Ireland* **31** (4), 404–30.

10. Community archaeology in the Sliabh Aughty uplands

CHRISTY CUNNIFFE

ABSTRACT

Through working with communities in the Sliabh Aughty uplands a suite of previously unrecorded archaeology has been recovered, adding to the extensive prehistoric layer already identified through the work of the Archaeological Survey of Ireland. Evidence for transhumance or booleying has emerged, and a completely new and unexpected layer of archaeology that can be directly associated with the migration of displaced Ulster Catholics in the aftermath of the Battle of the Diamond has been discovered. Local community involvement has been central to the success of this project.

This short paper is not intended to be an examination of the theoretical framework underpinning community archaeology or a commentary on the subdiscipline in general, but simply a review of some of the outcomes of fieldwork and research in and around the Galway section of the Sliabh Aughty uplands undertaken under the auspices of the Galway Field Monument Advisor, now the Galway Community Archaeology Advisory Project.

The Sliabh Aughty area has been quite silent in relation to the discovery of new archaeology. Several clusters of megalithic tombs, standing stones and related prehistoric monuments across the mountain are recorded in the Record of Monuments and Places (RMP), and a medieval zone was identified at a lower level, represented by the presence of a mix of ringforts, tower-houses, ruined parish churches, a religious house and a number of other contemporary sites, but for the most part the uplands appear to be empty. The time spent by the Community Archaeologist working with various communities and individuals in the Sliabh Aughty area has changed that fact, however, challenging this previously held misconception. Several new layers of archaeology in the landscape have been identified, leading to the development of a much greater appreciation and awareness of archaeology in general in the Sliabh Aughty region.

An interesting aspect of working in the realm of community archaeology is the friendships that one develops with individuals who share a common interest in human settlement patterns and historic landscapes. Local knowledge is a key component in finding hitherto unrecorded features in the landscape.

My first foray into the uplands was with Kevin Cunningham, an avid hillwalker and heritage and community activist from Kilchreest, a village at the foot of the mountain, south of Loughrea. Our initial discussion about the perceived lack of upland features took place after the winning of two awards by the Kilchreest/Castledaly Heritage Group at the Galway Golden Mile Awards in 2012. This initiative is similar in many ways to the Tidy Towns programme but is instead focused on a rural mile. After the ceremony we had a brief discussion about the absence of built heritage and archaeological features in their submission. Kevin related that there were all sorts of interesting features to be seen on the commonage but that they were too far removed from the chosen mile to be included in the application. Of course, the next step was to see this material firsthand for myself, so we arranged to undertake a stint of upland walking. This was to lead to repeated visits to those same uplands at regular intervals over the next two years. The initial outing was revealing, as we visited a deserted clachan and its associated rundale field system (Fig. 10.1). As we began to explore this landscape, we found hut sites associated with booleying, evidence of millstone manufacturing, the presence of stone-built turf stacks used for drying turf, limekilns, road systems and numerous other features, all associated with an earlier layer of settlement. This led to the discovery of an aspect of upland settlement completely forgotten about and not previously recorded (Cunniffe and Cunningham 2013).

On the back of this fieldwork we organised a series of public lectures, creating greater archaeological

Fig. 10.1—Kilnagappagh clachan settlement and its associated rundale field system in the uplands near Kilchreest.

awareness at local level. Each of the lectures was well attended and well received. In addition, the community held a weekend festival, *Féile na Sleibhte*, which included a one-day conference focused on the archaeology, geology, ecology and history of the Kilchreest uplands. This was a remarkable success and an example of how community-based archaeology can be a key influence for success.

Fieldwork continues around Sliabh Aughty. Following the success in Kilchreest, it was felt that a similar spate of fieldwork involving local volunteers should take place further east in the uplands around Woodford and Ballinakill in the region overlooking Lough Derg. The Field Monument Advisor/ Community Archaeologist once again sought out local activists and interested hill farmers. Similar to the situation in Kilchreest, there was no shortage of volunteers in Woodford. My good friend the late Dermot Moran was of huge importance to the project (Fig. 10.2). His knowledge of and love for the uplands and their many secrets were immense and inspiring. His death is a huge loss to the upland communities. He introduced the Community Archaeologist to numerous people and to out-of-the-way places where he had seen features of interest. In a similar fashion to

what took place in the Kilchreest area, the Community Archaeologist organised information courses for local people interested in learning about their archaeology and kept them abreast of what was happening by means of public talks and field trips. The goodwill generated amongst the local farmers is very important. A key aspect of successful fieldwork and field research is that it is undertaken with the consent and support of the landowners or others with an interest in the land in question. Though the upland areas are usually divided into commonage, this does not mean that they are freely accessible but rather that the land is held in commonage by a set number of farmers. Obtaining permission is essential; it is first of all good manners, and it also removes any possible tensions that may arise in relation to trespass.

Fieldwork undertaken on the commonage in the townland of Derryoober following a discussion with Michael Walsh has led to the discovery of a landscape literally alive with traces of past agricultural practice. From the archaeological and cultural evidence we know that the commonage was once used as a booley place (Cunniffe 2016). A spring well, known as the butter well, occurs in the townland—a reference to the practice of butter-making during the seasonal booley.

Fig. 10.2—The late Dermot Moran (looking away from camera) enthralling a group of people in Derryoober Commonage during a field trip in 2013; one of the many earth-cut structures recorded can be seen in the foreground.

A cluster of huts was discovered on the northern slopes of the commonage overlooking a marshy area, naturally drained by a small stream that in turn enters the Aghnamallaght River. The site containing the hut sites is enclosed on the east by a boulder wall, while the stream and the area of marshy ground form the western boundary. The landscape rises to the east outside the limits of the enclosure. The ruins of an abandoned house of later date survive to the north of the site. This house was built into a hillside, providing it with natural shelter. It is possible that it was constructed after the Big Wind of the night of 6 January 1839, although this is only a supposition. Many houses were purposely built into banks and sheltered hillsides after this devastating natural disaster. It was, according to local information, the house of a herder who settled here when a wave of pressurised Ulster Catholic families, known as Ultachs, settled in the Sliabh Aughty uplands following the famous Battle of the Diamond in 1795 (discussed below). The settlement or appointment of a herdsman in the commonage is of interest, as his presence likely marks the demise of the traditional summer booley whereby young people, often teenage girls, were sent up the mountains to look after the dairy cattle. With a full-time herdsman settled on the commonage, holding grazing rights for a set number of livestock in payment for acting as the communal herder, booleying was no longer necessary.

An opportunity presented itself in 2017 to make a short heritage-awareness film on the topic of booleying or transhumance. This was facilitated by Marie Mannion, Galway County Heritage Officer, who accessed funding for a short production by Paul Murphy of ID Films from the Heritage Council (link: https://vimeo.com/247176951). As the hut sites discovered in Derryoober, the townland where the film was focused, were quite ephemeral in the landscape, Paul asked whether we could construct a booley hut. The upstanding remains of many of the Sliabh Aughty huts consist of very simple doughnut-shaped rings of earth and stone. The Derryoober examples were also hidden in growth, making them difficult to capture on film. This turned out to be an interesting and worthwhile piece of experimental archaeology involving people from the local Sliabh Aughty community. A group of enthusiastic volunteers came together to build a simple tepee-style hut of timber poles and bog scraw, which we thatched with *fionnar*, a native long grass used locally in the past for thatching sheds, bedding livestock and similar uses. A dried-up lake referred to locally as 'the mire' was the major source of this grass in the past. The mire, like the upland commonage, was divided in shares among the local farmers, a further example of how the rundale system worked.

Fig. 10.3—One of the camp-sites associated with the first phase of Ultach settlement in the Sliabh Aughty uplands.

One of the great surprises that emerged from fieldwork in the uplands was the discovery of a large number of 'hut sites' arranged in a large cluster or settlement in the townland of Alleendarra East, south of Woodford village. As of now they have not been systematically recorded; it is assumed that in the initial area of discovery there are upwards of 40 individual features, but this figure will likely change when a fully measured survey is undertaken. When the landowner, Patrick McGann, first pointed them out to me I was amazed. He indicated the remains of what initially looked like a series of water- and sphagnum-filled pits. In fact, that is how he described them. Closer examination revealed, however, that they were actually a series of circular and subcircular platforms with penannular rings of stones on their outer edges, enclosed by an external wet ditch *c.* 1m in diameter and 0.5m deep (Fig. 10.3). Initial thoughts were that perhaps this was a large Bronze Age settlement, but the huts were too small and the wet ditch problematic. Discussion in the field with other archaeologists led to the conclusion that they were likely to be late in date but too numerous to have been associated with booleying. We were fortunate to have a site visit in 2014 by several members of the Irish Post-Medieval Archaeology Group (IPMAG), who kindly shared their

opinions on the upstanding archaeology. Other similar clusters have been recorded since in the townlands of Alleendarra West and Toorleitra, making this a significant and extended archaeological discovery.

Dr Theresa McDonald, the founder of the Achill Archaeological Field School, observed that the features in question looked more like camp-sites than hut sites. And on reflection, now that we have developed a greater understanding of the settlement history of this area, that is in fact what they appear to be. The post-medieval history of human settlement in this landscape is intrinsically linked to the outburst of agrarian unrest in the Ulster borderlands in the mid- to late eighteenth century. Following the so-called 'Battle of the Diamond', which took place in 1795 at Loughgall, Co. Armagh, it is argued that several thousand Catholics were forced to migrate southwards as a result of agrarian tensions and outrages that developed over flax-growing (Egan 1954; McGuire 2017). A large contingent of 'Ultachs', as the natives called them, arrived in the Sliabh Aughty region to take up land advertised for rent by John Burke of Marble Hill. Many of their descendants are still living in the area and have been actively involved in the project. The primary focus of Ultach settlement was in the townlands of Alleendarra East, Alleendarra West, Toorleitra and

Fig. 10.4—Locals attending open-air Mass at Loughatorick Mass rock on 15 September 2014.

Loughatorick in County Galway and in Slianoir, Co. Clare (that townland was in County Galway until the redrawing of the county boundaries in 1898). The earliest documented evidence for their presence in these townlands is recorded in the Tithe Applotment Books (1823–37) for Galway. The site in Toorleitra East is therefore probably best described as a refugee camp, a temporary makeshift settlement of tents or simple tent-like structures. It is likely that this settlement remained in place until the settlers laid out their suite of ladder farms, the traces of which we still see in the landscape today. Examination of the surviving archaeology in this group of townlands shows a strong cultural legacy. For example, two squat-type sweathouses recorded are typical of those found in the northern regions of the country. Evidence for flax-growing occurs by way of place-name evidence in the landscape; for example, the small farmstead of Tooreenmanus is associated with the flax industry. The 'toor' element in the name and the existence of the Bleach River nearby hint at the presence of flax-bleaching greens.

A strong religious belief was an important factor in the lives of these upland people. This is evidenced in the landscape by the presence of an interesting collection of religious sites associated with the practice of popular piety, such as Mass rocks (Fig. 10.4), inscribed stones, an unrecorded graveyard and a former chapel, all with clearly identifiable Ultach associations. When a new graveyard was eventually opened in Woodford in the 1850s, the Ultach families populated one section, distinguishable today by the presence of what are obvious Ulster names and a collection of high-status funerary monuments. They were, as the surviving archaeology shows, a resilient, self-reliant and progressive people.

Several other interesting features occur. In Alleendarra East an inscribed boulder bears a harp with a Maid of Erin and the word 'Erin', along with a series of acronyms with clear religious connotations (Fig. 10.5). The Latin words *Parentes Amamus* translate as 'parental love', while the letters 'FX' refer to the missionary St Francis Xavier, one of the founders of the Society of Jesus (Jesuits). The letters 'AMDG' stand for *Ad majorem Dei gloriam* ('For the greater glory of God'), the Jesuit motto. The date 1913 appears to mark the departure of M.J. Murray from the townland. Another inscribed stone in the commonage in Toorleitra townland bears a crudely cut IHS monogram, a small cross and the inscribed words 'Pray to God' (Fig. 10.6). This latter example is undated.

The three main strands of archaeology currently

Fig. 10.6—Inscription and cross on an earthfast boulder in Toorleitra townland.

Fig. 10.5—Inscribed boulder, Alleendarra East.

emerging from the Sliabh Aughty uplands are an expanding prehistoric layer, a previously undocumented layer associated with rundale and booleying, and the discovery of a rich settlement layer associated with the Ultach migrants who have contributed so much to the region. All three require further research. The wider Sliabh Aughty region would benefit very much from a targeted programme of research, but the key to successful survey and long-term conservation in the region is the involvement of local stakeholders; this can only be achieved by working in partnership with the local communities.

REFERENCES

Cunniffe, C.   2016   Looking for the booley: did Derryoober have a king? *Sliabh Aughty Journal* **16**, 13–19.

Cunniffe, C. and Cunningham, K.   2013   The secret landscape of the Sliabh Aughty. *South East Galway Archaeological Society Newsletter* **13**, 5–6.

Egan, P.K.   1954   Progress and suppression of the United Irishmen in the western counties in 1798–99. *Journal of the Galway Archaeological and Historical Society* **25**, 104–34.

McGuire, K.   2017   On the trail of the Ultachs: a multi-disciplinary exploration of the settlement of Ulster Catholics in East Galway. Unpublished BA dissertation, Galway–Mayo Institute of Technology, Castlebar Campus.

11. From mummified 'Barbies' to meteorites: fourteen years of the Belfast Young Archaeologists' Club

NAOMI CARVER AND EILEEN MURPHY

ABSTRACT

The Belfast branch of the Young Archaeologists' Club was set up in 2006 by staff from Queen's University Belfast. Almost fourteen years later the club is a well-established and vibrant organisation drawing members from across Northern Ireland. In this paper we set the scene by introducing the Young Archaeologists' Club, briefly examining its roots and the format of the Club network today. We then turn to the Belfast Young Archaeologists' Club, discussing the composition of the membership and leadership of the branch. We provide an overview of the workings of the Club and the nature of the activities in which we have engaged. We reflect on the Club's role in enabling young people to learn more about archaeology, a discipline that often falls under the auspices of history in Northern Irish schools. We also consider future directions that the Club may take in the interests of ensuring gender and age balance across its membership and leadership.

INTRODUCTION

Community can be defined in a number of ways—the wide and varied list of contributions to this volume is testament to this. *The Oxford Living Dictionaries* (Oxford University Press, n.d.) include two relevant definitions:

- A group of people living in the same place or having a particular characteristic in common.
- The condition of sharing or having certain attitudes and interests in common.

Within these two definitions are a range of classifications relating to community. Organisations such as the Belfast branch of the Young Archaeologists' Club (Belfast YAC) probably fall somewhere in between the two, with a leaning towards the second. Geographically, the Club's members are from the same area: Belfast and its environs, and other parts of Northern Ireland. It brings together, however, children and young people with a shared interest in archaeology and related subjects, such as geology, palaeontology and history, and it is for this reason that the dictionary's second definition of community is more relevant. In this way Belfast YAC forms its own community, positioned somewhere between school and youth club arenas at an intersection between formal learning and fun interaction. In post-Troubles Northern Ireland such shared spaces are of particular importance. A small number of articles have been written about the potential positive role that archaeology can play within the post-conflict society of Northern Ireland (e.g. Horning *et al.* 2015). We will not dwell further on this topic in the current paper, but we feel that the Club demonstrates the role that archaeology can play through its creation of a shared space where children and young people with similar interests can make friends while learning about the past, regardless of their community of origin. The Club also provides continuity rather than a one-off school trip to an excavation or archaeological site.

In this paper we will start by introducing the broader UK-based Young Archaeologists' Club before focusing on the Belfast branch. We will outline the structure of the Club and review the activities in which it has engaged over the past fourteen years. We will examine the demographics of its membership to see whether insights can be gained in relation to the characteristics of children and young people with a particular interest in archaeology. The role of the volunteer leaders, their age range and gender will also be examined. Following this analysis of the Club's members and leaders, we will provide an overview of the 129 sessions held during the period from 2006 to 2018. We will conclude with a review of the contribution that the Club can make to providing young people with an opportunity to learn about archaeology, a subject somewhat hidden within the school curriculum. We will also consider issues that this review has uncovered and how we might address these.

THE ROOTS OF THE YOUNG ARCHAEOLOGISTS' CLUB

The Young Archaeologists' Club (YAC) is a UK-wide organisation for children and young people from the age of eight up to seventeen years. The Club, initially known as 'Young Rescue', was established in 1972 by Kate Pretty, an archaeologist at Cambridge University (Henson 2007). She was later joined by fellow archaeologist Mike Corbishley, and both received an award at the British Archaeological Awards in 1998 for their work in initiating the Club. From the outset the Club was popular and its success was due in part to the occurrence of major archaeological discoveries at the time, such as the Chinese Terracotta Army in 1974. In addition, television programmes aimed at a young audience further whetted the imagination, from the drama of *Children of the Stones* (1977) to the reality show *Living in the past* (1978), which focused on the lives of a group of young volunteers who lived as Iron Age farmers for a year. The Club was overseen by the York Archaeological Trust from 1987 before becoming part of the Council for British Archaeology (CBA) in 1993. The CBA is a registered charity in England and Wales (No. 287815) and in Scotland (SC041971), while in Northern Ireland it has worked alongside its partner organisation, the Northern Ireland Archaeology Forum (NIAF). The CBA's mission statement is 'Archaeology for All' and it seeks to promote participation in archaeological research, education and the conservation of the built, buried, landscape and townscape heritage (CBA, n.d.).

The main aim of the original Young Archaeologists' Club was to provide access to archaeology for young people who wanted to pursue their interest in the subject, which is not widely taught in schools. YAC branches provide an opportunity to share in this experience and their members can discover just how much fun it can be to learn about the past. Until 2014 the Club took two forms: YAC UK, which was a magazine-based subscription package, and the network of local YAC branches. Regrettably, funding cuts necessitated restructuring of the organisation and it now consists solely of the YAC Branch Network with the support of 'YAC HQ'—a small number of staff and a website which was launched in 2015 (http://www.yac-uk.org). There are currently over 70 branches spread throughout the UK, based largely at museums and heritage centres. University-based clubs exist at Newcastle and Reading Universities, in addition to our branch at Queen's University Belfast, while two branches are also based

in schools but are not open to the wider public. All branches are run by adult volunteers and the majority meet once a month. Since 2015–16 there have been two types of YAC branch: CBA-managed branches and affiliated branches. The affiliated branches are administered and run by a partnership organisation which is responsible for the Club's child protection, health and safety and insurance policies. The inception of the affiliated branch option, which is a quicker and more straightforward way to set up a new branch, has resulted in a rise in the number of YAC branches (Nicky Milsted, pers. comm.).

In addition to Belfast YAC there are currently two other YAC branches in Northern Ireland, based at Down County Museum in Downpatrick, Co. Down, and the Tower Museum in Derry City. A branch was also based in Bangor at North Down Museum, but it sadly folded around 2006. The Downpatrick YAC branch has been in existence for almost sixteen years, while the newest branch, Derry and Strabane YAC, was set up in 2017. A unique combination of factors, including their geographical detachment from the rest of the UK, their location in a relatively small province (Northern Ireland is 14,130km^2) and their existence in a post-conflict society, have resulted in the YAC branches in Northern Ireland sharing a connectedness. Belfast YAC is in close contact with Downpatrick YAC and we have run a number of sessions together over the years. We hope to organise a session with the Derry and Strabane branch in the near future.

BELFAST YOUNG ARCHAEOLOGISTS' CLUB

Belfast YAC was established in June 2006 by members of staff from the then School of Archaeology and Palaeoecology at Queen's University Belfast (QUB), following a tradition of successful science-based open days within the School that demonstrated a clear appetite among children and young people for learning more about the past. The inaugural meeting took place on 17 June 2006 with a 'family field-walking' session in Ballydrain townland near Comber, Co. Down, which was followed up by an official launch at QUB during which a series of taster activities were organised.

It was envisaged from the outset that the Club would draw on the wide and varied areas of knowledge and expertise within Archaeology and Palaeoecology at QUB and beyond. From its early days it has been recognised an as official University outreach programme and has therefore been able to avail of the University's facilities and resources to support its activities. One of

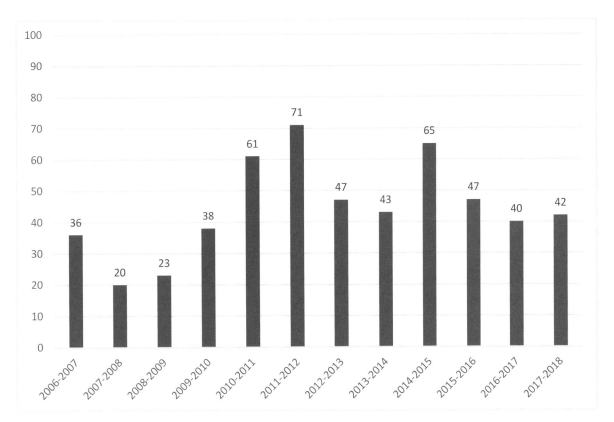

Fig. 11.1—Number of Belfast YAC members by membership year.

Belfast YAC's informal aims is to teach its members that archaeology is not simply about digging holes in the ground and that it has many transferable skills which can make it a valuable subject to study at university. The Club is now part of the Centre for Community Archaeology in the School of Natural and Built Environment (http://www.qub.ac.uk/sites/communityarchaeology/). It is run on a volunteer basis and the Branch Leader is Naomi Carver, who is supported by a team of Assistant Leaders that includes staff, postgraduate and undergraduate students, as well as a small number of external volunteers. Part of the process involved with becoming a Belfast YAC leader involves an Enhanced Access NI check, since the Club involves working with children. All leaders have the opportunity to avail of child protection and First Aid training courses.

Belfast YAC's membership year runs from 1 June to 31 May. The Club currently operates an annual subscription fee of £10 combined with a nominal fee of £1 per session. This money is used to purchase materials and refreshments for sessions, as well as to subsidise costs for field trips. The Club meets on the second Saturday of the month, with the exception of July and August in recent years, and sessions normally run from 2pm to 4pm. Over the years we have held a diverse array of classroom-based sessions in QUB in addition to those that involve visits to heritage-related institutions and archaeological sites and monuments. We have a strong working relationship with the nearby Ulster Museum and, thanks to Museum staff such as Science Education Officer Fiona Baird and Geology Curator Dr Michael Simms, many sessions have been held in the Museum. Further details about the Belfast YAC can be found at http://www.qub.ac.uk/sites/byac.

REVIEW OF 2006–2018

Membership

Throughout the Club's existence there has been an average of 44 signed-up members on the books per year. This number peaked at 71 in 2011–12, fluctuating in the earlier years when the branch was becoming established (Fig. 11.1). The peaks in membership numbers in some years were most likely a result of large, high-profile sessions that were advertised to the wider public through other external events. A session focused on mosaics that ran in June 2011 and was attended by almost 30 families, for example, was promoted as an official QUB Family Event (see below).

Table 11.1—Average number of members attending each Belfast YAC session and attendance expressed as a percentage of total member numbers per year.

Year	Average member attendance per session	Range	% of total membership
2006–2007	21	15–26	58
2007–2008	15	4–25	75
2008–2009	23	14–37	100
2009–2010	30	18–58	79
2010–2011	26	12–46	43
2011–2012	29	15–39	41
2012–2013	26	15–39	55
2013–2014	24	10–40	56
2014–2015	18	10–35	28
2015–2016	16	11–22	34
2016–2017	16	14–18	40
2017–2018	19	12–22	45

Several new member enquiries occur per month, and these generally stem from word of mouth, from advertisement in schools and at open days, as well as from internet searches and YAC UK website referrals. The natural turnover of members has meant that it has never been necessary to introduce a waiting list for Club membership.

The number of members attending individual sessions varies, with average attendances per year ranging from fifteen to 30 (Table 11.1). The average meeting attendance at Belfast YAC is generally above the mean average of ten of the UK YAC branch network, as recorded in 2015 (Milsted 2015, 3).

Age profile

Belfast YAC does not apply a strict lower age limit like most other clubs in the YAC UK branch network. The Club is advertised for children and young people aged from eight up to seventeen years; at the branch leader's discretion, however, slightly younger members (generally aged six or seven years) are permitted to attend sessions, provided they are accompanied by a parent or guardian. Indeed, it is often the case that younger siblings wish to attend, and in some cases whole families come along to Club sessions. We view this as a positive aspect of our Club, since it enables members to engage with archaeology with the support of their family and is a practice that hopefully extends beyond Club activities.

The age profile of the membership is displayed in Fig. 11.2 and it is evident that the majority of Belfast YAC members fall within the eight–ten years group, followed by those of eleven–thirteen years. During the twelve years between 2006 and 2018, membership of the eight–ten-year-olds has averaged at 49%, with a range of 34% to 65%, while the average proportion of members aged eleven–thirteen years was 27%, with a range of 19% to 35%. This trend correlates well with data from the 2015 YAC census, where most members were found to lie within the eight–twelve years age category. Nicky Milsted (2015, 4) goes on to say that in the preceding years when censuses were taken (2011, 2012, 2013) eight–twelve-year-olds represented approximately 75% of YAC members. Membership of those aged less than eight years has remained fairly constant over the years, with an average level of 16% and a range of 0% to 23%.

Those older than fourteen are the least well-represented group and on average during the period between 2006 and 2018 they have formed 8% of members, with a range of 0% to 15%. This drop-off is also reflected in the YAC census report, where only 14% of members fell into this age group. Here it is reasonably explained as a consequence of '[the] increasing pressures of school work for young people as they enter Key Stage 3, with GCSEs and coursework assessments' (Milsted 2015, 4). We are also increasingly of the view that activities enjoyed by younger age categories are less palatable to those older than fourteen years (see below). Most years only one or two

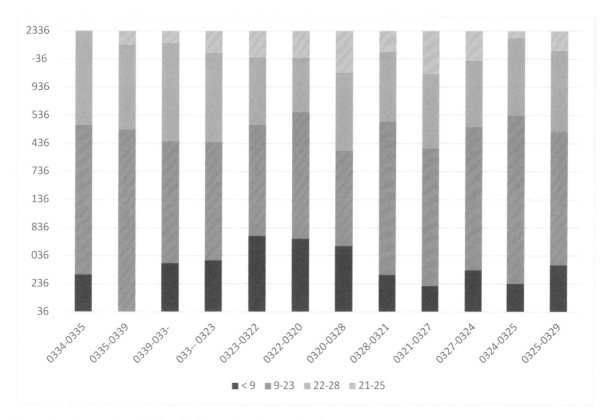

Fig. 11.2—Age profile of Belfast YAC members by membership year.

young people aged sixteen or seventeen have been Club members and this has been viewed as problematic, given the desire for it to be a mechanism of recruitment to archaeology degree programmes. The introduction of the Young Leader category in October 2013 for sixteen- and seventeen-year-olds was helpful, as it allowed the Club's older members to participate in the running of sessions as well as providing them with valuable experience that can help them to develop their CVs and personal statements for university applications.

Gender profile
From the outset, membership of Belfast YAC has been weighted approximately two-thirds male to one-third female (Fig. 11.3). In the 2006–7 membership year, for example, there were 64% males to 36% females. This trend has continued, rising as high as a 70:30 male to female breakdown in the 2007–8 membership year. Indeed, during the period between 2006 and 2018 there were only two membership years in which there was a more even split of males to females: in 2008–9 it was 52:48 and in 2012–13 it was 55:45. Across the YAC branch network there are more equal numbers of male to female members, roughly a 52:48 split according to the 2015 census (Milsted 2015, 7). The male

predominance does not appear to be mirroring the gender breakdown among the Level 1 intake to archaeology degrees in QUB, where the male:female ratios have varied greatly in recent years for which data are available—49:51 (2013–14), 56:44 (2014–15) and 32:68 (2015–16). It is possible that societal factors are at play and that, for some unknown reason, girls in Northern Ireland are less attracted to archaeology than boys. Gender stereotyping is a well-known issue among children of primary school age and studies have been undertaken to help challenge such behaviours, which can limit opportunities for both children and adults throughout their lives (NUT, n.d.).

Volunteer leaders
Young Archaeologists' Club leaders undertake the role in a voluntary capacity. At present some twenty volunteer leaders are attached to Belfast YAC, most of whom are staff and students from Queen's University Belfast, with a small number of external volunteers. YAC UK rules stipulate that there must be a ratio of one leader to every eight YAC members. In recent years an average of eight leaders participated in each Belfast YAC session, which is notably higher than the required ratio. Comparison of the number of volunteer leaders to the number of members attending Belfast YAC gives

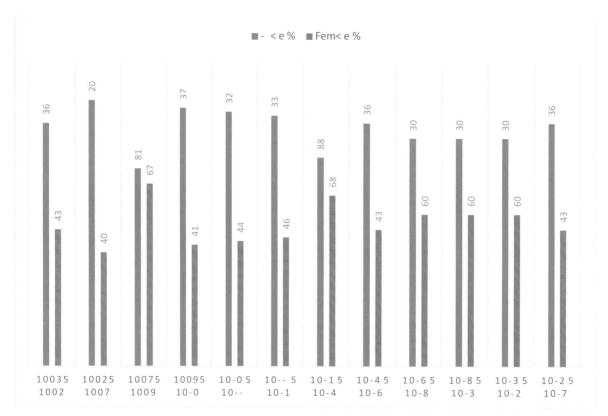

Fig. 11.3—Percentages of male to female Belfast YAC members per membership year.

a rough ratio of one leader for every two to three members. This is broadly equivalent to the numbers recorded in the 2015 YAC census, when the average ratio of volunteers to members was 1:3, with a range of leaders present from one to eight.

Two forms of information are available about the current volunteer leaders: gender and age. Female leaders notably predominate (76%), and the proportion of female to male leaders is slightly higher than the average reported in the 2015 YAC census, where volunteer leaders were recorded as 69% female compared to 31% male. The 2015 YAC census report acknowledges the need to encourage more male volunteers to participate (Milsted 2015, 7)

When the age spread of the twenty volunteer leaders at Belfast YAC is compared to that of the YAC branch network as a whole, some interesting differences are evident (Table 11.2). The YAC census report suggests that involvement with YAC appeals more to 'early career professionals across the heritage sector' (*ibid.*, 5) and this is evident in the data, with a peak in leaders lying within the 25–34 years (22%) and 35–44 years (23%) age groups. While the 25–34 years (25%) age cohort is high amongst the Belfast YAC leadership, the 18–24-year-old group (30%) predominates. This is

Table 11.2—Comparison of the age profile of the Belfast YAC volunteer leaders with corresponding data derived from the wider YAC branch network (Milsted 2015, 6).

Age group (years)	Belfast YAC (n=20)	YAC branch network (2015) (n=159)
16–17	10%	5%
18–24	30%	8%
25–34	25%	22%
35–44	15%	23%
45–54	20%	16%
55–64	0	18%
65–74	0	6%
75–84	0	2%
85+	0	0

a notable deviation from the trend for the broader network and it is undoubtedly a reflection of the Club's position within a university setting. The relatively high proportion of younger volunteer leaders comprises undergraduate or postgraduate students, supported by

Fig. 11.4—Studying rocks during a geology session at the Ulster Museum.

Table 11.3—Summary of the Belfast YAC sessions held between 2006 and April 2018.

Session type	No. of sessions
FIELD TRIP SESSIONS	
Local field trip (Belfast environs)	22
Non-local field trip (e.g. National Museum, Dublin)	19
Excavation	7
Total	*8 (37%)*
CLASSROOM SESSIONS **Cultural archaeology**	
Period-specific (e.g. medieval life)	12
Artefact-focused (e.g. pottery)	11
Site types/places (e.g. castles)	6
Rock & cave art	3
Introduction to archaeology	2
Archives	1
Maritime archaeology	1
Scientific archaeology/palaeoecology	
Human remains & burial practices	8
Environmental archaeology (e.g. insects)	6
Animal bones	3
Dendrochronology	3
Technological approaches, e.g. geophysics	2
Volcanoes	2
Experimental archaeology	1
Seasonal events	
Hallowe'en	4
Christmas	3
Winter solstice	2
Chinese New Year	1
Related disciplines	
Ethnography (e.g. body modification)	2
Folklore	2
Geology	2
Astronomy	1
Mythology	1
Palaeontology	1
Religion	1
Total	**81 (63%)**

a smaller number of staff, which has provided a level of continuity to the Club. It is interesting that none of the Belfast YAC leaders are aged over 55 years since these groups are represented in the broader branch network. It is possible that this situation has arisen because of the largely self-contained nature of the Belfast YAC within QUB—assistant leaders who leave the university and the Club, following completion of their studies, are generally replaced by new entrants to the university. In addition, the Ulster Archaeological Society (UAS), whose membership comprises approximately 400 individuals and who mainly identify as 'retired', caters extremely well for older individuals with an interest in the past (see McAlister, Conway and Welsh, this volume). While the UAS and Belfast YAC are both affiliated to the QUB Centre for Community Archaeology, there has been somewhat limited overlap between the two groups. This is something we intend to address in the future, however, since there is clearly scope for grandparents and grandchildren, for example, to gain much through a shared involvement in the Club.

Fig. 11.5—Making wattle-and-daub fences as part of an experimental archaeology session.

Sessions

The Belfast YAC runs sessions on a range of themes, including those that are not solely archaeological. The sessions are broadly interdisciplinary, and topics based on architectural history, folklore, geology (Fig. 11.4) and palaeontology, to name but a few examples, have all been enjoyed (Table 11.3). Some of the more unusual themes have included Pokémon, witchcraft and meteorites! One of our key aims is to demonstrate the breadth of archaeology, and the Club leaders are at pains to demonstrate that it is not limited to excavation. The sessions have been designed to show that archaeology is a wide-ranging subject area with many facets and transferable skills that can be readily applied to other disciplines. Feedback received indicates that Belfast YAC members enjoy the diversity of themes. Members are also afforded the opportunity to suggest ideas for sessions and, where possible, these topics are facilitated.

Belfast YAC sessions are normally two hours in length and generally follow a basic format in which the topic is introduced during a short PowerPoint presentation (lasting ten–fifteen minutes), designed to be interactive so that members can contribute and ask questions. Following the talk, the remainder of the session involves a bespoke practical activity related to the theme of the session. Some 129 sessions were held between 2006 and 2018. The majority have involved classroom-based activities, normally within QUB (63%). The indoor sessions can be broadly subdivided into those focusing on cultural archaeology (45%), scientific archaeology/palaeoecology (31%), seasonal events (12%) and a number that can be viewed as based on a related discipline (12%). The cultural archaeological sessions included those that examined a period, artefact or site type, while the more scientific topics covered included osteoarchaeology, technological approaches and experimental archaeology (Fig. 11.5). Seasonal events have been based on Hallowe'en and Christmas, but the festivals of other cultures, such as the Chinese New Year and the Mexican Day of the Dead, have also been represented.

As mentioned above, some of our most ambitious sessions have been run as part of larger events. Of particular note was a session on Egyptian mummies that ran in June 2009 as part of the sadly now-defunct Archaeology Days event run by the then Northern Ireland Environment Agency DOE: NI (now the Historic Environment Division). This session was inspired by a paper published by Lauren Talalay and Todd Gerring (2007) in which they described how they

Fig. 11.6—'Barbie' dolls with 'internal organs' and abdominal incisions as part of a session on Egyptian mummification.

used 'Barbie' dolls to teach children about Egyptian mummification in the Kelsey Museum of Archaeology at the University of Michigan. The internet is now awash with guidance on this topic but at the time this publication was highly innovative. The session involved a substantial amount of preparation that largely involved acquiring the necessary raw materials—cheap plastic dolls, tubs for canopic jars, sweets/dried fruit for internal organs, bandages, wax for seals, shoeboxes for the sarcophagi and printouts of various Egyptian motifs for decorative purposes. A considerable amount of time was invested in preparing shoeboxes by spraying them gold, and all dolls were afforded an abdominal incision prior to the session (Figs 11.6 and 11.7). The effort paid off, however; the session proved to be highly enjoyable for all and a great success, and we have emulated it at more recent outreach events as part of the NI Science Festival.

Another topic that required substantial planning but was particularly rewarding focused on mosaics. An initial session ran in June 2011 under the auspices of an official QUB Family Event. The session started with an introduction to mosaics through the ages, followed by a practical session in which participants had the opportunity to help with the creation of a large (120cm x 120cm) mosaic devised to celebrate the Belfast YAC that now takes pride of place in the foyer of the Archaeology and Palaeoecology Building at QUB. We were fortunate at that time to have an artist on the leadership team (David Withers) and he designed the mosaic. A substantial amount of preparation was required: drawing the sections of the mosaic and adding in details of colour schemes to small wooden blocks (40cm x 40cm) that would later be pieced together within a wooden frame to form the finished version (Figs 11.8 and 11.9).

Organising field trips can involve greater logistical issues, including health and safety matters, dealing with poor weather conditions (Plan Bs!) and transport costs. We have tried to ensure that we run at least one field trip and, more recently, participate in an excavation each year. In the period between 2006 and 2018 the Club undertook some 48 field trips, including local (46%) and non-local (39%) trips as well as excavations (15%) (Table 11.4). Local trips generally take place within the Belfast environs and have included repeat visits to a number of locations, including the Giant's Ring, the Ulster Museum and Friar's Bush Graveyard. Our September meeting normally coincides with the European Heritage Open

Fig. 11.7—Belfast YAC members proudly displaying their decorated mummy sarcophagi at the Egyptian mummies' session.

Fig. 11.8—Work in progress on the Medusa-inspired mosaic. Assistant Leader Matthew Adams is on the left.

Table 11.4—Details of the field trips undertaken by the Belfast YAC between 2006 and 2018.

Location	Year(s)
Local field trips	
Giant's Ring, Belfast	2006, 2012
Friar's Bush Graveyard, Belfast	2006, 2008
Ulster Museum, Belfast	2009, 2014, 2015
Divis Mountain field trip, Belfast	2010
Belfast ghost tour & Clifton Street Cemetery, Belfast	2010
Belvoir Forest Park, Belfast	2011
Friar's Bush Graveyard, Belfast (EHOD)	2011
Ulster Folk & Transport Museum	2012, 2017
NI War Memorial, Belfast (EHOD)	2012, 2015
Botanic environs, Belfast	2013
Graymount House, Belfast (EHOD)	2013
SS *Nomadic*, Belfast (EHOD)	2014
Slievenacloy, Co. Antrim, survey	2015
Belfast City Hall (EHOD)	2016
Clifton House, Belfast (EHOD)	2017
HMS *Caroline*, Belfast	2017
Non-local field trips	
Comber, Co. Down, field-walking	2006
Carrickfergus town, Co. Antrim	2007
Dunluce Castle, Co. Antrim	2007

Location	Year(s)
Navan Fort, Co. Armagh	2007
Newgrange, Co. Meath	2008
Devenish, Co. Fermanagh	2009
Greyabbey, Co. Down (EHOD)	2009
Slieve Croob, Co. Down	2010
Carrickfergus Gasworks Museum, Co. Antrim	2011
Medieval tower-houses in Co. Down	2011
Carrickfergus Castle, Co. Antrim	2013
Ballynoe stone circle, Co. Down	2013
Down County Museum, Co. Down	2013, 2016
UCD Centre for Experimental Archaeology and Material Culture	2014
The Somme Centre, Co. Down	2014
Carrickfergus Museum, Co. Antrim	2016
National Museum of Ireland, Dublin	2017
US Rangers Museum, Carrickfergus, Co. Antrim	2018
Excavation	
Dunluce Castle, Co. Antrim	2010
Dundrum Castle, Co. Down	2012
Divis Mountain, Co. Antrim	2013
Grey Point Fort, Co. Down	2014
Slievenacloy, Co. Antrim	2015, 2016
Aghagallon, Co. Antrim	2017
Total	**48**

Day (EHOD) weekend and we generally visit a historical property made accessible during the event. Non-local field trips have mostly been to sites around Northern Ireland, including Carrickfergus, Co. Antrim, Devenish, Co. Fermanagh, Greyabbey, Co. Down (Fig. 11.10), and Navan Fort, Co. Armagh, but we have also made a number of trips to the Republic of Ireland, where we have visited Newgrange, Co. Meath, University College Dublin's Centre for Experimental Archaeology and Material Culture and, most recently, the National Museum of Ireland. In recent years members have had the opportunity during the month of June to participate in an excavation which coincides with the QUB training excavation for undergraduate students (Fig. 11.11). The excavation is often preceded by a session that contextualises the site, or sometimes a visit to the site to carry out pre-excavation surveying.

Members also have the opportunity to learn about post-excavation processes and, when possible, a session will be run after the excavation that enables them to wash and investigate finds.

DISCUSSION

The importance of community and heritage outreach programmes such as the Young Archaeologists' Club cannot be overstated. The YAC annual report of 2016/17 noted that 70 local branches existed across the UK, associated with 500 volunteers, and that some 700 sessions had been run, with an average of thirteen children in attendance at each session. It was calculated that the volunteer time equated to £840,000 of monetary investment (Milsted 2017, 2). Belfast YAC is

Fig. 11.9—The Belfast YAC mosaic on display in the foyer of the Archaeology and Palaeoecology Building at Queen's University Belfast.

an inclusive organisation offering children and young people a chance to learn about archaeology. It has played an important part in its members' lives at a formative stage of their education and development. The members have established long-term friendships with others with similar interests, and the volunteer leaders have also benefited from their involvement with the Club. Student leaders can get formal recognition for their participation—for example, through the university's Degree Plus and Researcher Plus schemes, which provide official recognition for volunteering activities beyond their formal studies. All Assistant Leaders have the opportunity to avail of child protection and First Aid training. Being a Club leader thus provides numerous opportunities that can help enhance CVs, which is particularly important for early career individuals.

A number of the Club's members have gone on to study archaeology at university, both at QUB and further afield. Of particular note is one member who joined the Club at the age of eight years when it launched in 2006, came back as a helper and recently completed a degree in QUB. Other members have stayed on to become young leaders while studying archaeology-related subjects at different universities, including the Ulster University. It is heartening to hear

about the genuine benefits that the Club has had for one such individual:

'I joined the Belfast Young Archaeologists' Club in 2010 as a junior member. As a child my time with the Club was fun and educational, and when I was eighteen I was offered the chance to become an Assistant Leader. I leapt at the chance and have been serving in this position ever since. My experience in this role has been extremely positive, as it has developed my organisational and delegation skills as well as my abilities as a leader and responsible care-taker. I have been entrusted with the safety of the Club's junior members, which has provided a boost to my confidence and offers desirable traits that I can put on my CV for professional career applications. Furthermore, I have been able to use my time in Queen's to make connections with professors and lecturers to further my career path, even securing an industrial placement with Queen's Centre for Archaeological Fieldwork as part of my degree course. In all, my involvement with the YAC has been

Fig. 11.10—Exploring Greyabbey, Co. Down, as part of the European Heritage Open Day.

tremendously rewarding and will be well treasured' (Matthew Adams, 2018; see Fig. 11.8).

Opportunities for children and young people in Northern Ireland to learn about archaeology are, however, generally somewhat limited. The curriculum in Northern Ireland is coordinated by the Council for the Curriculum, Examinations and Assessment (CCEA), although at Key Stage 4 schools can opt to follow GCSE and GCE courses offered by other examination boards. Primary school education in Northern Ireland contains much of archaeological relevance through the 'World Around Us' Area of Learning, with suggested Key Stage 2 topics including the Celts, the Romans, the Vikings, the Victorians and studies of 'historical' sites in the local area and, more generally, investigation of 'some of the characteristics of past societies and distinctive features of life in the past' (CCEA 2007a, 89). Interestingly, there is a clear association of these topics with History rather than Archaeology in formal CCEA publications, but the connection with archaeology appears to be made

naturally, as witnessed by the peak in membership of the YAC by children of primary school age (see above).

During the first three years of secondary education in Northern Ireland topics of archaeological relevance are also represented within the 'Environment and Society: History' Area of Learning. Suggested examples used to address particular questions in Key Stage 3 include the Incas, Egyptians, Romans, Greeks and Aztecs, while some of the topics focus on plantation, emigration and public health over time (CCEA 2007b). Since 2006 Archaeology has not been offered as a separate GCSE subject by any examination board within the UK. The CCEA GCSE History curriculum largely focuses on Modern History (CCEA 2015), although the corresponding AQA curriculum, which is undertaken to a lesser extent in Northern Ireland, contains a substantial amount of Medieval 'History' (AD 500–1500) (AQA 2018).

Since 2018 Archaeology is no longer taught as an A-level anywhere in the UK following AQA's decision to withdraw the subject owing to concerns about the accuracy of assessment. Elements of the subject are taught within other subjects, such as Classical

Fig. 11.11—Excavating at an enigmatic enclosure at Aghagallon, Co. Antrim.

Civilisation, but AQA opted recently to discontinue this too (although it continues to be offered by Examination Board OCR). The decisions by AQA to drop both the Archaeology and Classical Civilisation A-levels were met with dismay in the archaeological community and beyond, with high-profile figures, such as YAC President Tony Robinson, voicing their outrage (Weale 2016). Archaeological topics are embedded within the curricula for other A-level subjects, however, including Biology, Geography, History and Sociology, but a major challenge for the discipline is to ensure that teachers and students recognise the archaeological relevance of these topics. It would seem that the breadth of the discipline, which is one of its strengths, can also be a threat in that its boundaries are not sufficiently well defined for those working outside the profession. As discussed above, the YAC is very well placed to help demonstrate that archaeology has a whole range of facets, from those that are arts-based to those in the scientific realm.

Belfast YAC provides children and young people with the opportunity to learn about archaeology and heritage in a broad sense, and the leaders work hard to connect the members to their shared history as well as to introduce them to a wide range of related subjects. The activities of the Club teach members that archaeology is not simply about digging holes in the ground and that it has many transferable skills which can make it a great subject to study at university. This is even more true in an age of increasing infrastructural development activities, both within Britain and Ireland, with an associated need for professional archaeologists. Indeed, there is a predicted shortage of archaeologists to work on such projects (e.g. Shepperson 2017). The Club is well situated within the Centre for Community Archaeology at QUB and it is anticipated that it will continue for many years, satisfying the appetite amongst children and young people for knowledge about the past that they can bring with them to adulthood, either through an appreciation and respect for heritage or by becoming archaeologists.

While there are many positive aspects to Belfast YAC, this review has enabled us to identify areas that we can work on for the future. Sadly, we have difficulty in maintaining the engagement of members older than fourteen years, which could perhaps be partly related to the invisibility of archaeology at Key Stage 4 in the national curriculum. This is a UK-wide problem and is referred to specifically in the YAC 2015 census report, where it is noted that:

> 'YAC members aged 14+ are likely to be those with most committed interest in archaeology. Potentially this can cause significant difficulties for volunteers, who need to balance the differing levels of ability between the majority of their members (who are likely to be <12) and a minority of older members who are looking for a deeper level of engagement' (Milsted 2015, 4).

Those individuals who have already identified their interest in archaeology are indeed highly committed to the subject, and we are working on solutions to maintain the engagement of our older members. We organise more challenging activities for them that involve more substantial projects that run over several sessions, such as undertaking research on a monument in their local area or helping with post-excavation analysis.

We are also mindful of the paucity of older (55+ years) volunteer leaders. Our positioning within the Centre for Community Archaeology at QUB, however, has enabled us to develop strong links with the Ulster Archaeological Society, which has a strong cohort of members in this age group. In the future we aim to hold an annual shared event that encourages grandparents and grandchildren to come together to learn about archaeology. We also need to address the gender bias within the Club, both in terms of volunteer leaders, who are predominantly female, and members, who are largely male. This may be possible through further promoting the Club both within the university and beyond, using positive male and female role models. In particular, we need to demonstrate that archaeology is not simply an outdoor 'dirty' activity and that it is an extremely broad discipline that has something for everyone, regardless of age or sex.

The Belfast YAC leaders are all highly committed to their discipline and thoroughly enjoy sharing the excitement of learning about the people of the past with the members and their families. The authors of this paper were both responsible for the foundation of the Club fourteen years ago and are very proud of its achievements to date. We have no doubt that it will continue to grow and develop for many more years to come, particularly in an era in which the importance and benefits of community archaeology are becoming increasingly recognised.

ACKNOWLEDGEMENTS

Thanks are due to Nicky Milsted (YAC Projects and Communications Officer) for advising on the history of YAC and answering our queries. We are extremely grateful to all those who have generously facilitated sessions for us over the years. We would like to take this opportunity to extend a huge thank-you to all of our volunteer leaders, past and present, for giving their time, their ideas and their enthusiasm to the running of the Club. Without them Belfast YAC would simply not be possible! Finally, thank-you to all our members—we hope that you enjoy the Club for years to come and that you become the next generation of archaeologists!

REFERENCES

AQA 2018 GCSE History (http://www.aqa.org.uk/subjects/history/gcse/history-8145; accessed 5 April 2018).

CBA (n.d.) About us (http://new.archaeologyuk.org/about-us/; accessed 12 April 2018).

CCEA 2007a The Northern Ireland curriculum—primary (http://www.nicurriculum.org.uk/docs/key_stages_1_and_2/northern_ireland_curriculum_primary.pdf; accessed 4 April 2018).

CCEA 2007b The statutory curriculum at Key Stage 3—rationale and detail (http://ccea.org.uk/sites/default/files/docs/curriculum/area_of_learning/statutory_requirements/statutory_curriculum_ks3.pdf; accessed 4 April 2018).

CCEA 2015 History (http://ccea.org.uk/history/; accessed 5 April 2018).

Henson, D. 2007 The Young Archaeologists' Club: a short history. Unpublished report for the Council for British Archaeology.

Horning, A., Breen, C. and Brannon, N. 2015 From the past to the future: integrating archaeology and conflict resolution in Northern Ireland. *Conservation and Management of Archaeological Sites* **17**, 5–21.

Milsted, N. 2015 Young Archaeologists' Club census 2015. Unpublished report for the Council for British Archaeology.

Milsted, N. 2017 Young Archaeologists' Club annual report, April 2016–March 2017. Unpublished report for the Council for British Archaeology.

NUT (n.d.) Practical strategies for challenging gender stereotypical choices and behaviours in primary schools—boys' things and girls' things? (http://www.teachers.org.uk/files/boys-things-revise-8875.pdf; accessed 8 April 2018).

Oxford University Press (n.d.) *Oxford Living Dictionaries* (https://en.oxforddictionaries.com/definition/community; accessed 10 April 2018).

Shepperson, M. 2017 British archaeology is in a fight for survival (https://www.theguardian.com/science/2017/jun/20/trouble-brewing-british-archaeology; accessed 8 April 2018).

Talalay, L.E. and Gerring, T. 2007 Eviscerating Barbie. Telling children about Egyptian mummification. In N. Galanidou and L.H. Dommasnes (eds), *Telling children about the past: an interdisciplinary perspective*, 226–40. University of Michigan Press, Ann Arbor.

Weale, S. 2016 Scrapping of archaeology and classics A-levels criticised as 'barbaric act' (https://www.theguardian.com/education/2016/oct/17/scrapping-archeology-classics-a-levels-barbaric-tony-robinson; accessed 28 March 2018).

12. The Adopt-a-Monument experience

NEIL JACKMAN

ABSTRACT

In recent years community archaeology has become a common way for the general public to engage with their history and archaeology in Ireland, with a number of successful public and community excavations, surveys and conservation projects. Arising from successive strategic plans, 'Adopt a Monument' is an initiative of the Heritage Council and is project-managed by Abarta Heritage. It follows the successful model created by Archaeology Scotland in the 1990s. The Adopt-a-Monument scheme aims to empower local communities to take an active role in understanding, protecting and engaging with their local heritage, while collaborating with stakeholders and State bodies, as well as following best practice and abiding by National Monuments legislation. Since the inception of the scheme in late 2015, thirteen groups across Ireland have been selected for participation, with a further seven sites recently added to the scheme in 2019. This paper outlines the scheme and introduces the different community groups and their varied monuments, from an ancient stone fort on a hidden island in Donegal to a twentieth-century handball alley. Their experiences are detailed, along with insights into the selection process and some common themes and challenges experienced by the participants.

THE ADOPT-A-MONUMENT SCHEME

'Adopt a Monument' is an initiative of the Heritage Council. The scheme aims to empower communities to become more involved in the conservation and protection of their local monuments for future generations, and to help them to raise awareness about the diverse heritage in their locality.

Adopt a Monument endeavours to bring monuments and local heritage from the periphery into the heart of a community. It is a democratising process for heritage that encourages, mobilises and engages with a variety of people from across the community. It aims to provide a powerful mechanism to connect monuments with communities for the benefit of both. The Adopt-a-Monument scheme offers participants opportunities to work collaboratively together as a community, to get active and to participate in community development, to boost regional tourism and business and employment opportunities, and to develop and understand the story of their locality. For the monuments, the scheme has the potential to ensure ongoing maintenance and care, increased protection through increased civic value, and increased standards of interpretation and understanding.

The scheme takes its inspiration from the successful 'Adopt a Monument Scotland' scheme, established in the 1990s by Archaeology Scotland, and a similar programme in Finland. The scheme in Ireland began in late 2015, when the Heritage Council appointed Abarta Heritage to project-manage Adopt a Monument, to help design the application process and to provide mentoring and support for successful groups.

One of the core aims of the Adopt-a-Monument scheme is to assist in creating positive partnerships between local community groups and State organisations, heritage professionals, archaeologists, academia and other experts working in the heritage and cultural sector. The advice, mentorship and training that are part of the scheme are designed to help the groups navigate their way through funding, organisational and legislative matters. A critical part of heritage and archaeological management is understanding the range of protective legislation measures that are in place to preserve our heritage for the future. The Adopt-a-Monument team works closely with community groups and State authorities such as the National Monuments Service to ensure that any approach to monument protection and conservation is undertaken in a best-practice and sustainable way that will not cause damage to our built or natural heritage. Each of the Adopt-a-Monument groups is supplied with a Management Plan template and they are given assistance and guidance to help complete this important document. Meetings are held with the group to explain aspects of the plan but it is entirely up to the group to decide amongst themselves what their own priorities and ambitions for the site are. The experience of Adopt a Monument thus far has reflected a true diversity both in the monuments themselves and in the aims and objectives of the participants.

Application process

The application process for Adopt a Monument was designed to be as thorough and transparent as possible. There are five key criteria that must be established for an application to proceed to the second round of evaluation.

Landowner and consent: The group must establish who owns the site. Has the landowner (such as the County Council, Coillte, the relevant church authority or a private landowner) given consent for the monument to be put forward for the Adopt-a-Monument scheme and for access to the monument? Do they agree with your long-term aims and objectives (such as tourism etc.) as this may have an impact on them for the future?

Site status: The scheme is unable to consider applications from National Monuments under the ownership or guardianship of the Minister for Culture, Heritage and the Gaeltacht.

Community involvement: This seeks to understand the make-up of the proposed community group. Applicants should be an established group with a clear organisational structure, with the potential for a positive and inclusive steering committee that will drive the project to success. As heritage projects are often far too onerous and demanding to fall on the shoulders of one person, an ideal group would be made up of a diverse section of the community who all bring their different interests and strengths to the project.

Safety and access: This seeks to understand whether there is safe access to the monument. Is the access through agricultural lands? Are there issues with livestock? Is the site structurally safe? Will the site itself be put at risk through any of the proposed works?

Environmental impact: Occasionally (often in an urban environment) a historical monument, e.g. a neglected and overgrown graveyard, can become a haven for wildlife and biodiversity. The nature of some conservation or vegetation management works, or the increased footfall during the project and from potential visitors, can have a negative impact on the natural environment of the site. The scheme can assist with methods to understand and mitigate such impacts on biodiversity by obtaining expert advice and works, but the group need to demonstrate that they have considered the natural as well as the cultural heritage when devising their application and plans.

With the exception of ownership and site status, failure to meet one of the five criteria does not necessarily exclude an application from being considered, but it does help to identify any potential issues that must be addressed. If the initial criteria are successfully met, the application is then scrutinised by a panel of heritage experts. The panels include representatives from the staff and board of the Heritage Council, academia and heritage practitioners, the National Monuments Service, Archaeology Scotland and others with an interest in heritage and community development. Each application is discussed in detail, the applications' stated aims and objectives are reviewed and compared, and a short list of the most promising applications is agreed upon. Abarta Heritage then visit every community on the short list, to discuss the scheme and application in detail and to visit the site to gain a firsthand impression of both the community and the monument. This information is then discussed again with the Heritage Council and a final decision is made on the most appropriate sites for selection. A key determinant that has been part of the ethos of the scheme since its inception is that we do not select a monument on its own archaeological or historical merits; we select a community. The group is always of the utmost importance, and we choose those who are sustainable (where the workload is not all going to fall on one person), groups who have clear and appropriate

Fig. 12.1—Location map of Adopt-a-Monument sites.

Fig. 12.2—The stunning Doon Fort, adopted by the Ardara, Glenties and Portnoo (GAP) Heritage and History Group (Abarta Heritage).

aims and objectives and are willing to adhere to best practice, and those communities who can work together as a group with outside stakeholders to give their project the very best chance of success.

In 2016, the initial year of the programme, Adopt a Monument received over 90 applications from around the country, and in the second year a further 60 applications were made by groups wishing to participate in the scheme. A number of the applications were immediately found to be ineligible, as they failed to meet the above criteria. The most common reasons for rejection were failure to establish permission from the landowner, that the application was on behalf of an individual rather than a community or group, and that the aims and objectives of the applicants were not wholly aligned to the ethos of Adopt a Monument.

Six communities and monuments were selected in the inaugural year of 2016, and a further seven were chosen for participation in 2017. These thirteen groups are representative of sites around Ireland, with monuments ranging from early medieval stone forts to a handball alley that dates from the 1930s. This diversity in monuments within the scheme reflects the wide scope of what our 'heritage' really is (Fig. 12.1).

PARTICIPANT ADOPT-A-MONUMENT GROUPS

Doon Fort, Ardara, Co. Donegal ('adopted' by the Ardara, Glenties and Portnoo (GAP) Heritage and History Group in 2016)

Dating from the early medieval period, Doon Fort (Recorded Monument DG064-011) is undoubtedly one of the most spectacularly picturesque heritage sites in Ireland (Fig. 12.2). It is situated on a small island in the middle of Loughadoon, just outside the charming village of Ardara in County Donegal. The fort was 'adopted' by the Ardara, Glenties and Portnoo (GAP) Heritage and History Group, who wish to help the landowner to preserve this stunning site for future generations.

The site has suffered in recent decades from the vigorous growth of ivy, which threatens to undermine the walls and has already led to collapse of part of the stone wall. Safe and appropriate access to the monument has been another problem that the group wanted to solve in conjunction with the landowner. As it is such a beautiful and otherworldly place, visitors are understandably keen to experience it for themselves. The waters of the lake are full of hidden

Fig. 12.3—Killeshandra Tidy Towns during Heritage Week (Abarta Heritage).

rocks, however, and the site itself is in a precarious condition. The increased pressure of tourism puts the safety of both the visitors and this vulnerable monument at risk.

Since becoming part of the Adopt-a-Monument scheme, the group have worked tirelessly to raise awareness about the importance and vulnerability of the site and to ensure its preservation. In 2016 Heritage Council funding was secured to commission an environmental and conservation report on the site, and a successful training weekend was held in Ardara, where the group came together to discuss the tourism potential of the area. The Adopt-a-Monument scheme has been working with the local community group to help record the site, to manage the vegetation that threatens to undermine the walls, to establish a conservation plan, to improve access and interpretation and to help raise awareness of the fort. Thanks to funding from the Heritage Council, a geophysical and photogrammetry survey was carried out by Earthsound Geophysics in 2017 to cast new light on this important monument. This was enabled by a careful cut-back of the dense ivy growth by the group, with the support of the Dry Stone Wall Association of

Ireland and the McHugh family and under the supervision and guidance of conservation engineer Duncan McLaren and the National Monuments Service. The work was featured on RTÉ *Nationwide*, which captured the real essence of the tremendous commitment of the local community and landowner in protecting and preserving this beautiful and unique monument.

Church of the Rath, Killeshandra, Co. Cavan ('adopted' by Killeshandra Tidy Towns in 2016)

The town of Killeshandra takes its name from the historic church and graveyard known as the 'Church of the Rath'. This wonderfully atmospheric monument has ancient origins and is thought to have been constructed on the site of an early medieval ringfort. The church (National Inventory of Architectural Heritage Reg. No. 40309001) is one of the few Jacobean-style churches remaining in Ireland and is of national architectural importance. The old brick vaulted roof of the church is in a desperately precarious condition, however, and the site was 'adopted' by Killeshandra Tidy Towns, who were concerned about the future of the monument.

Since participating in the scheme, the group held

Fig. 12.4—Excavation under way at Gallows Hill, Co. Waterford (Abarta Heritage).

a successful information and storytelling evening, where people from all around the locality came to share their stories and discuss the future of the monument. The group have also received training on the best-practice care and maintenance of historic graveyards. They held a very successful Heritage Week event in August 2016, when over 600 people visited the graveyard over the weekend to hear about the history of the site and come face to face with occupants of the graveyard who had risen from the dead to tell their tales (Fig. 12.3). The group continue to host events and activities to raise awareness about the monument and to carry out fund-raising. In 2018, with the support of Cavan County Council Heritage Officer Anne Marie Ward, they were awarded significant funding from the Department of Culture, Heritage and the Gaeltacht and Cavan County Council's Structures at Risk Fund, as well as Heritage Council funding. This will enable conservation works with conservation engineer Kevin Blackwood, and the erection of a new roof to protect the monument. The group have also installed interpretative signage to help tell the story of this once-forgotten but now greatly cherished monument.

Gallows Hill, Dungarvan, Co. Waterford ('adopted' by the Gallows Hill Community Archaeology Group in 2016)

Gallows Hill in Dungarvan, Co. Waterford (Recorded Monument WA031-067), is a large defensive motte or earthen castle site dating from the twelfth or thirteenth century. The motte in Dungarvan is surrounded by housing estates on the outskirts of the town, and over the years it had become neglected, with anti-social behaviour, dumping and large fires lit on its summit. The motte was 'adopted' by the Gallows Hill Community Archaeology Group, in partnership with Waterford County Museum, in order to raise awareness of the monument, to help limit illegal dumping and bonfires, and to engage the local community in discovering the story of this important historic site. The group were awarded funding by the Heritage Council for geophysical surveys, carried out by Kevin Barton, and they held a number of public engagement events—including a medieval fair—to help raise awareness. The fair featured demonstrations of life in the past by the Déise Medieval re-enactment group, and the local Men's Shed group created a set of stocks. The group had a local artist working with children to create chalk

Fig. 12.5—A guided walk to Roundhill motte, Lismore, by Lismore Heritage Centre during Heritage Week (Abarta Heritage).

murals of life in Viking and medieval Dungarvan, and with funding and assistance from Waterford County Council the wonderful Big Dig gave the local children an opportunity to get hands-on with archaeology.

In recognition of their efforts and superb work, the group won the Culture & Art Award at the 2017 Waterford Public Participation Network Community Awards. In 2017 they raised funds and carried out a targeted archaeological test excavation of the monument under the guidance of archaeologist Dave Pollock (Fig. 12.4). The dig uncovered fascinating new insights into the story of this monument, revealing that long after it was erected by the Anglo-Normans it was reused in the seventeenth century as a fort (Knight-O'Connor and Cantwell, this volume). The group's work was featured in *Archaeology Ireland* magazine, and they have presented their findings at the Community Archaeology Conference at Rathcroghan and the annual conference of the Group for the Study of Irish Historic Settlement. They plan to carry out further surveys and excavation to reveal more of the story, along with hosting an Archaeology Festival with re-enactments and displays.

Roundhill, Lismore, Co. Waterford ('adopted' by the Lismore Heritage Company and Lismore Tidy Towns in 2016)

The large Anglo-Norman motte at Roundhill (Recorded Monument WA021-022) is spectacularly sited beside the River Blackwater just outside Lismore,

Co. Waterford. The monument was 'adopted' by a group formed of the Lismore Heritage Company and Lismore Tidy Towns. Thanks to funding and support from the Heritage Council, the group commissioned a number of detailed surveys on the history, biodiversity and geology of the monument, and they have carried out topographical and geophysical surveys with geophysicist Kevin Barton and Simon Dowling. In 2017 the group carried out a successful folklore project with local secondary school students, who captured the stories and traditions of Roundhill and Lismore. This project led to an art competition with the Heritage Council, where the efforts of the students were judged and prizes awarded. Future plans include the creation of a safe walking route around the base of this enormous monument, with interpretative signage both on site and at the Heritage Centre to help visitors understand its story (Fig. 12.5).

Baravore Ore Crusher Building, Glenmalure, Co. Wicklow ('adopted' by the Glenmalure PURE Mile Group in 2016)

The New Crusher building at Baravore is a two-storey edifice of cut-stone granite constructed in 1859–60. It stands as a testament to the entrepreneurs of the nineteenth century who sought to exploit the rich mineral lodes that lay hidden deep in these beautiful valleys of County Wicklow. The building was 'adopted' by the Glenmalure PURE Mile Group, who wished to conserve this important building and to help raise

Fig. 12.6—Glenmalure PURE Mile Group with the Mining Heritage Trust of Ireland and participants at Baravore for Heritage Week (Abarta Heritage).

awareness about and tell the story of the industrial heritage of Glenmalure. Having secured funding from the landowners, Coillte and Wicklow County Council, conservation works were successfully carried out on the crusher building to stabilise and repoint the walls and to make the building safe for future generations. Experienced stonemason Kevin Carrigan carried out the work under the direction of conservation engineer Ivor McElveen.

Supported by Adopt a Monument, the Mining Heritage Trust of Ireland, Wicklow County Council and Coillte, the group have been tireless in their efforts to raise awareness of the story of this beautiful valley, and they have held a number of successful Heritage Week events (Fig. 12.6), tours and a celebratory weekend when visitors enjoyed demonstrations by the stonemasons and witnessed a small archaeological excavation to uncover the original floor surface of the building. Local children also had the opportunity to experience an archaeological 'dig in a box'. Throughout the project the community at Glenmalure displayed a true passion for their place, and a key determinant for their success has been their focus on building positive and proactive partnerships with stakeholders and other local heritage groups and organisations like the Glens of Lead. Now visitors can enjoy the beautifully conserved building as part of a looped walk with

interpretative signage that was designed with the assistance of the Mining Heritage Trust of Ireland.

Handball Alley, Ballintleva, Co. Roscommon ('adopted' by the Ballintleva National School Board of Management in 2016)

The handball alley at Ballintleva, Co. Roscommon, is undoubtedly the most modern monument selected to be part of this scheme (Fig. 12.7). Though it was constructed relatively recently, in the 1930s, the structure is of great social and community significance, as it was a focal point for the community for generations until it was recently deemed unsafe. Handball is similar to squash, with players using their bare hand or fist to strike a ball against a wall in such a way that the opponent cannot return the shot.

The handball alley was 'adopted' by the Ballintleva National School Board of Management, who manage the National School next door to the alley. The group aim to revive the long-standing tradition of handball in the area, as handball was once a very popular sport across Ireland, and in particular in this area. The group have carried out successful folklore projects in the National School to help the children gather stories from their parents and relatives. They have also held successful Heritage Week tours to help raise awareness of the wealth of heritage in the locality.

Fig. 12.7—Handball alley at Ballintleva (Abarta Heritage).

Fig. 12.8—The precarious ruins of Kilbarron Castle, Co. Donegal (Abarta Heritage).

Fig. 12.9—The line of bushes and trees marks St Moling's Millrace.

Kilbarron Castle, Co. Donegal ('adopted' by the Kilbarron Castle Conservation Group in 2017)

Located near Ballyshannon, Co. Donegal, Kilbarron Castle (Recorded Monument DG103-043002-) is the ruin of a late medieval castle and the birthplace of Mícheál Ó Cléirigh (the chief author of the famous Annals of the Four Masters). The ruins are currently in a very precarious condition and the Kilbarron Castle Conservation Group 'adopted' the monument to protect, conserve and interpret the remains of the site (Fig. 12.8).

The group at Kilbarron have taken a number of steps forward on the path towards the conservation of this important monument. The works are now planned for 2019, if funding can be secured. The group have received guidance in best-practice conservation and management from Pauline Gleeson (National Monuments Service) and Ian Doyle (Heritage Council). They have been active in seeking to raise awareness of the site and have engaged with the landowner and Donegal County Council, especially Heritage Officer Joseph Gallagher, throughout the year. The group are also interested in genealogy and helping to tell the story of the Cleary family. They undertook a well-attended Heritage Week walk and tour and continue with the popular Michael O'Cleirigh Summer School.

St Moling's Millrace, St Mullins, Co. Carlow ('adopted' by the St Mullins Amenity and Recreational Tourism Group Ltd in 2017)

St Moling's Millrace (Recorded Monument CW026-006) is a stream leading to a historic mill which was dug by the saint's own hands, according to folklore. Today the remains of the millrace are heavily overgrown (Fig. 12.9). The St Mullins Amenity and Recreational Tourism Group Ltd 'adopted' the site, as they wished to develop an understanding of the archaeology, pilgrimage traditions and folklore related to the monument, and to ensure its protection for future generations.

The group at St Mullins have been working to deepen their understanding of this monument, and have met with Dr Colin Rynne, University College Cork, who specialises in the archaeology of milling. The group have also been working hard to engage with local landowners and the broader local community. They held a successful Heritage Week event that focused on the natural heritage of the millrace and how it has become recognised for its biodiversity value.

Old St Peter's Church, Portlaoise, Co. Laois ('adopted' by Portlaoise Tidy Towns in 2017)

Old St Peter's Church (Recorded Monument LA013-041002) is one of the oldest buildings surviving in Portlaoise and dates back to the middle of the sixteenth century (Fig. 12.10). The church and graveyard were

Fig. 12.10—Old St Peter's Church, Portlaoise, Co. Laois, adopted by Portlaoise Tidy Towns (Abarta Heritage).

'adopted' by Portlaoise Tidy Towns, who wish to conserve the historic fabric of the site and to recreate a place for peaceful reflection within the busy town centre of Portlaoise. The group created a collaborative steering group consisting of members of Portlaoise Tidy Towns, Laois County Council Heritage Officer Catherine Casey, the Irish Wildlife Trust and archaeologist Colm Flynn. The group successfully applied for Heritage Council Grant funding and have had the iron gates to the graveyard beautifully conserved. They have also cut back excess vegetation and ivy in accordance with best practice, and have carried out small amounts of conservation work to the tower and graveyard wall. They have been very proactive in securing funding, and plan to work with local schools and the broader community to protect this important site and to help tell its story. The application came at an exciting time for heritage in Portlaoise. The Council's new Public Realm Plan, *2040 and beyond: a vision for Portlaoise*, emphasises the value of heritage to public well-being. The plan has designed a 'Cultural Quarter' and has led to investment in a conservation plan for the sixteenth-century Fort Protector as well as Old St Peter's Church, with a view to helping residents and visitors to appreciate the story and origins of the town.

Earlshill Colliery and Powder House, Co. Tipperary ('adopted' by the Slieveardagh Mining Group in 2017)

The Powder House is part of an enormous industrial coal-mining landscape that once stretched from Tipperary to Castlecomer in County Kilkenny. The Slieveardagh Mining Group want to preserve and protect the important industrial heritage of the locality, and to raise awareness of the social history of the area.

The group have hosted successful Heritage Week events, with a tour of the industrial complex and an exhibition with beautifully designed models to show locals how the area once appeared. They have engaged with bodies such as the Mining Heritage Trust of Ireland, and they have continued their important work in collecting the stories of the miners who once lived and worked here. They have held discussions with academics such as Dr Colin Rynne (Fig. 12.11) and Dr Richard Clutterbuck, and it is hoped that this will lead to a detailed study of the industrial heritage of the region.

Kilfinane Motte, Co. Limerick ('adopted' by Kilfinane Community Council in 2017)

The large monument, recorded as a castle or motte (Recorded Monument LI056-024), consists of a large motte-like mound that appears to be positioned on the

Fig. 12.11—The Slieveardagh Mining Group with Dr Colin Rynne at the Powder House of Earlshill Colliery.

Fig. 12.12—The motte of Kilfinane, adopted by Kilfinane Community Council (Abarta Heritage).

banks and ditches of an early medieval ringfort, though the mound and ditches may be contemporaneous (Fig. 12.12). The monument was 'adopted' by Kilfinane Community Council, who wish to develop an understanding of the archaeology and heritage through survey and geophysics to better promote and protect this important monument for future generations.

The group have conducted research on the history and folklore of the monument and its surrounding archaeological landscape. Over the course of their time in the Adopt-a-Monument scheme, they have had assistance from County and City Archaeologist Sarah McCutcheon and have enjoyed ongoing support from Ballyhoura Development CLG.

The group were awarded Heritage Council funding to commission a detailed geophysical survey by Earthsound Geophysics in 2017. The survey revealed a complex concentration of archaeological features, providing evidence that the site was a place of importance even before the arrival of the Normans. Further survey work is planned for the coming years to help establish the full nature and extent of this significant archaeological landscape.

Knockboy Medieval Parish Church, Co. Waterford ('adopted' by the Knockboy Church Conservation Group in 2017)

The medieval church and graveyard at Knockboy (Recorded Monument WA013-034001) (Fig. 12.13) is home to seven ogham stones that were built into its walls. Perhaps the chief conservation issue facing this site for a number of years has been the vigorous ivy growth on the surviving church remains. The local community came together to form the Knockboy Church Conservation Group with Dr Nora White (the principal investigator on the 'Ogham in 3D' project).

Since their participation in the Adopt-a-Monument scheme, the group have taken important steps along the path to conservation. They were awarded grant funding from the Heritage Council to erect scaffolding and have the dense cover of ivy professionally removed, under the supervision of archaeologist Dave Pollock. The site was subsequently recorded using photogrammetry techniques by Simon Dowling and assessed by conservation engineer Ivor McElveen. The group were further assisted by additional funding from Waterford County Council, and Heritage Officer Bernadette Guest and Conservation Officer Rosemary Ryall have both been of great help to the group. They have also received advice and support from Fionnbarr Moore and Pauline Gleeson of the National Monuments Service. In 2018 the gable ends of the church were conserved by stonemason Tom Pollard under the direction of conservation engineer James Powell.

The group intend to continue the work of protecting this important monument and to continue to engage with the local authority and national bodies

Fig. 12.13—Knockboy medieval church, Co. Waterford (Abarta Heritage).

Fig. 12.14—Mountbellew Walled Garden, Galway, adopted by the Mountbellew Heritage and Tourism Network (Abarta Heritage).

to ensure that all works are carried out according to best practice.

The group has helped to raise awareness by hosting successful Heritage Week events, where visitors learned about the archaeology and history of this fascinating site, along with demonstrations on medieval building techniques and mortar by stonemason Tom Pollard.

Mountbellew Walled Garden, Mountbellew, Co. Galway ('adopted' by the Mountbellew Heritage and Tourism Network in 2017)

The early nineteenth-century walled garden of Mountbellew (National Inventory of Architectural Heritage Reg. No. 30404617) was once part of the Bellew Estate (Fig. 12.14). The garden was 'adopted' by the Mountbellew Heritage and Tourism Network, who wish to conserve the large stone walls that surround the gardens and to restore the features of the garden to their original glory. They hope that the process will lead to the garden becoming a popular tourism attraction and a positive local amenity for the area. Since they joined the scheme, the group have achieved much. Perhaps most importantly, they have developed very positive collaboration with the landowners (Coillte),

the local authority, Galway County Council, especially Heritage Officer Marie Mannion, Conservation Officer Máirín Doddy and Biodiversity Officer Elaine O'Riordain, the National Monuments Service, local councillors and businesses, and the broader local community. The group were awarded funding through the Built Heritage Investment Scheme administered by Galway County Council and used it to carry out a conservation and specification plan of works for the entrance archway. Following the report, the group had the archway and parts of the wall repaired by a professional stonemason on behalf of the Department of Culture, Heritage and the Gaeltacht.

In 2018 the eminent garden historian Finola Reid produced a detailed report and assessment of the garden that lays out clear strategies for the sensitive restoration of this important site. The group have also greatly benefited from the advice and support of Galway Community Archaeologist Dr Christy Cunniffe, who has demonstrated archaeological techniques and methods by helping the group to uncover the original features of the garden. They also received training in research techniques and practice, and in tourism, public engagement and outreach. As a group, they have been proactive in raising funds, and they have hosted a number of events and Heritage Week activities, along with developing a website and Facebook page to help raise awareness of the project and to keep the local community informed of their progress. Like the other groups, Mountbellew Heritage and Tourism worked on a management plan to help them set out the short-, medium- and long-term steps to achieve their ambitions.

Other groups

Seven new groups were accepted into the Adopt-a-Monument scheme in the summer of 2019: a nineteenth-century limekiln at Kilmurry, Co. Clare; a Napoleonic-era battery fort that guarded the Shannon Estuary at Kilkerrin, Co. Clare; an unusual 'moated' site on the shoulder of Brandon Hill, Co. Kilkenny; the historic Malin Well Old Church at Malin Head, Co. Donegal; a medieval church in Lucan, Co. Dublin; Moygara Castle, Co. Sligo; and the intriguingly named 'Graves of the Leinstermen' in County Tipperary.

Like the other Adopt-a-Monument sites, each of these monuments comes with its own particular challenges, but in common with the others they all share a committed community who are determined to protect, promote and preserve their local heritage.

THE ADOPT-A-MONUMENT MANUAL—GUIDANCE FOR COMMUNITY ARCHAEOLOGY PROJECTS

In addition to the provision of ongoing mentoring, training, support and advocacy for the participant groups, a guidance manual was created and published in 2017 to help any community or voluntary group to engage with their heritage (Burke *et al.* 2017). The manual covers a range of core aspects, such as advice on how to conduct research, fund-raising, organisational development, health and safety, recording, promotions and outreach, and care and conservation. It was awarded the 'Mary Mulvihill Media Award' by the Industrial Heritage Association of Ireland in 2017. The manual is available free of charge in print or as a free PDF download from the Heritage Council.

THE ADOPT-A-MONUMENT EXPERIENCE

From the experience of Adopt a Monument to date, one of the key learning outcomes both for us as practitioners and for the community participants is that there are few 'quick wins' in heritage. By its very nature, the conservation and understanding of our monuments can involve a gradual, and an occasionally glacial, process. It can take time to create a sustainable group or team, to agree on approach and plans, to raise funds, to build a support network and to engage with appropriate practitioners and specialists. It can also take time to obtain the necessary permissions to build awareness and momentum, but all of that time is well spent. There are no short cuts in heritage, but if a group embraces the 'journey' as being a necessary and essential part of the process the project has a much higher chance of success, as the process becomes an enjoyable experience in itself.

Adopt a Monument is a truly rewarding and important project. Local communities play an increasingly important role in the ongoing care and conservation of our cultural environment. With support, funding and training, the communities can be empowered to become a truly vital force in the preservation of our national heritage.

FURTHER READING AND SOURCES

Burke, R., Jackman, N. and Ryan, C. 2017 *Adopt a Monument: guidance for community archaeology projects*. The Heritage Council, Kilkenny.

Internet resources
Adopt a Monument Ireland: http://www.heritage council.ie/projects/adopt-a-monument and https://www.abartaheritage.ie/adopt-a-monument-ireland/.
Adopt a Monument Scotland: https://archaeology scotland.org.uk/adopt-a-monument/.
Adopt a Monument Manual: http://www.heritage council.ie/content/files/Guidance_for_communit y_archaeology_projects.pdf.

13. The Ulster Scots Archaeological Services Project—encouraging community engagement with the study of Plantation-era archaeology

JAMES LYTTLETON AND NEIL MACNAB

ABSTRACT

The Ulster Scots Archaeological Services Project was a three-year project commissioned by the former Department of Culture, Arts and Leisure in Northern Ireland. Its purpose was to raise awareness of Ulster Scots history, heritage and culture, and to provide a clearer understanding of the archaeology of the Plantation era. The project brought together all the evidence for archaeological sites and monuments dating from the Plantation period (1600–50), relating not just to the Ulster Scots but also to the Gaelic Irish and English. The project was managed by archaeologists from AECOM, an engineering and environmental consultancy firm, and involved extensive research, field survey, excavation and community outreach. A key objective of the project was to promote cross-community co-operation and engagement through involvement in the archaeological excavations and outreach events. The project had a strong research focus, being led by academic advisers under the direction of a project steering group with members drawn from the Historic Environment Division and the Department of Culture, Arts and Leisure. The team undertook three set-piece community-based archaeological excavations and prepared a teachers' education pack, popular publications and public outreach, including a weekly online diary or blog that shared the day-to-day events and findings of the excavations. The team also engaged with a number of cross-community groups in North Belfast and Carrickfergus, bringing archaeological workshops to their door. The project culminated with a unique landmark publication documenting all of the known archaeological sites from the period in Northern Ireland. The project was covered by television programmes on the BBC and UTV. Re-enactors also brought the open days to life, with the construction of a creat house (Gaelic Irish cabin) and the preparation of displays of finds, period costumes, armour, weapons and a blacksmith. The open days also had the benefit of having the fortified houses at Derrywoone and Monea as archaeological backdrops.

INTRODUCTION

The Ulster Scots Archaeological Services Project was a three-year project undertaken by AECOM, a multinational environmental consultancy firm, and commissioned by the former Department of Culture, Arts and Leisure (now assimilated into the Department for Communities) following the advice of the Ministerial Advisory Group for the Ulster Scots Academy (MAGUS). Its purpose was to raise awareness of Ulster Scots history, heritage and culture, and to provide a clearer understanding of the impact of the Ulster Plantation on the landscape, peoples and architecture of the province. The project brought together for the first time all the evidence for archaeological sites and monuments dating from the Plantation period (1600–50) across Northern Ireland. It involved extensive research, field survey and excavation. A key objective of the project was to promote cross-community outreach and engagement through involvement in archaeological excavations and other events. It has been observed that archaeological

fieldwork can facilitate a degree of community empowerment among participants and promote dialogue and greater understanding between groups from different political traditions (Breen *et al.* 2015, 920). The project had a strong research focus, being led by academic advisers under the direction of a project steering group, with members drawn from the Historic Environment Division and the Department of Culture, Arts and Leisure in Belfast.

THE ARCHAEOLOGICAL EXCAVATION OF THREE ULSTER SCOTS SITES

A core component of the AECOM-led project was the identification of three archaeological sites suitable for excavation as part of the project's agenda to identify and study the domestic dwellings of the new Scottish tenants (Fig. 13.1). All three of the archaeological excavations undertaken for the project were carried out by Irish Archaeological Consultancy (IAC) and directed by Fintan Walsh. The first excavation was

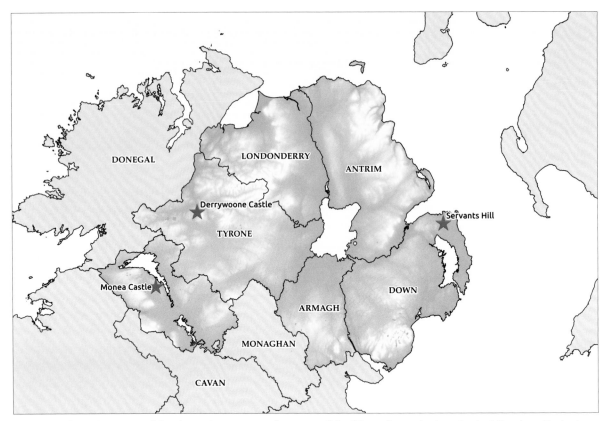

Fig. 13.1—Location map of the three sites excavated as part of the Ulster Scots Archaeological Services Project: Servants Hill, Co. Down, Derrywoone Castle, Co. Tyrone, and Monea Castle, Co. Fermanagh (courtesy of IAC).

carried out at Servants Hill, located in the suburbs of Bangor, on a small farm surrounded by modern housing and the Bloomfield Shopping Centre. Pictorial maps produced by the cartographer Thomas Raven in 1625 clearly illustrate four houses at this location, together with their garden plots, beside a watercourse that still flows by the site today (Fig. 13.2). The place-name suggests that the houses were occupied by tenants of James Hamilton, a prominent Scottish landowner at the time. The houses are illustrated as being essentially Gaelic Irish in architectural form— single-storey, possibly of oval or subrectangular plan, with a thatched roof—but also with a centrally placed chimney-stack. Few examples of such houses have been excavated, and their investigation on a greenfield site provided a rare opportunity to explore such structures. A geophysical survey identified several anomalies which reflected the presence of what was believed to be one of the houses, as well as field ditches or boundaries and rubbish pits. Subsequent excavation failed to reveal any evidence for Plantation-period settlement, but it did uncover houses dating from a much earlier period—the Bronze Age (Walsh 2014) (Fig. 13.3).

The second excavation took place in the early summer of 2013 at Derrywoone Castle in County Tyrone. This fortified house was built in 1622 by a Scottish planter, Sir George Hamilton, on a raised plateau overlooking Lough Catherine, and is now surrounded by mixed open farmland and woods within the Baronscourt estate (Fig. 13.4). The house is L-shaped in plan, with a west and a south wing, and consists of three floors and an attic, with the most important room, the great chamber, on the first floor. The timber floors would have been supported on wooden joists, the sockets for which are still evident in the walls today. The windows around the house are particularly large and it is thought that they may have been half-glass, half-shutter, covered by iron grills for additional protection. A flanker tower on the north-east corner of the castle featured gun loops at ground-floor level. At first-floor level, in the re-entrant angle between the two wings, is a corbelled stone turret that contained a stairwell allowing access to the upper floors. The turret's appearance, with its carved curving corbels, is directly influenced by the Scottish masonry tradition. The primary aim of the excavation at Derrywoone was to locate the dwellings of the ordinary people who lived as tenants on Sir George Hamilton's estate. A geophysical survey identified several areas with strong archaeological potential, although there

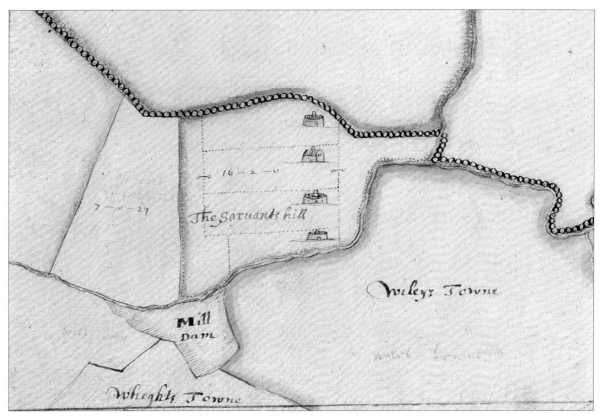

Fig. 13.2—Thomas Raven's map of the houses at Servants Hill outside Bangor, Co. Down, in 1625 (PRONI T510/1) (courtesy of the Deputy Keeper of the Records).

Fig. 13.3—Archaeological excavation at Servants Hill uncovered the remains of Bronze Age houses, but nothing of the early modern houses depicted by Raven in his 1625 map (courtesy of Ards and North Down Borough Council).

Fig. 13.4—A school group is shown how a historic building like Derrywoone Castle, Co. Tyrone, is studied by archaeologists (courtesy of IAC).

were no clear indicators of any domestic settlement. A total of fifteen cuttings were excavated across the site, uncovering traces of the surrounding courtyard wall (also known as a bawn), a cobbled stone surface within the same bawn, and pits that may be related to the construction of the castle (Walsh 2016a).[1]

The final excavation was carried out during the summer of 2014 at Monea Castle, Co. Fermanagh. The castle was built between 1618 and 1622 by a Scottish clergyman, Malcolm Hamilton, who later became the archbishop of Cashel, Co. Tipperary. It is one of the best-preserved examples of a fortified house in Ulster. The three-storey building features two circular towers on its western front façade and exhibits various aspects of Scottish architectural form and layout, including crow-stepped gables. The ground floor had vaulted ceilings and contained the kitchen and stores. The windows at this level were of small size, a feature designed to prevent unwanted visitors from gaining access. The castle stands in the south-east corner of a bawn, protected by two corner gun turrets or flankers—a circular flanker to the north-west and a D-shaped flanker to the north-east.[2] The north-western flanker was redesigned as a dovecote at an unknown

date and several nesting boxes are still evident inside. Gun loops can be seen around the castle.[3] As at Servants Hill and Derrywoone, the main objective of the excavation at Monea was to locate and investigate the tenants' houses that would have been situated in the surrounding area of the castle. A geophysical survey was undertaken around the grounds of the castle, to the north, south and west of the bawn wall. A total of eight cuttings were excavated around the castle (Fig. 13.5). While the investigations failed to reveal any evidence for the tenants' houses, they did uncover some artefacts such as musket-balls and a prehistoric axe (Walsh 2016b).

While certain areas of Monea and Derrywoone Castle were investigated to answer questions of architectural interest, the main aim of the fieldwork was to throw light on the material culture of the ordinary people who once lived on these Scottish-owned estates. The potential locations of their housing in the vicinity of the fortified houses and a group of four tenant houses in Servants Hill recorded on one of Raven's maps of the Hamilton estate were investigated. While artefacts such as window fragments, iron nails, metal slag, ceramics, tobacco pipe fragments and

Fig. 13.5—Members of Cavanaleck Community Association excavate in the shadow of Monea Castle, Co. Fermanagh (courtesy of IAC).

musket-balls were recovered, along with animal bone, no structural evidence for any seventeenth-century house was found (even though a couple of Bronze Age houses were found at Servants Hill). This highlights the challenges faced in trying to identify non-élite settlement from this period, with houses made of clay and post-and-wattle with no deep foundations, or dwellings made of timber framing supported on sill-beams, not leaving substantial remains to be uncovered in later centuries. Other archaeological approaches could be used in the search for such ephemeral house remains, including field-walking and phosphate analysis, followed up by further targeted test-pitting.

ON-SITE COMMUNITY ARCHAEOLOGY

The investigations at Derrywoone, Monea and Servants Hill provided an opportunity for the project archaeologists to be involved in a programme of community outreach, school involvement and cross-community inclusion. Heather James from Northlight Heritage, an independent archaeological company and charitable trust based in Glasgow that specialises in

community engagement, was commissioned by AECOM to co-ordinate the community archaeology activities. A blog was posted to share the day-to-day events and findings of the excavations (http:// ulsterscotsarchaeologicalproject.blogspot.co.uk), and local schools and community groups were actively engaged and encouraged to visit the sites during the course of archaeological fieldwork. Along with site tours and artefact displays, activities were arranged to familiarise schoolchildren with the range of work carried out by archaeologists: surveying exercises using a theodolite, planning using tapes, trowelling for artefacts, drawing plans of buildings, sieving for and washing artefacts, and photographing features and deposits. It was noted by the archaeologists that the children quickly understood what was being looked for and how the excavation process worked (James 2012; 2014; 2015). The artefacts found, such as the pottery, a quern-stone, a clay pipe and roofing material, also gave the pupils an insight into what life was like in the seventeenth century.

School feedback forms provided useful information by which to gauge the suitability of the various on-site activities and to inform the following year's outreach. At Monea Castle, for example, digging proved to be the most popular activity with the children (43%), followed by drawing (19%), participation in the site tour (15%) and sieving for artefacts (14%) (James 2015, 8). A total of 115 drawings were made of Monea Castle by schoolchildren during their visit; the process of drawing required the children to engage with the past in an imaginative way and to explore certain scenarios inspired by the ruins (*ibid.*, 10). The popularity of sieving and drawing demonstrates the importance of including a wide range of activities for children, to take into account personal interests and strengths (*ibid.*, 9). The castles at Derrywoone and Monea also provided a suitable backdrop to the fieldwork, which assisted in capturing the children's imagination.

Efforts were made to engage with local community groups, while further publicity was generated by engaging with newspaper and television outlets, as well as by visiting local schools to give presentations on the project. At Servants Hill, the project archaeologists received visits from the Little Diggers YAC group (North Down Museum), Downpatrick YAC group (Down County Museum), the Ulster Archaeological Society and the Bangor Historical Society (James 2012). In November 2012, as part of its first ever 'Night at the Museum' event, North Down Museum invited the project archaeologists to participate with a contribution on the Servants Hill excavation involving a poster session and a number of talks. The museum recorded over 180 visitors to the event, including parents and children who had participated in the excavations. Exchanges were lively, and some of the children attended more than one talk, obviously delighted to recognise themselves and their friends in photographs. Some clearly remembered their on-site lessons on Pythagorus' Theorem and on the distinction between natural subsoil and archaeological strata, as well as the range of different artefacts that could be uncovered by excavation (*ibid.*). The excavation at Derrywoone received visits from staff from the Ulster American Folk Park and the Ulster Archaeological Society (James 2014). The excavation at Monea Castle, in turn, attracted visits from the Cavanaleck Community Group, the Monea Parish Youth Group and the Clogher Historical Society (James 2015, 16).

In a Northern Irish context, it was important to reach out to communities on both sides of the political divide in order to provide opportunities for communities to come together and explore their shared heritage. It has been remarked that the perceived neutrality of an archaeologist can transcend community divisions (Horning 2013, 22). At Servants Hill, thirteen schools (including cross-community or integrated and those with religious affiliations) were initially invited, following the advice of staff at the North Down Museum. Both of the YAC groups and the Ulster Archaeological Society also encouraged cross-community participation (James 2012). At Derrywoone, the initial invitation of twelve schools (five of which attended) took into consideration the names of the schools and the information available on their websites to ensure that both communities were represented (James 2014). At Monea, an initial invitation was extended to fifteen schools (thirteen of which attended) to be involved in the project, again enabling cross-community representation and participation (James 2015, 1–2).

Open days were also held at the three sites, hosted by staff members from IAC and Northlight Heritage. Members of Claíomh, a military 'living history' group, were also involved, displaying period dress, weaponry and armour, as well as demonstrating seventeenth-century blacksmithing and leather-working (Fig. 13.6). The employment of a re-enactment group who used period-specific replica artefacts and clothing provided an excellent way of engaging adults and schoolchildren in the past history of the sites that they were visiting (James 2012; 2014; 2015, 17). At Servants Hill visitors also got to experience some experimental archaeology thanks to Bruce Crawford, who constructed a willow and turf shelter in an effort to replicate the cabins known as *creats*, which were commonplace in Ulster at the time. The open day at Monea Castle attracted over 150 visitors and a reporter from the local newspaper (James 2015, 20). Owing to issues of public access, the open day at Servants Hill only targeted those groups and individuals who had already been involved or shown an interest in the project, attracting about 40 people (James 2012). Similarly, the open day at Derrywoone Castle proved problematic, as concerns with young pheasants nearby precluded the hosting of large groups of visitors; consequently only the children from the schools already hosted at the site, plus their parents, a small number of local interested parties and some archaeologists, were invited, amounting to ten children and 22 adult visitors (James 2014).

Given the significant role of the Ulster Plantation in the history of Northern Ireland, it was considered important to reach the widest audience possible, informing people about the location and nature of Plantation-era sites to be found in their midst. Whether Ulster Scots, English or Gaelic Irish, such sites

Fig. 13.6—A member of Claíomh, a military 'living history' group, displaying seventeenth-century blacksmithing in the grounds of Monea Castle, Co. Fermanagh, during an open day for members of the public to view the results of the excavation there (courtesy of IAC).

represent a valuable cultural and historical heritage—a resource to be valued, cherished and shared—the continued survival of which in today's landscape is contingent on the support of the general public. This necessitated an approach that also maintained community archaeology off site, long after the actual field investigations had concluded.

OFF-SITE COMMUNITY ARCHAEOLOGY

The Ulster Scots Archaeological Services Project has also engaged with the wider public beyond hosting site visits. The results of the archaeological excavations carried out at Servants Hill, Derrywoone Castle and Monea Castle form the basis of an education resource pack entitled *Discovering the Ulster Scots Plantation* (Walsh *et al.* 2015a). This education resource is aimed at Key Stage 2 (7–11-year-olds) and Key Stage 3 (11–14-year-olds) in the Northern Irish school system, and it is envisaged that it will eventually be made available online to schools. It is hoped that the education pack will play a role in providing a resource for teachers to draw on as they help children to develop an awareness

of the Ulster Plantation as a part of their shared history. The pack is divided into three modules: Module 1 provides a background to the Plantation and the archaeological process, Module 2 covers the fieldwork at Servants Hill, and Module 3 deals with the excavations at Derrywoone and Monea (Fig. 13.7). In one of the exercises, teachers are encouraged to arrange small discussion groups to inquire into the sorts of challenges that would have been faced by Scottish tenants moving to a new land, how the Irish people would have reacted to the new arrivals, and how the two communities might have worked together (*ibid.*, 28). This exercise is designed to stimulate enquiry about the past, including discussion of how the events of the Plantation shaped the future of Northern Ireland. Another exercise is to compare two images, a reconstruction drawing of what Monea Castle would have looked like in the early seventeenth century and a photograph of the same building today, and to discuss the changes that the building has undergone over time (*ibid.*, 88–9). The philosophy of the school curriculum in Northern Ireland embraces active learning, independent thought and questioning, and collaborative learning — educational principles

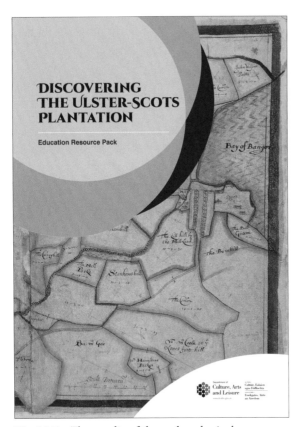

Fig. 13.7—The results of the archaeological excavations carried out at Servants Hill, Derrywoone Castle and Monea Castle formed the basis of an education resource pack for use within the Northern Irish school system.

embraced in the design of the three modules in the education pack.

Furthermore, the results of the excavations have been combined into another publication called a 'general reader'. This provides the public with details of the Ulster Scots Archaeological Services Project in an effort to promote the research and community engagement. The historical backgrounds to Servants Hill, Derrywoone Castle and Monea Castle are discussed, followed by post-excavation research and analysis. The nature of community involvement in the field projects is also outlined—open days, society visits, school groups, actor re-enactments and experimental archaeology (Walsh *et al.* 2015b). It is envisaged that this will be published online by the Department for Communities to facilitate public access. The education pack and general reader were developed and written by Fintan Walsh and Christina O'Regan from IAC, with input from Northlight Heritage, AECOM and the Department of Culture, Arts and Leisure (as mentioned above, since absorbed into the Department for Communities). Such publications can help to raise

awareness of Ulster Scots history, heritage and culture, and of the impact that the Plantation had on the landscape, peoples and architecture of Ulster. They can also help to develop a clearer understanding of the historical legacies and shared heritage of this period for communities living today in Northern Ireland.

INCLUSIVE WORKSHOPS

The on-site community engagement created the basis for a programme of social inclusion and schools outreach workshops. This involved the hosting of twelve workshops between December 2015 and March 2016, six in North Belfast and six in Carrickfergus (Donaghy 2016, 1). The aim of the social inclusion workshops was to create opportunities for people to learn about and participate in archaeological work on the Ulster Plantation. This was carried out in a practical and engaging 'hands-on' manner, allowing people to become involved in the study of their shared heritage (Fig. 13.8). This in turn cultivated an appreciation of Plantation-period sites, encouraging a greater understanding of the monuments and promoting them as assets to local communities. This would help to promote initiatives which would build social capacity within communities, including those in areas of deprivation, and to engage specifically with groups with special needs, working in partnership with existing community organisations and statutory agencies (*ibid.*, 2).

The workshops were designed around the education resource pack (Walsh *et al.* 2015a), with the exercises modified and adapted to address the specific needs of the participating groups. Three types of social groups were targeted, those with special needs, the elderly and inner-city schools (Donaghy 2016, 9), all of whom can be isolated from and unable to participate in archaeological outreach such as site open days. The workshop content was kept to a similar structure for each of the groups that were visited, with variations allowed for physical and cognitive ability. A talk was given about the Ulster Scots Archaeological Services Project, with special emphasis placed on the archaeology uncovered at Servants Hill, Derrywoone Castle and Monea Castle. The exercises were geared towards building empathy with the Plantation settlers, describing their lives and asking people to understand what life was like during the seventeenth century. Interpreting maps is an important skill for an archaeologist and these workshops explained how maps are used to help reconstruct past landscapes.

Fig. 13.8—Students in Carrickfergus handling artefacts recovered from the excavations of seventeenth-century sites, as well as replica weapons from the early modern era (courtesy of IAC).

Using Thomas Raven's maps from the 1620s, participants tried to work out what a Plantation-period house was constructed of and, on the basis of their analysis, to assess whether it would still survive today. They also had to work out the changes in the landscape that had occurred by comparing older and newer maps (*ibid.*, 10). Another exercise used the artefacts recovered from the excavations to tell how people would have lived on these sites in the past. Participants were split into groups and given cloth bags containing five artefacts. By using their sense of touch, they had to identify what the object was, what it was made from and what its function may have been. The artefacts were then revealed to the participants and they were able to re-evaluate their initial interpretation. Participants were also given the opportunity to draw the artefacts, going through the actual function and material of each item, explaining its history, how it had been used and where it had been found (*ibid.*, 10).

These workshops proved to be an excellent medium for disseminating the information gathered during the archaeological investigations. Participants responded positively to the information and the way in which it was delivered, paving the way for similar schemes to be established in the future. The local community groups and organisations were successfully engaged, and a foundation for future work and partnerships has been laid, with groups now equipped with the tools necessary to start research into their local

heritage (*ibid.*, 11–13).

One aspect of the outreach programme that proved difficult was attempting to include participants from nationalist and republican areas. Although the project focused on cross-community activities and promoted social inclusion, there was a lack of interest in the workshops among groups from this side of the political divide. The Catholic schools that were approached did not touch on the subject in their syllabus, and therefore the workshops were not considered relevant to their students (*ibid.*, 14). Research on education in Northern Ireland has revealed a tendency among teachers at all levels of the education system to avoid examining certain historical periods in case they cause antagonism within communities (Breen *et al.* 2015, 924).

MONUMENTS SURVEY AND LANDMARK VOLUME

As part of the project, an archaeological survey of Plantation-period sites dating from *c.* 1600–50 was carried out across Northern Ireland. The main objective was to identify the contribution that the Scots had made to the development of society at the time through the survey of archaeological sites and monuments related to their daily lives, traditions and culture. Given the presence of the Gaelic Irish and

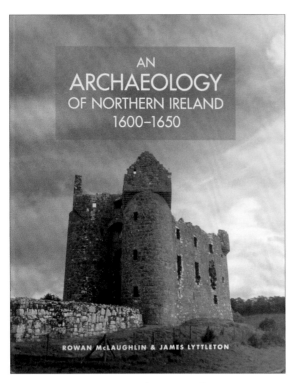

Fig. 13.9—One of the chief outputs of the project was the publication of a gazetteer in 2017, entitled A*n archaeology of Northern Ireland 1600–1650.*

English populations in Ulster, it was considered important to include settlement associated with those ethnic groups as well, addressing concerns that the project would focus solely on the Ulster Scots population and in the process ignore the complexities of the social and cultural interplay between the different ethnic groups (Horning 2013, 24; Breen *et al.* 2015, 925). The relevant archaeological sites (e.g. fortified houses, bawns, churches, farmsteads and mills) were identified using the Northern Ireland Sites and Monuments Record held by the Historic Environment Division in the Department for Communities, along with detailed research into archaeological, historical and literary sources. This desk-based assessment was followed by field inspections to gauge the current condition of these archaeological sites and to confirm their identification as being of the Plantation period. The desk-based research, data management, GIS work and site inspections were managed and undertaken by AECOM, with assistance for the site inspections provided by IAC. Remarkably, some 600 such sites were identified across the province—a significant survival of buildings from a period marked by rebellion, dislocation and destruction. Over 70 new sites from the period were discovered during the course of the project

and were assigned SMR numbers by the Historic Environment Division. Numerous sites were also identified where no upstanding traces of buildings survived but where documentary and cartographic sources suggested the presence of buried archaeological remains.

This corpus of Plantation-period archaeological sites and buildings provided the basis for a landmark publication, a gazetteer or inventory of various site types dating from the first half of the seventeenth century. This gazetteer, compiled by Rowan McLaughlin and James Lyttleton, was published in 2017 by the Department for Communities as a book entitled *An archaeology of Northern Ireland 1600–1650* (Fig. 13.9). Unlike previous county surveys published by the Historic Environment Division, like those for County Armagh in 2009 and County Fermanagh in 2014, where sites were arranged in chapters dealing with specific monument types such as megaliths, castles and churches, it was decided to group the early seventeenth-century buildings according to the respective historic estates in which they were situated. This was to encourage local people to seek out and visit the archaeological sites in their neighbourhood, as well as to promote research on the various estates that made up the Plantation. Another aspect of the gazetteer was the inclusion of six case-studies: the excavations at Servants Hill, Derrywoone Castle and Monea Castle, along with studies of Ballygally Castle and Dunluce Castle, Co. Antrim, and Dungiven Castle and Priory, Co. Londonderry, which were included owing to their significance in our understanding of the Ulster Scots archaeological and architectural heritage. The chief source of information on the types of buildings erected on these estates consisted of the official surveys that were carried out periodically to review progress, beginning in 1611 and followed by others in 1613, 1618/19 and 1622 (McLaughlin and Lyttleton 2017, 10–12). In addition, Thomas Raven's maps of the London Companies' settlements in County Londonderry in 1622 and the Hamilton estate in northern County Down in 1625 were of considerable assistance in identifying the spatial layout of settlements, as well as the physical appearance of individual buildings.

Other settlement was also included in the gazetteer, such as sites outside the Plantation estates, including those located on church lands, which were still an integral part of the landscape at the time. Knowledge of such sites provides for a greater understanding of the political, cultural and social processes involved in the transformation of Ulster by plantation. The physical appearance of the different building types used during the period—their form, layout and situation in the surrounding landscape—can tell us much about how people lived their daily lives. By studying these monuments it is possible to infer how households were organised, how people expressed their religious beliefs, and what sort of contacts they had with the outside world through travel and trade. This can enable a better understanding of the lives of people at the time and encourage reflection and debate.

CONCLUSION

While it is too early to speak of legacy, the Ulster Scots Archaeological Services Project touches upon many fronts—academic research, community archaeology, education and inclusion. A key objective of the project was to promote cross-community outreach and engagement through involvement in archaeological excavations and other events. The excavations at Servants Hill, Derrywoone and Monea provided an opportunity for just such a programme of community outreach, engaging with local schools and community-based groups. In a Northern Irish context, it was important to reach out to both unionist and nationalist communities, and the excavations were successful in attracting schools from both sides of the political divide.

The publication of *An archaeology of Northern Ireland 1600–1650* is an important benchmark in the archaeological study of the Plantation period. The comprehensive nature of the survey has identified all known sites dating from the first half of the seventeenth century, associated not only with the Ulster Scots but also with the English and the Gaelic Irish. The provision of a gazetteer, with the monuments documented in their respective estates, offers an appropriate baseline for future academic research into the nature of settlement in Ulster. The publication of this gazetteer also offers a template for the survey of Plantation-era settlement in the other counties that were covered by the Ulster Plantation, namely Donegal and Cavan, but which are now in the Republic of Ireland and hence outside the remit of the Ulster Scots Archaeological Services Project. A similar approach could be taken for other parts of the island of Ireland that saw English and Scottish plantation, such as counties Laois and Offaly in the 1550s and 1620s, or the province of Munster in the 1580s. Aside from being a research resource, the gazetteer is also an important tool in educating the wider community about their local history and heritage, and provides a starting point for archaeology and history groups to explore their local shared heritage that is related to the Plantation period. It is envisaged that this book will also encourage the promotion of heritage assets for tourism and education in Northern Ireland.

The Ulster Scots Archaeological Services Project is an exemplar in the development and running of community engagement projects, something that was recognised by its inclusion as a finalist in the category of best archaeology project in the British Archaeological Awards for 2016 (http://www. archaeologicalawards.com). The project was significant in its cross-community approach to shared heritage, tackling an important but divisive and emotive period in Irish history, and was underpinned by a strong and inclusive public archaeology and community engagement strategy. Such work can play a role in providing a more nuanced understanding of the complexities of life in early modern Ireland and contribute to some form of shared understanding between the unionist and nationalist traditions.

REFERENCES

Breen, C., Reid, G. and Hope, M. 2015 Heritage, identity and community engagement at Dunluce Castle, Northern Ireland. *International Journal of Heritage Studies* **21** (9), 919–37.

Donaghy, G. 2016 Report on schools outreach and social inclusion workshops for Department for Communities (NI). Unpublished report by IAC Archaeology.

Horning, A. 2013 Exerting influence? Responsibility and the public role of archaeology in divided societies. *Archaeological Dialogues* **29** (1), 19–29.

James, H. 2012 Ulster Scots 2012 Community Engagement Report. Servants Hill, Bangor, Co. Down. Unpublished report by Northlight Heritage.

James, H. 2014 Ulster Scots 2013 Community Engagement Report. Derrywoone Castle, Co. Tyrone. Unpublished report by Northlight Heritage.

James, H. 2015 Ulster Scots 2014 Community Engagement Report. Monea Castle, Co. Fermanagh. Unpublished report by Northlight Heritage.

McLaughlin, R. and Lyttleton, J. 2017 *An archaeology of Northern Ireland 1600–1650*. Department for

Communities, Belfast.

Walsh, F. 2014 Final report of excavation of Bronze Age settlement and site of Plantation houses, Ballymagee, Co. Down, Belfast. Unpublished report in the archives of the Historic Environment Division, Department for Communities.

Walsh, F. 2016a Final report for excavations at Derrywoone, Baronscourt, Co. Tyrone, Ulster Scots Archaeological Research Project, Belfast. Unpublished report in the archives of the Historic Environment Division, Department for Communities.

Walsh, F. 2016b Final report for excavations at Monea Castle, Co. Fermanagh, Ulster Scots Archaeological Research Project, Belfast. Unpublished report in the archives of the Historic Environment Division, Department for Communities.

Walsh, F., O'Regan, C., James, H., Brannon, N., Tobin, M., Macnab, N. and Kelly, G. 2015a *Discovering the Ulster Scots Plantation. Education Resource Pack*. Department of Culture, Arts and Leisure, Belfast.

Walsh, F., O'Regan, C., Macnab, N., Brannon, N., James, H. and Tobin, M. 2015b *Ulster Scots Archaeological Project. Excavations at Servants Hill, Co. Down, Derrywoone, Co. Tyrone, and Monea, Co. Fermanagh* (general reader to be published online by the Department for Communities).

NOTES

[1] A bawn is a walled courtyard of a tower-house or fortified house, commonly provided with gatehouse and corner flankers; the word is derived from the Irish *bádhun* or 'cattle fort', an enclosure where cattle could be corralled.

[2] A flanker is a tower, typically circular or rectilinear, placed at the corners of bawns or fortified houses to cover the perimeter.

[3] A gun loop is an opening for a gun or musket. They are found within the walls of tower-houses and fortified houses, and can also be found in the walls of bawns and flankers.

14. Blackfriary, Trim: the field school experience

FINOLA O'CARROLL, RACHEL E. SCOTT, LAURA CORRWAY AND IAN KINCH

ABSTRACT

The Blackfriary Community Heritage and Archaeology Project (BCHAP) is centred around the medieval Dominican friary in Trim, Co. Meath. Lacking any significant above-ground remains and having been consistently used for casual rubbish-dumping and anti-social behaviour, the site presented the opportunity to create a research and teaching project that would transform the Blackfriary into a space that is welcoming, educational and of benefit to the community. Archaeological excavations since 2010 have uncovered remains of the friary buildings plus areas of the cemetery and medieval gardens. The majority of this work has been carried out as part of an archaeological field school, designed to train undergraduate students in excavation techniques. The field school not only produces the archaeological material necessary for the interpretation of the site but also plays a key role in community engagement. By boarding the students with local families, the field school both provides a direct economic benefit to the community and creates personal ties that generate interest and support for the project. A variety of outreach activities target different groups within the community. Regular community events include site tours, talks and family days scheduled throughout the year, along with a community dig during Heritage Week in August. The BCHAP has also conducted an oral history project, created a pop-up museum in Trim Library and supported the building of a community garden on site. This paper reflects on the differences between running an archaeological field school and a community dig, as well as on the outreach efforts required to develop community interest in a largely forgotten site.

INTRODUCTION

The Blackfriary Community Heritage and Archaeology Project (BCHAP) is a collaboration between a private company, the local authority and local community groups. It is located on the site of a Dominican friary at Blackfriary, Trim, Co. Meath, founded in 1263 to the north of the medieval town wall by the then lord of Trim, Geoffrey de Geneville (Fig. 14.1) (see O'Carroll *et al.* 2018; O'Carroll 2019). The friary buildings stood until the mid-eighteenth century, when they were quarried out for building stone, and today only occasional pieces of masonry survive above ground. The site, a six-acre field to the north of the town, is surrounded by housing and situated behind the local supermarket. It is in the ownership of the local authority, Meath County Council, and is a National Monument subject to a Preservation Order (No. 4 1972) that prohibits its damage or development. Despite this protected status, the Blackfriary's identity as a historic monument was being eroded to the point of being lost entirely from local memory. Lacking any significant above-ground remains, the site was being consistently used for casual rubbish-dumping and anti-social behaviour.

The BCHAP came about because the project founders (Finola O'Carroll and Dr Stephen Mandal) had carried out a lot of work in Trim as a commercial archaeological consultancy (CRDS Ltd) and were interested in developing projects in the area of education and tourism. Although the Blackfriary was not an obvious heritage attraction (Fig. 14.2), the site presented an opportunity to create a research and teaching project that would help develop its potential to become a tourist destination. The resulting project is centred on an archaeological field school but also involves community outreach. Earlier work by Professor William J. Kennedy of Florida Atlantic University had helped establish the location of the remains of the buildings. In June and July 1988 he conducted a geophysical survey consisting of soil resistivity, proton magnetometry and low-altitude infrared aerial photography of that part of the site where the buildings were likely to have been. The survey results showed subsurface features, outlined by Kennedy as foundations of the kitchen, living quarters, refectory, cloisters, church tower, chancel and entrance (Potterton 2005; Potterton and Seaver 2009)— identifications now broadly confirmed by our excavations (Fig. 14.3). While excavations were proposed at the time, they were not undertaken for logistical reasons and the site was left as it was. Although Kennedy's survey generated some interest and expectation of future work, there was no impetus locally to carry this further. The present excavations are therefore not a 'bottom-up' project led by local

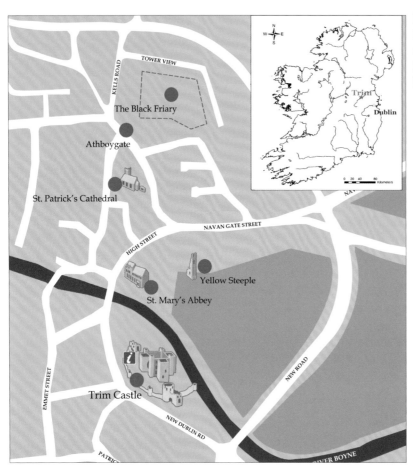

Fig. 14.1—Location of the Blackfriary within Trim (base map of Ireland kindly provided by Mary Valante and the map of Trim by the Tourist Information Office).

Fig. 14.2—View from the tower of St Patrick's Church of the Blackfriary (looking north-north-east), showing its location behind the local supermarket and with housing around its perimeter.

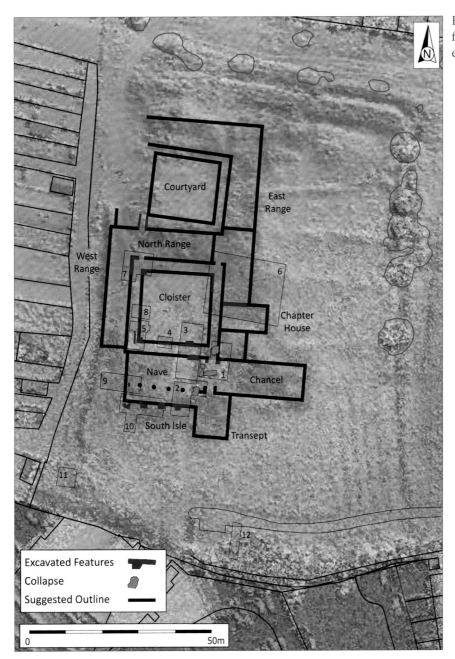

Fig. 14.3—Footprint of the friary as revealed by excavation.

community interest in the heritage of the site. Rather the local interest is growing in step with the continuing development of the project.

Community archaeology as a term is applied to a very broad spectrum of initiatives founded within a range of theoretical frameworks and, as Suzie Thomas (2017, 16) notes, 'in practice [it] is greatly affected by the social, cultural, economic and legislative settings in which it takes place'. In its simplest definition community archaeology refers to archaeological projects, frequently excavations but also other recording/survey projects, that are carried out in collaboration with members of a local 'host' community. There can be inherent conflicts of interest:

which community is being served? Is it the community of archaeological researchers that, as an aside, educates (or entertains) a local community through its work? Or is such work envisaged as a service to a community that through mutual co-operation both meets the needs of that group and fulfils the goals of the archaeologists, which may include providing a valid service to the community (see Agbe-Davies 2010)? In practical terms, there is a division between the top-down (professionally designed and led) and bottom-up (community-designed and led) approaches (see Baker 2016, 37; Thomas 2017). Another key distinction is whether the project is an excavation, a field survey, an oral history or another form of enquiry.

Situating a field school, which generates income through charging fees to students, within the framework of community archaeology seems at face value to go against the accepted definitions. Community archaeology is not usually seen as being an economic activity, but we contend that the economic benefit flowing to the community is an important driver of local engagement with our project. In addition, archaeological excavation imposes an obligation to carry out the work to professional standards, to conserve and analyse the materials uncovered and to disseminate the results—all of which require both time and money. Other forms of community archaeology also bring costs, including professional fees, in their wake. Because such costs have to be met regardless of the genesis of the project, funding inevitably becomes a major issue in any community project, especially one involving excavation.

THE BLACKFRIARY ARCHAEOLOGY FIELD SCHOOL (BAFS) AND COMMUNITY ENGAGEMENT

The field school was established in 2010 under the auspices of CRDS Ltd but is now run by the authors as the Blackfriary Archaeology Field School (www.bafs.ie). Excavations are carried out under Ministerial Consent (C420; Registration No. E4127), issued to the local authority and Finola O'Carroll as archaeological director. In 2011 the BCHAP was awarded funding by the Archaeological Institute of America as part of its site preservation programme to assist with the preservation and presentation of the site (Mandal and O'Carroll 2011). The Blackfriary Archaeology Field School (BAFS) attracts fee-paying students from around the world (Fig. 14.4). Their fees provide the funding to keep the project going and, crucially, they stay with local families, who are paid for this service. This, in turn, engages those families with the activities of the project and helps generate interest in the excavations. The student fees, together with support and input from Meath County Council—including funding for site-specific works and specialist post-excavation costs, facilitated by the Heritage Officer, Dr Loreto Guinan, and the Council CEO, Ms Jackie Maguire—have ensured the continuance of the project to date.

While the focus of the authors has primarily been on the teaching and research activities of the field school, the project also possesses a strong community component. The long-term goal of the BCHAP is to transform the Blackfriary into a space that is welcoming, educational and of benefit to the community. In the shorter term, multiple engagements with the community take place every year—principally site tours, talks and family days. In addition, we carried out an oral history project (Living Among the Monuments, https://trimstories.wordpress.com/) funded by Meath County Council, and created a pop-up museum in Trim Library funded by the Heritage Council through the Irish Walled Towns Network. Since 2016 we have also run a community dig during Heritage Week in August (Fig. 14.5). Furthermore, the three Ireland-based authors have gained additional experience in community excavations with the Community Archaeologist in Fingal, Christine Baker, at digs in Swords, Bremore and Drumanagh, Co. Dublin. Our time running both a field school and community digs at the Blackfriary, as well as supervising community projects in County Dublin, allows us to compare and contrast the field school and community excavation experiences.

The majority of the participants in the Blackfriary Archaeology Field School are undergraduate students, while a small percentage are postgraduates, retirees or other. Most students, especially those from the US, Canada and Australia, study anthropology, with archaeology as a subdiscipline. Many are coming from a learning environment where theoretical frameworks rather than the actual physical activity of an excavation inform much of their studies. They fill this gap in their practical knowledge through the field school experience. Taking part in a field school is for many their first introduction to the excavation process, which cannot be fully replicated in the classroom. For those who undertake this venture, it may be the deciding factor in pursuing a career in the profession. 'Participation in an archaeological field school is often considered as a definitive moment in life, when students decide during its short timeframe whether to pursue archaeology professionally or to relegate it to a hobby, memorable story or simply something in the past' (Perry 2004, 236).

Possessing a theoretical framework that shapes their expectations and potentially a career goal to work towards, our students are generally eager to learn as much as they can. Those with prior experience at excavations that use different methodologies sometimes find the modified single-context recording practised at the Blackfriary to be disconcerting. It can be a challenge to assure them that when, for example, excavating tons of rubble overburden or finely graduated layers, the square or box methods with

Fig. 14.4—Some of the field school students at work.

Fig. 14.5—Participants in the 2018 Blackfriary community dig, with Ian Kinch (middle left, with mattock).

Fig. 14.6—Ian Kinch instructs students in soil and feature description.

which they are familiar are not appropriate for our recording standards and methodology. Recording and interpretation of single-context stratigraphical relationships using the Harris Matrix is not only better suited to this kind of excavation but also, in the setting of a field school, can help involve students because it is relatively easy to explain and understand (Fig. 14.6). With some training and supervision, our students can accurately complete the necessary feature sheets to record archaeological contexts.

Students at the field school are expected to interact with the community and also with tourists visiting the area. For example, local children come to the Blackfriary daily and use the site as a playground of sorts during the summer. Interacting with them on a regular basis means that they are being educated to some degree in their own heritage, which is clearly valued by the students and other visitors to the site. Visits from tourists and members of the local community cause the students to engage more deeply with the site, as they are encouraged to talk about the archaeology and explain what they are doing (Fig. 14.7). This has a positive effect on the visitor experience, as they see how enthusiastic the students are about the Blackfriary. That the majority of our students are international visitors who come a long way

for this experience reinforces the value of the site for the local audience.

THE BLACKFRIARY COMMUNITY DIG

By contrast, the community excavations at the Blackfriary attract a mixture of individuals, with the largest proportion being those who are retired or close to retirement and have the time to pursue their interests. While people on the community dig possess the desire to participate in an excavation, we have found that few are interested in developing actual excavation skills. Most just want to take part in the process of digging. The community excavations are thus primarily about participation. Nevertheless, some training must be provided, both to protect the archaeology and to ensure an intelligible and enjoyable experience.

We as archaeologists have a responsibility to the archaeology to ensure that it is excavated to the best professional standards and recorded correctly. This goal can be more difficult to attain on a community excavation than on a field school dig. Teacher/student relationships and the formal courses of the field school help to structure the excavation. In addition, students

Fig. 14.7—Students interacting with visitors on site.

are there for a set number of weeks and have a duty to show up on time every day. Even though we have a set daily start time on the community dig and one of the director's duties is to ensure that all new people attend an induction, it can be difficult to ask people to commit to a given number of days on the excavation. For example, 70% of the participants in the 2018 community dig worked on site for only one or two days. Moreover, people like to 'pop in and out' whenever they can fit time into their schedules. This can slow the pace of excavation and make it challenging to predict how much can be achieved. On the other hand, students attending the field school are also taking a structured training course that may include academic work. This is run in conjunction with the excavation and necessitates that we prioritise students' learning, so the excavation pace can similarly be affected by the teaching of this course. Consequently, although the field school students may have a more regimented approach to their work than their counterparts from the community, they have their own agendas and requirements that must also be met. In both cases, the objectives of the archaeologists in terms of reaching specific goals to fulfil a research aim have to be tempered by the needs of the groups who are participating.

EXPECTATIONS OF THE STUDENTS VS THE COMMUNITY

In our experience, the expectations of students and the public can differ. We see this difference in how they think about both the field of archaeology and specific aspects of the Blackfriary excavation. Students are often more realistic in their expectations, as they are usually working towards being professional archaeologists, though the majority aim to be employed in academia or public service rather than the commercial sector. We are very frank with students about what it means to be a professional archaeologist, as we want them to know about career prospects and the realities of the life. For some students, for various reasons, the field school experience may not be what they hoped and they decide not to pursue archaeology any further. The physical demands of the manual labour involved in excavation may be a factor, or the fairly onerous requirements of the paperwork. For others, the experience is an affirmation of their goal to become an archaeologist and provides a springboard for their future career.

In comparison, members of the public often view archaeology as an exciting hobby but not a profession. They can therefore be surprised that archaeologists are

Fig. 14.8—Excavation of human remains as part of the field school.

hired and paid as supervisors on community projects, when their expectation is that everyone is volunteering their time and labour. While this may occasionally be the case, it is an unsustainable position for all archaeological projects that require funding and professional expertise. The sheer physicality of the work can come as a shock to both students and the general public, and having a variety of tasks that can be performed regardless of physical ability is important. For both groups, participants need to know and believe that their contribution is valid and meaningful.

Given that the Blackfriary is a medieval religious foundation, the excavation of human skeletal remains is part of the field school's research and teaching (Fig. 14.8). Burial occurred within the cemetery and the church during the late medieval period and following the friary's dissolution in 1540. After the destruction of the buildings by quarrying in the eighteenth century (and, indeed, probably before that time), the place became a burial ground for unbaptised infants, a *cillín*,

Fig. 14.9—Children excavating in the 'mock dig' at the Blackfriary.

a well-known site type in Ireland (see Finlay 2000; Murphy 2011). We carefully explain to students and the wider public that we are excavating the burials for a number of explicit reasons formulated through the research design. We plan to excavate a sample of the burials, not the entire population, sufficient to address the research questions. Because the location—and, indeed, any knowledge—of these burials had been effectively lost, one of our main objectives is to determine the limits of the graveyard. We now know that the burials have been severely disturbed by farming activities in the eighteenth and nineteenth centuries, by construction of the houses along the Kells road and the erection of electricity poles in the twentieth century, and most recently by an extension to the local supermarket. A second objective is to recover a sample of the buried population in order to study the nature of the people's lives through the analysis of their physical remains.

Students frequently come to the field school specifically to receive formal training in the excavation of human remains, which is the remit of one of the authors, Dr Rachel Scott of DePaul University, Chicago, who is the project bioarchaeologist (osteoarchaeologist). Many students are less interested

in the research framework of this aspect of the project and are more concerned to ensure that they get the opportunity to excavate a burial. This focus can bring its own problems and students sometimes have to be reminded of the ethics of the situation. Excavating human remains is a privilege that is only legitimised by the need to preserve and record burials that might otherwise be under threat, and/or where valid research questions are being pursued. In all instances, it is important to excavate burials to the highest professional standards.

For the wider community, the knowledge that human remains are being excavated may provoke in some no more than mild curiosity, but others may feel uneasy that the burial place of these people is being disturbed. Many have become accustomed to the idea of the excavation of human remains through media coverage. Popular television programmes such as *Time Team* have introduced huge audiences to the process of field research and excavation, and projects such as the finding of the remains of Richard III have captured the public imagination. Nevertheless, the sight of skeletal remains can be upsetting for some individuals, and for others a source of fascination that is not tempered by the constraints imposed by scientific enquiry. For these reasons, we ensure that the burials are fully protected when we are not on site and that any exposed burials are excavated and lifted before the weekends. Excavation of the human remains at the Blackfriary thus requires respecting the varying perspectives of students, visitors and the local community.

BCHAP'S MULTI-FACETED OUTREACH PROGRAMME

Why do we define an archaeological field school as a community project? We do so because the underpinning ethos of the BCHAP is that it will benefit the community by preserving, recording and interpreting the archaeological site. We believe that the monument's long-term security can be ensured by developing a heritage-based enterprise run by and for local individuals and organisations. Generating local interest in this endeavour has entailed a variety of outreach efforts that target different groups within the community. This community outreach is ongoing alongside the field school's main activity of training students in excavation techniques.

In addition to interacting with neighbourhood children who play around the site, we host school visits on a regular basis. Interactive facilities for children include a fully excavated cutting repurposed as a learning space, complete with a mock town wall, where simulated excavations can take place (Fig. 14.9). The South Meath Area Response to Teens (SMART), a local project that works with teenagers who have come to the attention of the Gardaí, obtained a grant to build a community garden at the Blackfriary. Meath County Council funded the design, commissioned from landscape gardener Jane McCorkill. The installation of the garden near the site's entrance involved the labour of the SMART, the BCHAP (for archaeological monitoring and general help), the local Men's Shed group and the Gateway Scheme (see below). A group of home-schooling parents and their children now maintain the garden, and it is well used as an amenity by local people, including many young children and teenagers. The SMART garden has won the Meath Pride of Place Award for four years in a row, 2015–18 (Fig. 14.10). Additional work on site has been carried out as part of the Gateway Scheme, an employment scheme for the long-term unemployed under the remit of the local authority. The Blackfriary was seen as an ideal locus for such a project, as landscaping and wall-building needed to be done but fell outside the

ordinary course of council work. These efforts to educate primary school children about the value of archaeological heritage and to involve local groups in the development and maintenance of the site have resulted in a marked decline in vandalism and anti-social behaviour at the Blackfriary. The use of the site for drinking and other activities in the evenings and at weekends, and the deliberate disturbance of excavation cuttings and facilities, has almost entirely ceased.

Since 2015, the majority of students who attend the field school have been found accommodation with local families. These families in turn visit the site, engage with the many community events held throughout the year and in effect become supporters and advocates of the project. The homestay programme has significantly contributed to a positive view of our work and has increased willingness on the part of the local community to engage with ancillary projects. The latter include the community garden and the oral history project, which seeks to capture people's memories and experiences of the site prior to the excavations. Our outreach endeavours thus arise from the underpinning ethos of the BCHAP—to make the town a better place for people to live through meaningful and positive engagement with their heritage, including both economic and social benefits. Improving the quality of life in a town like Trim not only benefits its residents but also makes it more attractive to visitors.

It can be questioned whether the project has succeeded in involving local people in the actual excavation activity on the site. While locals have always been encouraged to take part in the excavations, only a small number of 'regulars' have come to dig, and at sporadic times that suit their own schedules. Admittedly, not everyone is interested in digging. Many prefer to attend open days at the Blackfriary, when they can learn about our results and be shown artefacts and areas of the excavation. A specific community dig, held during Heritage Week, has attracted a lot more active participation, however. In 2018, 64 individuals joined the community dig, with nine (14%) coming from Trim and twenty in total (31%) from County Meath. We anticipate being able to increase these numbers by making the community excavation available at the weekends, often the only free time that people have. This greater level of participation suggests that local people connect more freely with the site when it is not perceived as being dedicated to the field school students. It is also easier for staff to engage more fully with the community members during this time. In our experience, therefore, separating the field school and

Fig. 14.10—Community event at the judging of the IBP Pride of Place Award in 2017.

community digs is a more effective way to include community members in the excavation process.

Over the last ten years the BCHAP has developed a multi-faceted engagement with the local community. Informal visits to the site by neighbourhood children, local residents and international visitors are complemented by more formal school visits, site tours, community talks and family open days. Community members are involved in the archaeological excavation through both the homestay programme for the field school students and the community dig held during Heritage Week. In addition, the BCHAP has implemented or supported a number of ancillary projects, such as the oral history project, the pop-up museum in Trim Library and the SMART community garden. The next stage is to develop an understanding of how best to protect, present and utilise the site into the future. Ideally, we hope to create a sustainable social enterprise that offers employment or creative business opportunities and ensures the preservation of the archaeological heritage.

ACKNOWLEDGEMENTS

A large-scale and long-term project like the BCHAP can only be realised with the support and assistance of many people. We are grateful to the site owners, Meath County Council, for permission to excavate the site, and we especially thank the CEO, Jackie Maguire, and the Heritage Officer, Dr Loreto Guinan, for their continued support. We thank the National Monuments Service of the Department of Culture, Heritage and the Gaeltacht and the National Museum of Ireland, who oversee respectively the conduct of all archaeological excavations and the treatment and curation of archaeological finds. The Heritage Council has assisted with training and grant funding for the project, and we are grateful to Liam Mannix of the Irish Walled Towns Network and Ian Doyle from the Heritage Council for this. The staff of Trim Municipal District, especially Anthony Conlon, have always been extremely helpful, and we have also received much practical assistance from Trim Tidy Towns. The community garden was an initiative of the SMART project (South Meath Area Response to Teens), led by Cathreen Sherrock, and is now maintained by an enthusiastic group of families, coordinated by Carmel Duffy. Finally, we thank our neighbours in Griffin Park and Tower View, the people of Trim (especially the homestay families) and all our students, volunteers and supervisors who make this project possible.

REFERENCES

Agbe-Davies, A.S. 2010 Concepts of community in the pursuit of an inclusive archaeology. *International Journal of Heritage Studies* **16**, 373–89.

Baker, C. 2016 Community archaeology: more questions than answers. *Archaeology Ireland* **30** (3), 37–40.

Finlay, N. 2000 Outside of life: traditions of infant burial in Ireland from cillín to cist. *World Archaeology* **31**, 407–22.

Mandal, S. and O'Carroll, F. 2011 A new model for site preservation and archaeological practice. In *Archaeological Institute of America Site Preservation Program: Heritage, Conservation & Archaeology Series Paper* (https://store.archaeological.org/sites/default/files/files/Mandal and O'Carrol v_3.pdf; accessed 15 July 2019).

Murphy, E.M. 2011 Children's burial grounds in Ireland (*cillíní*) and parental emotions toward infant death. *International Journal of Historical Archaeology* **15**, 409–28.

O'Carroll, F. 2019 The Blackfriars preachers, Trim, Co. Meath, and the legacy of Geoffrey de Geneville. In E. Bhreathnach, M. Krasnodębska-D'Aughton and K. Smith (eds), *Monastic Europe AD 1100–1700: landscape and settlement*. Brepols, Turnhout.

O'Carroll, F., Kinch, I. and Corrway, L. 2018 Digging the past, growing the future: the Blackfriary project. *Ríocht na Midhe* **29**, 27–38.

Perry, J.E. 2004 Authentic learning in field schools: preparing future members of the archaeological community. *World Archaeology* **36**, 236–60.

Potterton, M. 2005 *Medieval Trim: history and archaeology*. Four Courts Press, Dublin.

Potterton, M. and Seaver, M. (eds) 2009 *Uncovering medieval Trim: archaeological excavations in and around Trim, Co. Meath*. Four Courts Press, Dublin.

Thomas, S. 2017 Community archaeology. In G. Moshenska (ed.), *Key concepts in public archaeology*, 14–30. UCL Press, London.

15. The work of the Ulster Archaeological Society Survey Group and the National Trust

GRACE McALISTER, MALACHY CONWAY AND HARRY WELSH

ABSTRACT

The following paper details the work of the Ulster Archaeological Society's (UAS) Survey Group, which, having been established in late 2005, provides UAS members with the opportunity to participate in archaeological monument survey and research. Over the past fourteen years the Survey Group have surveyed 94 sites, and this paper will summarise some of the wide range of surveys and projects undertaken. The majority of the sites surveyed have been within the landholding of the National Trust for Northern Ireland, and the paper will highlight how the collaboration with the Trust has been not only fundamental to the Survey Group's success but also of real value to the National Trust in regard to heritage management and conservation. It will also consider how the Group's skill set has developed over the years and reflect on some of the challenges they have encountered along the way. The paper will ultimately highlight how engaging members of an archaeological society can and has contributed to archaeological research and community archaeology in Ireland.

INTRODUCTION

The Ulster Archaeological Society (UAS) is the leading and largest archaeological society in Northern Ireland. It was originally set up in 1947 to support the *Ulster Journal of Archaeology*, the longest-established and foremost repository of excavation reports and other papers on archaeological research in Ulster, the first series of which was published in 1853. As well as producing the journal, the UAS holds monthly lectures, local field trips, international study tours, workshops and an annual conference, with the aim of educating and promoting public involvement in local archaeological activity. Since its beginnings, the UAS has had a strong association with Queen's University Belfast (QUB) and has been affiliated with the University's Centre for Community Archaeology since 2017; as such, it is ideally positioned to bridge the gap between archaeology as an academic discipline and the interpretation of our heritage to the wider public. In late 2005, keen to develop fieldwork opportunities for members, the UAS established a Survey Group (Welsh 2009), a collective of UAS members interested in learning surveying skills and surveying historic monuments.

ESTABLISHMENT OF THE GROUP

The Survey Group was initiated by long-standing member Dr Ann Hamlin OBE, who on her death in 2003 bequeathed a sum of money to the UAS for this purpose (Welsh 2015). In 2005, at the planning stage of the group, the UAS committee consulted with the National Trust Regional Archaeologist, Malachy Conway, and it was agreed that a programme of archaeological surveys would commence to record monuments that had not previously been investigated on National Trust properties.

The National Trust is a charity founded in 1895 to protect and preserve the nation's heritage and open spaces for everyone to enjoy. Over 100 years later these values are still at the heart of everything the Trust does. In total, across England, Wales and Northern Ireland, the National Trust looks after over 255,000 hectares of land, 1,195km or 742 miles of the UK coastline, and over 73,000 archaeological sites, of which 1,283 are designated Scheduled Monuments. In Northern Ireland the Trust cares for some of the region's most iconic places—from the Giant's Causeway World Heritage Site to our highest mountain, Slieve Donard—as well as about one third of the coastline, some 40 square miles of countryside, and houses and gardens such as Mount Stewart, Co. Down, and Castle Coole, Co. Fermanagh. In terms of the historic landscape there are over 2,500 Historic Environment records in the National Trust database for Northern Ireland, including over 30 Scheduled monuments, 442 Recorded monuments and 232 Listed buildings.

Volunteering and community projects are a key and important component in how the Trust delivers its conservation mission. In terms of volunteering, the National Trust benefits from over 70,500 volunteers each year, 6,500 of whom are based in Northern Ireland. As an example of this contribution, in 2012/13

Fig. 15.1—The Survey Group at Forthill Rath, undertaking their first survey.

some 3,770,630 volunteer hours were logged across the organisation, encompassing everything from helping in gardens, historic houses, countryside management and, of course, archaeology. Collaboration between the UAS Survey Group and the National Trust is therefore significant, helping the organisation to record in detail many of its historic and archaeological assets, assessing condition and evaluating and mitigating threats in line with the organisation's key conservation principles.

Advice on the type of equipment required by the survey group was provided by Barrie Hartwell, then Research Officer at the Archaeology Department of QUB and a long-time member of the UAS. As a result of this advice, a range of equipment was purchased by the Society, including a Leica Sprinter electronic distance-measuring device, hand-tapes of various lengths, ranging poles and other ancillary equipment. Over time the amount of equipment has increased, with the addition of a second Sprinter on long-term loan from QUB and a Distomat from the Environment and Heritage Service (now Department for Communities: Historic Environment Division). There are also hand-held two-way radios, a GPS recorder, survey flags and a weatherproof digital camera.

It was decided that the Survey Group would meet on the last Saturday of each month, with surveys being carried out during the summer months. During the winter months, the information gathered by the Group during each survey would be compiled into a report to be made available to the public via the UAS website (http://www.qub.ac.uk/sites/uas/SurveyGroup/Survey Reports/). Copies would also be given to the National Trust and the Environment and Heritage Service (now Department for Communities: Historic Environment Division), with annual summaries published in the *Ulster Journal of Archaeology*.

Having purchased the equipment and undertaken some basic training in its use, the Survey Group carried out their first survey in Forthill Rath at Rowallane, Saintfield (Fig. 15.1), on 29 April 2006 (Welsh 2007). Eleven members attended and completed a plan and profile drawings, accompanied by a photographic survey of the monument, as well as completing a Condition and Management Survey of the Archaeological Resource (CAMSAR) form.

THE SURVEY GROUP IN ACTION

Over the past fourteen years there have been 179 Survey Group meetings and a total of 94 sites of varying type and period have been surveyed, ranging from megalithic tombs to twentieth-century military defences. Only three surveys have had to be abandoned owing to poor weather conditions since the project began. Of the 94 sites surveyed, 74 have been within

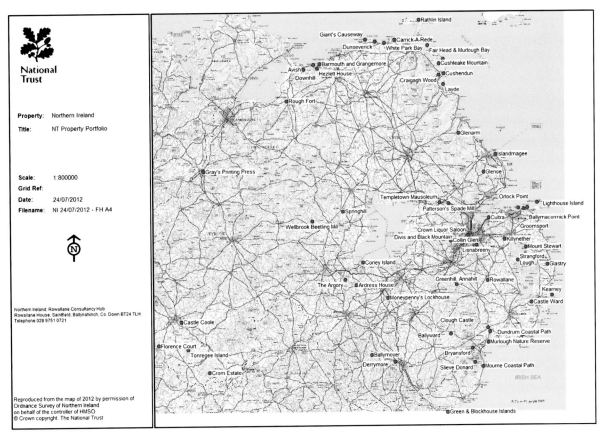

Fig. 15.2—Locations of National Trust property in Northern Ireland.

Table 15.1—Number of sites surveyed and reports completed by the Survey Group.

County	Number of sites surveyed	Surveys on NT property	Completed reports
Antrim	29	23	28
Armagh	5	5	4
Down	47	36	39
Fermanagh	4	4	3
Londonderry	7	6	7
Tyrone	2	0	2
Total	94	74	83

the landholding of the National Trust for Northern Ireland (Fig. 15.2; Table 15.1), and 83 reports have been completed and are available to consult or download from the UAS website. Most of the surveys are carried out within a day, but occasionally the complexity of a monument makes it necessary to revisit a site.

Below are summaries of three key projects that best encapsulate the ethos and varied work of the Group: Divis and Black Mountain, Co. Antrim; Mount Stewart, Co. Down; and Drumgath, Rathfriland, Co. Down.

Landscape survey at Divis and the Black Mountain

One of the most extensive archaeological landscapes surveyed by the UAS is the National Trust property of 'Divis and the Black Mountain', on the outskirts of Belfast. The 1,500-acre area of upland heath and bog was previously under the ownership of the UK Ministry of Defence (MoD), who, having initially leased the area in 1953 during the Cold War, purchased it in 1986 and used it for communications during the Troubles. As a result, the landscape was inaccessible to local communities for over 50 years, and the area's rich heritage had gone largely unrecorded. This changed when the National Trust, with the support of the Heritage Lottery Fund, purchased the land in 2004 for £3 million, opening up the area to the public and facilitating environmental and heritage surveys. The MoD presence in the area had mixed effects on the landscape. On the one hand it could be said that archaeological sites were somewhat protected from the erosion associated with intensive farming or footfall, while twentieth-century defensive structures have added to the archaeological heritage of the area. On the other hand, military operations carried out there have undoubtedly damaged some sites, most notably at the

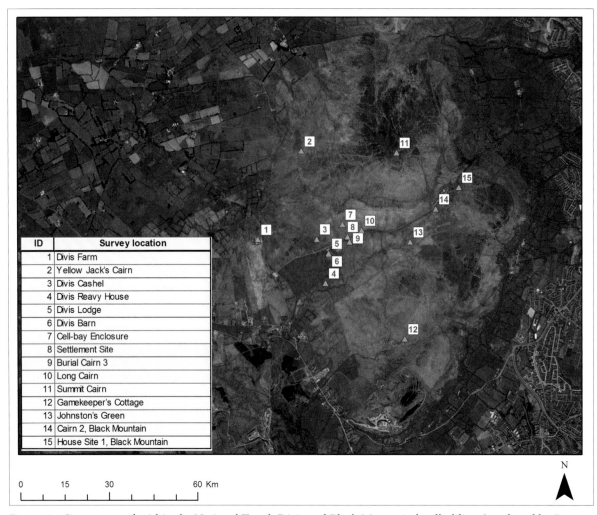

ID	Survey location
1	Divis Farm
2	Yellow Jack's Cairn
3	Divis Cashel
4	Divis Reavy House
5	Divis Lodge
6	Divis Barn
7	Cell-bay Enclosure
8	Settlement Site
9	Burial Cairn 3
10	Long Cairn
11	Summit Cairn
12	Gamekeeper's Cottage
13	Johnston's Green
14	Cairn 2, Black Mountain
15	House Site 1, Black Mountain

Fig. 15.3—Sites surveyed within the National Trust's Divis and Black Mountain landholding (produced by Dr Siobhán McDermott, QUB).

summit of Divis Mountain, where the construction of a military base has removed any of the archaeological sites that might be expected to be present in such an eminent position (Conway 2005). Prior to the National Trust's acquisition of Divis and Black Mountain, only five archaeological sites had been recorded (*ibid.*). Following a comprehensive landscape survey undertaken by the Trust from 2006 to 2008, the number of archaeological sites and other heritage features of anthropogenic origin, including ruined farm buildings, rose to 200, all of which were recorded in the Trust's own Sites and Monuments database. The Survey Group carried out their first survey on the property in 2006 and since then have surveyed a total of fifteen sites, which have ranged from prehistoric cairns to nineteenth-century farm buildings (Figs 15.3 and 15.4). In addition, through their established links with the National Trust, they have been able to forge links with other independent charities, such as the Belfast Hills Partnership (BHP), who seek to improve how the hills around Belfast are managed (Belfast Hills,

n.d.). The links with the BHP have resulted in two seasons of excavation at Divis; the first, in 2013, was in advance of a new car park (Fig. 15.5) and the second, in 2017, investigated two sites previously surveyed by the Survey Group, a probable cashel (McAlister 2012) and a collection of hut circles (Gillespie 2009). Members of the Survey Group were invited to participate in the excavations; while some members had extensive previous experience, for most it was their first time to take part in an archaeological excavation. The sites surveyed and interpreted by the Survey Group are also a significant feature in the National Trust's walking trails on the site and form part of the BHP cultural and heritage focus across the wider Belfast Hills.

Encouraging historical research at Mount Stewart
Mount Stewart is an eighteenth-century mansion set within a large walled demesne on the shores of Strangford Lough, Co. Down. The National Trust owns the majority of the demesne, having gradually acquired

Fig. 15.4—Surveying the 'Reavy' House at Divis.

Fig. 15.5—The Survey Group excavating at Divis.

ID	Survey location
1	Fort Hill rath
2	RAF Site
3	Ice House
4	Rose Garden
5	Bridge Mountstewart
6	Motte
7	Cottage Ornee
8	Templecrone

Fig. 15.6—Sites surveyed within the National Trust's Mount Stewart landholding (produced by Dr Siobhán McDermott, QUB).

different areas and buildings since 1955 and in 2015 acquiring the remainder of the demesne land and buildings for £4 million, bringing its total ownership of Mount Stewart to *c*. 800 acres. With this most recent purchase of land, additional archaeological sites were brought under the National Trust's protection and several sites were discovered. To date the Survey Group have surveyed eight sites across the demesne (Fig. 15.6), ranging from a rath to a Victorian ice house. One of the most notable sites surveyed by the group was a motte, which was recorded in advance of clearance to remove invasive trees and scrub growing on this scheduled monument (Fig. 15.7). Although the site was recorded on the Northern Ireland Sites and Monuments Record (DOW 011: 006), little was known about its history. Two of the Survey Group's members, Randal Scott and Chris Stevenson, undertook historical research into the site and were able to link it to a Robert de Sengelton, who held the land or estate

that included the Mount Stewart motte in 1333 (Scott and Stevenson 2016). In November 2016 Randal delivered a lecture to the UAS, presenting the survey results and the historical research; this was significant, as UAS lectures are normally given by professional archaeologists and historians. The research carried out by the Survey Group, more specifically Randal and Chris, has added significantly to the interpretation of the site, highlighting the need for further landscape survey of the demesne land and the potential for future excavation to verify results.

Community group collaboration at Drumgath

As the Survey Group has evolved and the confidence and competency of its members has grown, the Group have been able to work with other smaller community groups who are interested in learning more about specific sites within their community. In 2016 the Survey Group were approached by Drumgath Ladies

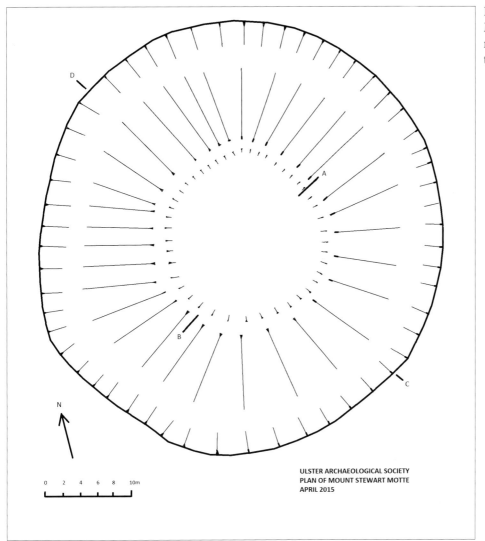

Fig. 15.7—Plan of Mount Stewart motte, produced by the Survey Group.

ULSTER ARCHAEOLOGICAL SOCIETY
PLAN OF MOUNT STEWART MOTTE
APRIL 2015

N

0   2   4   6   8   10m

Group to carry out survey work at their local graveyard, Drumgath, near Rathfriland, Co. Down. Drumgath Ladies Group is a small community group set up in 2010 to provide a social outlet for women in the area. Having 'tidied up' the neglected graveyard, they were interested in mapping the site and in carrying out further historical research with the intention of erecting a storyboard (Welsh *et al.* 2016). The graveyard at Drumgath is a large, circular enclosure approximately 70m in diameter, and in the late eighteenth century a bronze hand-bell was found in the enclosing hedgerow by a local woman named Peggy McGivern (Bourke 1980). The hand-bell, which is now on display in Down County Museum in Downpatrick, is thought to date from around AD 700–900 (Hamlin 1997, 60), indicating that Drumgath was once a monastic site. The Survey Group completed two surveys at the site; the initial survey in May 2016 produced elevation and plan drawings of the structural elements remaining in the graveyard. A drone survey

was also carried out, which resulted in a digital elevation model of the graveyard (Fig. 15.8) and revealed the remains of an additional structure located within the graveyard enclosure. The structure, which was not visible at ground level, was aligned east/west and measured 56.7m by 17.7m. It was interpreted as a probable ecclesiastical building (Stevenson and Scott 2017). In July 2016 the Survey Group returned to Drumgath, this time to complete a survey of the headstones, helped by members of Downpatrick's Young Archaeologists' Club. A total of 194 headstones or grave-markers were recorded but only 26 of these bore any inscription, while at least nine were thought to be reused architectural features (Welsh and Craig 2016). The survey results and research were used to encourage local groups and schoolchildren to visit the site. The children subsequently completed projects, which were then put on display at both Rathfriland Parish Centre and Rathfriland Library (Welsh *et al.* 2016).

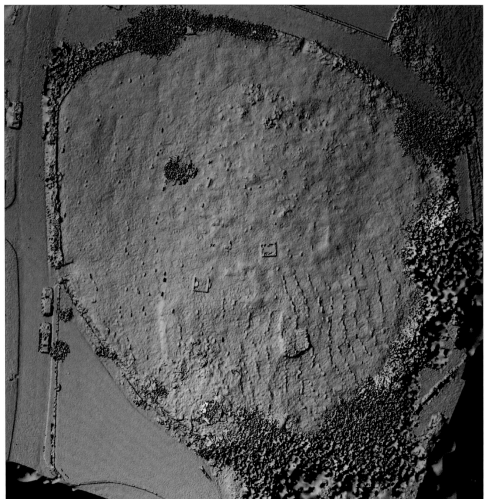

Fig. 15.8—Drumgath Graveyard: hillshade derived from digital elevation model (produced by David Craig).

THE MEMBERS

The activities of the Survey Group are coordinated by two UAS members who are also professional archaeologists, Dr Harry Welsh (Centre for Archaeological Fieldwork, QUB) and Malachy Conway (National Trust Regional Archaeologist for Northern Ireland). Both Malachy and Harry have been enthusiastic supporters since the Survey Group's establishment, giving up one Saturday each month, all year round, over the last thirteen years to facilitate the activities of the Group.

The other members of the Survey Group are mostly amateurs in archaeology, hailing from a variety of backgrounds and professions; although the majority are of retirement age, the age ranges from the mid-twenties to the mid-eighties. An average of sixteen members participate every month, with up to 50 members 'on the books'. Members are not obligated to attend every survey day, and monthly attendance can be affected by factors such as site condition and the weather. The wide and varied skill set that the group members bring from their professional lives is of considerable value to the Survey Group. This can be anything from practical survey skills, interesting perspectives on the interpretation of a site, local knowledge or even archival information. An example of important archival information supplied by the members is a photo taken by original Survey Group member Billy Dunlop of his brother standing on top of the summit cairn at Divis (Fig. 15.9). The summit cairn was destroyed during the MoD use of the site and the photo, which is thought to be the only surviving image, provides not only invaluable historical information but also confirmation that a cairn, most likely of prehistoric origin, once stood on the summit.

Members can get involved at whatever level they choose and, as numbers have increased, it has been possible for members to focus on the specific tasks that they enjoy, whether that be drawing/planning, measuring, note-taking or photography. For some it is the practical and teamwork nature of the surveying that attracts them to the group. For others the social aspect and interaction with other members is what keeps them coming back month after month. It is inspiring

Fig. 15.9—Photo of the now-destroyed cairn on the summit of Divis (taken by original Survey Group member Billy Dunlop).

Table 15.2—Monetary value of Survey Group volunteer time to the National Trust. [*'Working days'* = *total number of attendees throughout year;* *'Monetary value'* = *no. working days x £50 daily rate.*]

	No. of survey meetings	Working days	Monetary Value
2006	9	91	£4,550
2007	14	119	£5,950
2008	11	120	£6,000
2009	12	133	£6,650
2010	10	124	£6,200
2011	10	133	£6,650
2012	21	256	£12,800
2013	10	158	£7,900
2014	13	194	£9,700
2015	12	153	£7,650
2016	14	182	£9,100
2017	12	180	£9,000
2018	15	198	£9,900
2019	16	231	£11,550
Totals	179	2,272	£113,600

to see the friendships and bonds that develop quickly between the Group members over their mutual interest in archaeology.

SUCCESS

With 94 monuments surveyed and 83 survey reports completed, the Survey Group has inadvertently become the leading group carrying out monument survey in Northern Ireland. The majority of the surveys have been carried out on National Trust properties, and having such a high level of support from the National Trust has been fundamental to the success of the Group for a number of reasons. Firstly, it removes the necessity to look for sites suitable for survey; secondly, there is no need to obtain permission from landowners for access; finally, the National Trust has a vast archive of maps and documentary records that can be accessed for research purposes. In addition to facilitating the monument surveys, the National Trust has also provided premises for the autumn and winter sessions of research, report-writing and training. As the Group is registered as a

volunteer group with the National Trust, members are covered by the Trust's insurance while on site. Both charitable organisations benefit from the association; the UAS provides opportunities for its members to become involved in archaeological activities while the National Trust meets its core conservation objectives of managing, protecting and presenting the plethora of sites, monuments and buildings for which it cares. Over the last fourteen years, the quantity of volunteer time dedicated by the Survey Group can be seen as providing a significant financial contribution (Table 15.2). If the number of attendees at each Survey Group meeting is totalled, it amounts to 2,272 working days dedicated by the Survey Group. If the number of working days is then multiplied by a wage, for example a £50 daily rate as suggested by the Heritage Lottery Fund (Heritage Lottery Fund 2017), this amounts to a financial contribution of £113,600. Given that the majority of surveys are completed on National Trust properties, the Trust has recently acknowledged the contribution of the Survey Group by recognising them as official National Trust volunteers. Members are also entitled to claim mileage for their travel to survey sites, although none have ever done so.

While there are numerous archaeological and historical societies throughout Ireland, it has been

Fig. 15.10—Survey and community excavation at the Queen Anne House, Castle Ward.

pointed out that activities organised by such groups can be quite passive as regards encouraging public participation in archaeology (Kador 2014). This is not, however, the case for the UAS, and ultimately one of the biggest successes of the Survey Group is the opportunity it has provided for the general public to contribute and become involved in meaningful archaeological recording and research. It has given members the confidence and skills not only to survey historic monuments but also to complete archival and cartographic research and subsequently offer interpretation. This is particularly evident when members are able not only to complete a report on the site but also to present the research to their peers in a formal lecture setting.

The Group has also enabled members to become involved in other aspects of fieldwork. By tradition the UAS have not carried out their own excavations, but over the last nine years, through collaborations with the Centre for Archaeological Fieldwork (QUB), the National Trust, the Historic Environment Division (HED) and the Belfast Hills Partnership, members have had the opportunity to participate in two field-walking exercises (Ballytaylor, Co. Antrim, and Ballygarvan, Co. Down) and eight seasons of excavation. These have

included community excavations at the site of the Queen Anne House, Castle Ward, Co. Down, in 2008 and 2009 (Fig. 15.10); the Bishop's Palace, Downhill, Co. Derry, between 2009 and 2012; and excavation of a flint-knapping site, cashel and hut circles at Divis, Co. Antrim, in 2013 and 2017 (see above). These community excavations have given Survey Group members the opportunity to experience the full cycle of the archaeological process—excavating at sites that they had previously surveyed, observing how their initial research informed the excavation and witnessing how the excavation results differ from the original survey interpretation.

The Survey Group's repertoire of survey skills has developed over the years, and in 2016 the UAS purchased geophysical survey equipment, specifically a resistivity meter, on the Survey Group's behalf. This was a TAR-3 Resistance Meter from RM Frobisher Ltd. Training was provided by the supplier and the Group have now completed three geophysical surveys, with the results processed by a technologically minded member, David Craig, who carries out commercial drone surveys. In addition to aerial photographs, David is able to apply various techniques to the data captured to produce some spectacular results, such as at the early ecclesiastical site at Drumgath. Working at sites like Drumgath with smaller, rural community groups has also given members of the Survey Group the opportunity to teach other enthusiasts about survey, and to pass on the skills they have learned over the years.

Within the community archaeology sector, there is much discussion about 'top-down' (professional/archaeologist-led) and 'bottom-up' (non-professional/community-led) approaches (Simpson and Williams 2008; Thomas 2016; Baker 2016). Undoubtedly, in its beginnings the Survey Group was very much 'top-down', having been initiated and set up by professional archaeologists within the UAS, the National Trust and QUB. This was intrinsic to the Group's success in the early years, in terms of both training members and gaining access to sites. As the Survey Group has developed, however, there has been a conscious decision to encourage amateur members to be more involved in the leadership and organisation of its activities. For example, on each survey day a different member of the Group takes on the role of 'site director'—deciding how the survey will be carried out, delegating tasks and collating all the information at the end of the survey. Similarly, one of the Group's amateur members takes on the responsibility of ensuring that the sites are written up, by encouraging members to complete their reports.

CHALLENGES

As with any community archaeology initiative, the Survey Group face challenges, which they continue to address as best they can. With regard to report-writing, some members enjoy the research element of the process and actively seek to write up sites of personal interest to them, while other members need more encouragement to participate. It would be easy for the professional archaeologists working within the group and familiar with research and publishing to take control of the write-ups, but it is important that amateur members are encouraged to be involved in this part of the process too. It is necessary to point out that any reluctance on the part of members to write up reports stems not from a lack of enthusiasm but from a lack of confidence. To make the task less daunting, members are encouraged to work in pairs if they wish, and during the winter months the indoor meetings give members a chance to discuss research and write-ups, and to chat to the archaeologists about ideas and interpretations. A template is provided for the report,

which provides prompts and suggestions to the author(s) and also ensures that there is an element of consistency to the report format to assist with the final dissemination of the results. Training is provided on how to use historical sources such as Griffith's Valuation, sometimes by external providers and occasionally by amateur members of the Group who have gained expertise through carrying out their own research. Visits have been organised to the Public Records Office of Northern Ireland (PRONI) and local libraries, all to encourage and empower members to carry out the research themselves. Certain members will be more inclined to research and will write lengthy, in-depth reports. This should not be discouraged but equally it is reinforced to other members not so inclined that any plan or brief description of a site is meaningful, especially if it is the first time a particular site has been recorded.

A recurring issue faced by the Group, and by the UAS in general, is the demographic of their members. While the Society is open to anyone aged sixteen and over (children under sixteen can be members through family membership), the majority of UAS members are of retirement age. This is to be expected, as the activities of the UAS are more accessible to people with more free time, whereas attending a Saturday survey is not always practical for those who have work commitments or young families. This problem is not unique to the UAS and is an issue throughout heritage volunteering, with research by the Council of British Archaeology suggesting that the average age of archaeological volunteers is 55 (Thomas 2010). Interestingly, this differs from the Belfast Branch of the Young Archaeologists' Club, which has no volunteer leaders over the age of 55 (see Carver and Murphy, this volume). Both the UAS and Belfast YAC are part of the QUB Centre for Community Archaeology and, while both groups have participated on community excavations together, collaborating more formally may help to counteract this age discrepancy. By pursuing relationships with other organisations outside of QUB, the UAS and the Survey Group could appeal to other members of the public not traditionally involved with archaeological projects.

Another challenge encountered is the geographical scope of our surveys. Despite the Survey Group's being a part of the Ulster Archaeological Society, there is a Northern Ireland bias as regards the location of our surveys, and to date no surveys have been carried out in the counties of Cavan, Donegal and Monaghan. Moreover, the majority of survey locations are in counties Antrim and Down, where 29 and 47 sites respectively have been surveyed (Table 15.1). There are two reasons for this. Firstly, the National Trust own an extensive amount of land in these counties, especially around Strangford Lough and the Belfast Hills. Secondly, sites within this area are usually no more than a one-hour drive from Belfast. This is particularly relevant to volunteer groups, as longer journeys entail much more cost in terms of travel, and a journey of two hours each way immediately reduces the survey time on site by four hours. It is important that the Survey Group and the UAS avoid being Northern Ireland- or Belfast-centric and appeal to and serve the whole community while continuing to meet one of the UAS core objectives, which is to advance the education of the public in archaeology and history particularly with regard to Ulster, which includes promoting the involvement of the public in local archaeological activity.

The Group have also been approached to undertake surveys by governmental bodies and private landowners, and this has increased since the purchase of the geophysical equipment. Carrying out such work may be seen as the UAS encroaching into the arena of commercial archaeologists and might be considered by organisations with limited budgets as a cheap alternative. The Group need to remain aware that their work is limited by the time available to volunteers and the expenses of the team (travel).

LOOKING TO THE FUTURE

As the Survey Group progresses further into its second decade of existence, it is hoped that its contribution to heritage research in Ireland will continue and develop further through use of UAV/aerial drone and geophysical survey. The work of the Group demonstrates that voluntary participation in archaeology is a necessity within Ireland, both to engage communities and the general public with their heritage and to benefit the archaeological resource by increasing knowledge for future researchers, both academic and amateur. As highlighted above, the Survey Group have carried out survey work on behalf of a wide range of groups and are willing to help anyone in furtherance of archaeological research. The Group, however, are increasingly aware that they need to be careful not to step into the realm of commercial archaeology. The collaboration with charitable organisations such as the National Trust has proven to be intrinsic to the success of the Survey Group. By further pursuing collaborations with smaller charitable

or community groups, members of the Survey Group can utilise the skills they have learned over the last fourteen years and engage in peer-to-peer learning to teach others about archaeological survey and research. Perhaps this could even inspire other archaeological or historical societies across the province to start their own survey groups and, in the long term, overcome some of the UAS Survey Group's own challenges with regard to geographical scope and reach.

ACKNOWLEDGEMENTS

Thanks to all the members of the Survey Group, whose time and enthusiasm throughout the years have ensured the Group's longevity and continued success. Thanks are also due to the UAS Committee and the National Trust for Northern Ireland, whose support from the Group's beginnings has been invaluable.

REFERENCES

Baker, C. 2016 Community archaeology: more questions than answers. *Archaeology Ireland* **30** (3), 37–40.

Belfast Hills (n.d.) About us (http://belfasthills.org/about-us/, accessed 31 March 2018).

Bourke, C. 1980 Early Irish hand-bells. *Journal of the Royal Society of Antiquaries of Ireland* **110**, 52–66.

Conway, M. 2005 *Divis and Black Mountain, an archaeological update.* National Trust.

Gillespie, I. 2009 *Survey of Divis settlement site.* Survey Report No. 16. Ulster Archaeological Society, Belfast.

Hamlin, A. 1997 The early church in County Down to the twelfth century. In L. Proudfoot (ed.), *Down: history and society*, 47–70. Geography Publications, Dublin.

Heritage Lottery Fund 2017 How to calculate volunteer time (https://www.hlf.org.uk/community/general-discussions-forum/how-calculate-volunteer-time; accessed 2 April 2018).

Historic Monuments and Archaeological Objects (Northern Ireland) Order 1995: *Restrictions on possession and use of detecting devices* (http://www.legislation.gov.uk/nisi/1995/1625/article/29/made, accessed 23 February 2018).

Kador, T. 2014 Public and community archaeology— an Irish perspective. In S. Thomas and J. Lea (eds), *Public participation in archaeology*, 35–48. Boydell and Brewer, Woodbridge.

McAlister, G. 2012 *Survey of Divis Cashel, County Antrim.* Survey Report No. 36. Ulster Archaeological Society, Belfast.

Scott, R. and Stevenson, C. 2016 *Mount Stewart Motte, Co. Down.* Survey Report No. 53. Ulster Archaeological Society, Belfast.

Simpson, F. and Williams, H. 2008 Evaluating community archaeology in the UK. *Public Archaeology* **7** (2), 69–90.

Stevenson, C. and Scott, R. 2017 *Early ecclesiastical site at Drumgath, County Down.* Survey Report No. 60. Ulster Archaeological Society, Belfast.

Thomas, S. 2010 *Community archaeology in the UK: recent findings.* Council for British Archaeology, York.

Thomas, S. 2016 Community archaeology in the UK: looking ahead. In M. Nevell and N. Redhead (eds), *Archaeology for all: community archaeology in the early 21st century: participation, practice and impact*, 159–67. Centre for Applied Archaeology, University of Salford.

Welsh, H. 2007 *Survey of Forthill Rath, Creevyloughgare, Saintfield, County Down.* Survey Report No. 1. Ulster Archaeological Society, Belfast.

Welsh, H. 2009 Accessible archaeology. *Archaeology Ireland* **23** (4), 10–13.

Welsh, H. 2015 Still going strong! *Archaeology Ireland* **29** (4), 30–1.

Welsh, H. and Craig, D. 2016 *Drumgath Graveyard, Co. Down.* Survey Report No. 62. Ulster Archaeological Society, Belfast.

Welsh, H., Craig, D. and Dickson, B. 2016 An ecclesiastical site investigated at Drumgath, Co. Down. *Archaeology Ireland* **30** (3), 17–20.

16. Rathcroghan Visitor Centre—community custodians of *Cruachan Aí*

DANIEL CURLEY

ABSTRACT

The Rathcroghan Visitor Centre, Tulsk, Co. Roscommon, is a community-run interpretive experience and resource hub for the Rathcroghan Archaeological Landscape. Established in 1999, it serves to create awareness of a unique collection of archaeological monuments, regarded as the provincial royal site for Connacht. In 2014 the visitor centre completed a substantial upgrade to the interpretive rooms, directed by the visitor centre staff. This development of ownership over the centre has led to a number of innovations, resulting in the improved sustainability and growth of the visitor centre and increased awareness of and interest in the Rathcroghan Archaeological Landscape. Embracing community archaeology has been a key aspect of this growth, leading to the delivery of a successful annual community archaeology conference, entitled 'Archaeology Above & Below'. The production of interactive information panels and archaeological trail booklets have assisted in overcoming the challenge of interpreting such a vast archaeological landscape, while current projects, on such diverse topics as improving farming livelihoods, guidebook production and artefact acquisition, are all part of a striving towards sustaining a community social enterprise based around archaeology.

BACKGROUND

The Rathcroghan Visitor Centre, Tulsk, Castlerea, Co. Roscommon, opened in 1999 as a community-run interpretive experience and resource hub for the Rathcroghan Archaeological Landscape (Fig. 16.1). Rathcroghan is one of a number of provincial royal sites in Ireland. It is traditionally seen as the symbolic capital of Connacht and the site of great communal gatherings or *aénaige*. It is also currently part of a serial nomination for inscription on the UNESCO World Heritage Site (WHS) list, under the heading 'Royal Sites of Ireland', together with Navan Fort, Co. Armagh (*Emain Macha*), Knockaulin, Co. Kildare (*Dún Ailinne*), the Rock of Cashel, Co. Tipperary, the Hill of Tara, Co. Meath, and the Hill of Uisneach, Co. Westmeath.

Gaining a full understanding of the Rathcroghan landscape involves interacting with two intertwined elements. On the one hand, Rathcroghan is the location of a vast array of archaeological monuments, ranging in date from the Neolithic to the late medieval period, with the Iron Age (*c.* 500 BC–*c.* AD 400) as a period of particular focus. Each period is represented in the archaeological record at Rathcroghan, which includes funerary monuments, settlement sites, ritual enclosures, ceremonial linear embankments and even

Fig. 16.1—Rathcroghan Visitor Centre, the interpretive experience and resource hub for the Rathcroghan Archaeological Landscape.

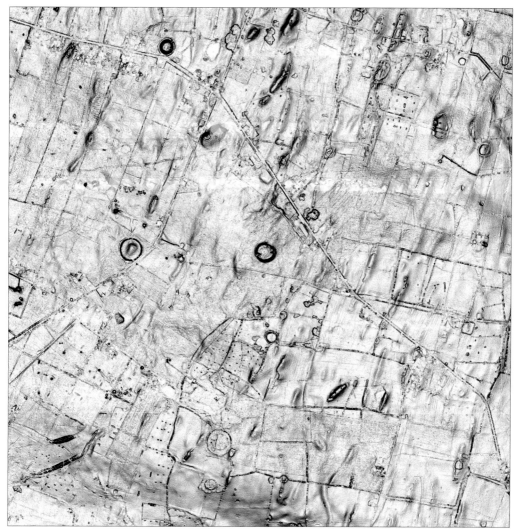

Fig. 16.2—Digital terrain model (DTM) of the core of the Rathcroghan Archaeological Landscape, derived from LiDAR data (data courtesy of Ordnance Survey Ireland).

a reputed entrance to the 'Otherworld'. The significance of this multi-period landscape does not diminish in the high and late medieval era, as witnessed by the vast expanse of pre-modern field boundaries which cover the plain, while in the wider region of *Machaire Connacht* archaeological remains at Cloonfree, Tulsk, Ardakillin, Ogulla, Carns, Ballintober and Roscommon, among others, testify to a continued societal interaction with the fringes of this symbolic capital into the early modern period at least.

On the other hand, there is the Rathcroghan that is attested in the manuscript tradition. It is often referred to as *Cruachan Aí* in the literary and historical sources, where it also serves as a central location for an extensive corpus of medieval Irish epic literature. For instance, Rathcroghan and Carnfree are central locations in the Finn Cycle tale *Acallam na Senórach* (Dooley and Roe 1999). Chief among these medieval

tales, which in some cases may hold veiled ancestral truths about the use of many of these monuments in the prehistoric period, is the *Táin Bó Cúailnge* or 'Cattle Raid of Cooley' (Kinsella 2002; Carson 2009). The epic literature presents Rathcroghan as the location and residence of the great warrior queen Medb of Connacht, and the setting for a number of the stories that comprise what is known as the Ulster Cycle. The combination of these two elements formed the inspiration for a community project which came to fruition in 1999.

The Rathcroghan landscape consists of over 240 visible archaeological sites, 60 of which are recorded as National Monuments, scattered over a landscape of approximately 6.5km^2. The interpretation of the landscape presents a challenge for the Rathcroghan Visitor Centre in Tulsk village, some 4km from the core area of the landscape (Fig. 16.2).

When the *Cruachan Aí* Heritage Centre opened in 1999, the display relied heavily on the presentation of material from traditional archaeological and historical academic sources, including work in the 1980s by Mary Gormley (1989), Michael Herity (1984; 1985; 1988; 1989) and John Waddell (1983; 1988). The only scientific archaeological excavation to have been carried out at Rathcroghan up to that time was a test excavation undertaken by Waddell (1988) on a monument known as Dathí's Mound.

The traditional source material presented in the display was supplemented by results from the ArchaeoGeophysical Imaging Project (AGIP), the Republic of Ireland's first large-scale, multi-method, archaeological remote-sensing survey, which commenced in 1994. The project, undertaken by NUI Galway with Heritage Council funding, carried out a programme of intensive topographical and geophysical survey at eleven monuments in the Rathcroghan area. The objective was to demonstrate the purpose and significance of these diverse monuments through non-invasive, non-destructive and cost-effective geophysical means that might also identify future targets for possible excavation or more refined remote-sensing survey.

The main results are discussed and illustrated in a monograph published in 2009 (Waddell *et al.* 2009) but AGIP also had a number of unexpected positive outcomes in the local community. During the course of the AGIP remote-sensing fieldwork, the landowners at Rathcroghan were happy to grant permission for access. They enthusiastically offered their time in aiding data collection, as well as taking great interest and pride in considering the results recorded for the monuments on their land. The remote-sensing techniques are non-invasive and non-destructive in terms of the landscape and any subsurface archaeological features and thus did not affect the fields or crops grown, as might be the case with excavation. The digital images and visualisations produced showed the farmers what lay beneath the soils of their fields.

The establishment of the Tulsk Action Group Ltd in 1996, as AGIP was drawing to a close, marked the coming together of a section of the local community in order to use the Rathcroghan narrative as an economic and tourism resource for the area, building on interest generated by the academic work in the 1980s and 1990s as well as the results from AGIP. The objective was to use the archaeological landscape as a resource to develop a long-term revenue and employment enterprise in the village of Tulsk. The community decided that there was a need to present the Rathcroghan landscape in a museum context. After much endeavour, Tulsk Action Group Ltd obtained funding from the Irish Tourist Board, now Fáilte Ireland, who saw the provision of a museum as a flagship project in an area which had seen little tourism development.

The first iteration of the museum was called the *Cruachan Aí* Heritage Centre. The exhibition largely utilised graphic panels to narrate local mythology and folklore, traditional landscape ground and aerial photography, and some of the AGIP remote-sensing results. It presented the current understanding of the archaeological and mythological landscape through the panels, some audio-visual presentations and innovative display of some of the more surprising and intriguing results of the remote-sensing investigations. The first interpretive expression of the remote-sensing results was rather soberly presented, however, playing a secondary role to the more 'popular' epic literature and mythological connections.

Between 1999 and 2018, continued academic investigation of the monuments in the Rathcroghan landscape has been undertaken almost exclusively through the use of a suite of remote-sensing techniques. Advances in technology have resulted in the use of new techniques and repeat surveys at higher spatial resolution. Recent work by academic researchers and professional practitioners has assisted in the visualisation and presentation of Rathcroghan mound and its surrounding landscape in new ways.

REVITALISATION OF THE RATHCROGHAN VISITOR CENTRE

The availability of more detailed survey methods, coupled with the embrace of new techniques, provided the foundational data when the heritage centre, renamed the Rathcroghan Visitor Centre, embarked on an upgrade of the public presentations in 2014. This upgrade had a number of direct aims, chief among which was the requirement to replace what was a fifteen-year-old interpretive space that had received few updates over such an extended period. Another aspect that required improvement was the aforementioned sober presentation of the archaeology, which was pitched to a narrow, more academic audience. This slightly alienated more general visitors to the Rathcroghan landscape and, by extension, the younger demographic. Indeed, general visitor feedback on the first iteration of the exhibition found that the high dependency on ground and aerial photography was difficult to relate to and failed to offer a meaningful impression of the Rathcroghan landscape.

As a result of these issues, as well as an academic desire to bring the display into line with up-to-date research, an approach was arrived at which allowed the new interpretive exhibition to serve as a platform to bring Rathcroghan to a wider and more diverse audience. This in turn served as a stimulus to reinvigorate the centre and its services, to re-engage with tourism markets which had moved away from the area as well as to attempt to interact with new markets.

The reinvigoration of the centre occurred in a number of ways. The displays were developed directly through a collaboration between the staff of the visitor centre, academic researchers and professional practitioners that has brought forward knowledge of the Rathcroghan landscape informed by historical sources and remote-sensing techniques. The active involvement of the centre's staff in the redevelopment of the interpretive facilities gave them a sense of ownership of the public presentation of the Rathcroghan landscape.

The planning of the upgrade to the facility also enabled the visitor centre to actively engage with school groups from primary level up, allowing us to tell the unique mythological and archaeological story of Rathcroghan while also introducing the next generation to the remote-sensing technology that is contributing to sustainable progress of the archaeological discipline.

Once the interpretive rooms had been upgraded, the staff wanted to ensure that all other elements of the social enterprise were brought up to the same standard. Within nine months they had repainted all interior and exterior public spaces in the centre and had decided on a theme that would more directly connect the café service, now called the 'Táin Café', with the rest of the facility. The retail offering was made more streamlined, and the major focus was on developing the shop into a rare and specialist bookshop, as well as engaging with local craft businesses and operators so that their products could be showcased.

This sense of ownership and associated striving for quality have also had a practical effect on the other services that the centre provides, from the guided site tours through to the production of information panels and archaeological trail booklets. The unique value of this approach is borne out when interested and proactive individuals and community groups visit the Rathcroghan Visitor Centre and the Rathcroghan landscape.

The Rathcroghan Visitor Centre employs nine people in a combination of full-time and part-time contracts, and is open year round. The Pobal Community Services Programme (CSP) provides a contribution towards the payment of the wages, and all other aspects to do with the maintenance, upkeep and progress of the centre are funded through the income generated from service-users. As a result, the effort of the staff and their pride in the continued operation of the Rathcroghan Visitor Centre are vital. This effort has been rewarded, and can be seen in the upturn in the number of visitors to the centre and its facilities from 2014 through to 2018 (Table 16.1).

Table 16.1—Visitor, tour and income statistics for the Rathcroghan Visitor Centre (2014–18).

	2014	2015	2016	2017	2018*
Number of service-users	7,507	9,065	10,106	13,325	18,760
% annual increase in number of service-users	N/A	21%	11.50%	32%	40%
Number of tour visits	1,600	2,321	2,604	3,327	3,760
% annual increase in number of tour visits	0.50%	45%	12%	28%	13%
% annual increase in income generated	62%	35%	30%	33%	21%

* For months Jan.– Nov. only

The Rathcroghan Visitor Centre is striving to expand its engagement beyond the static environment of the indoor interpretive exhibition. This is achieved by organising and hosting a number of outreach events throughout the year.

RATHCROGHAN CONFERENCE: ARCHAEOLOGY ABOVE & BELOW

It is through the annual Rathcroghan Archaeology Conference that the Rathcroghan Visitor Centre most actively seeks to engage with community archaeology and remote sensing, attempting to increase awareness and understanding of their merits and uses in Ireland and further afield. The importance of the Rathcroghan

Fig. 16.3—Clockwise from top left: kite aerial photograph (KAP) of Roscommon Castle (courtesy of Jim Knowles); drone photograph of Dumha Selga conjoined earthworks (courtesy of CopterView); KAP of Rathbeg ring-barrow (courtesy of Landscape & Geophysical Services); KAP of Rathra multivallate enclosure (courtesy of Christy Lawless); digital elevation model (DEM) of Lissacurkia townland (courtesy of IrishSights).

Conference, within the frame of the community use of remote sensing and in generating a discussion on community archaeology in Ireland, has been explored by Barton and Curley (2018).

Since 2014 the conference has sought to harness and embrace the two central themes that have sustained the Rathcroghan Visitor Centre: (i) community input and (ii) remote sensing to visualise and interpret the monuments and the surrounding landscape. The focus of the conference, that of community archaeology, fits perfectly under the new title of 'Archaeology Above & Below'.

The non-adversarial conference format comprises a combination of talks, workshops and practical demonstrations on the use of remote sensing, primarily in a community setting, and the visualisation, analysis and presentation of results. It is delivered by community group representatives, academics and professional practitioners alike, which in turn creates a vibrant and refreshing forum for three sometimes divergent areas of the discipline to interact, discuss and progress.

The conference, now in its fifth year under the banner of community archaeology, has had presentations from groups from across the country, with counties Roscommon, Mayo, Galway, Sligo, Waterford, Cavan, Wexford, Louth, Dublin, Donegal, Meath and Westmeath all represented in the past five years. The conference has also received presentations from Scottish, English and European groups, thus underlining the national and European credentials of the Rathcroghan Conference.

This format has a number of benefits. It provides an opportunity for community groups to 'cut their teeth' in terms of presenting their projects to a new audience of interested conference-goers. This plainly has played a role in increasing the confidence and experience of the presenters, and has led to a number of the previous community contributors going on to speak in a number of professional lecture and conference environments both nationally and further afield.

Owing to the range of contributors who generously give their time each year, from backgrounds of amateur interest, the professional archaeological spectrum and academia, the conference serves as a unique melting pot for ideas and for progressing projects, and allows 'traditional' academic researchers and professional practitioners to see the invaluable work being undertaken by motivated community groups. The latter are essentially serving a vital purpose for the discipline in a manner that 'traditional' archaeology cannot, owing to various constraints such

as possible difficulty in access to private land, lack of sustainable funding for small-scale projects, short-term projects not being practicable within an academic timetable, and unavailability, in certain cases, of remote-sensing resources. The conference also serves as an effective networking opportunity and sounding board for contributors and attendees in order to discuss one another's projects as well as possible future collaboration and assistance.

Finally, the conference helps to inspire interested parties in the audience to engage with remote sensing and to develop their own community remote-sensing projects. It provides information about the remote-sensing tools available. Combining cost-effective remote-sensing techniques with ready (and, in some cases, intimate) access to local knowledge of the areas that are being surveyed allows community groups to explore their own localities. This can have a number of direct and indirect benefits for a community group and the local area as a result.

A practical outcome of the conference each year is to target a monument or collection of monuments in the area for aerial survey, enabling kite aerial photography (KAP) and other aerial photography practitioners to photograph archaeological landscapes which do not routinely get explored by the general public. Since 2014, Rathcroghan, Carnfree, Rathra, Lissacurkia and the wider *Ard Caoin* ridge have been the subject of aerial survey (Fig. 16.3). In certain cases, where access allows, the conference field trip also takes place at these locations. The value of this approach is that we can bring the conference attendees to an important archaeological monument or collection of monuments not usually publicly accessible. It also contributes important aerial surveys of monuments of which there has previously been limited coverage. In certain instances, it also offers the opportunity for demonstration of remote-sensing techniques. This has important benefits for future research into these areas, as well as showing community groups the practical research possibilities available to their own projects.

The Rathcroghan Conference is complemented throughout the year by archaeology and heritage-based events which seek to continue the conversation in the disciplines. These come in the form of the now-annual Prof. Michael Herity Memorial Lecture, which serves as the centrepiece of our Heritage Week events each August, as well as the Winter Lecture Series, which runs over the month of November. Both series are heavily subscribed and allow the centre to welcome academics from Ireland and further afield to present their current work in a rural community setting.

THE RATHCROGHAN EXPERIENCE— PRESENTING AN ARCHAEOLOGICAL LANDSCAPE TO THE VISITOR

Community engagement at Rathcroghan is developing out of an interest in harnessing the physical archaeological resource that exists in the area in a very deliberate manner. The experience of the Rathcroghan landscape for the general-interest visitor is currently best achieved through an exploration of the indoor interpretive exhibition, coupled with a guided tour of a select number of the important visible monuments that comprise the archaeological landscape. A number of ideas have recently converged, however, in order to inspire a different way of enjoying and understanding the archaeology of Rathcroghan.

One of these ideas is that the 6.5km² Rathcroghan landscape can be thought of as an 'outdoor museum', with the 'exhibits' being the visible and invisible (subsurface) monuments in the landscape. These range from enclosures to burial mounds, and from ringforts to linear earthworks. This results in a new way of appreciating the broad and varied narrative which is presented in the Rathcroghan Visitor Centre.

The idea of the 'outdoor museum' is one that intrigues those seeking to develop this resource. The challenge that faces the small museum concerns the need to ensure that the exhibition remains relevant to visitors, particularly the younger, 'digital native' generation (Calvi and Vermeeren 2015). There is also a need to create a link between the outdoor visible and subsurface archaeology (visualised by remote sensing) and the narrative and interpretation offered indoors in the Rathcroghan Visitor Centre, which is some 4km from the Rathcroghan landscape.

One idea developed from the use of QR codes on a poster. The poster was first displayed at the final ArchaeoLandscapes Europe Project (ArcLand) conference in Frankfurt, Germany (Barton *et al.* 2015):

> 'The target of the ArchaeoLandscapes project is to address existing imbalances in the use of modern surveying and remote sensing techniques and to create conditions for the regular use of these strikingly successful techniques across the Continent as a whole. It aims to create a self-sustaining network to support the use throughout Europe of aerial survey and "remote sensing" to promote understanding, conservation and public enjoyment of the shared landscape and archaeological heritage of the countries of the European Union' (ArcLand, n.d.).

The positive reception of this method of interpretation at the conference was evidence of the value of the use of QR codes.

In association with Roscommon County Council Heritage Office, the Rathcroghan Visitor Centre has developed a series of interactive information panels that provide a summary narrative for individual monuments in the Rathcroghan Archaeological Landscape. Each panel contains text in both Irish and English, as well as ground and aerial photographs of the monument in question. These photographs are complemented by interpretive images, which provide a conjectural interpretation or reconstruction of the monument and its use (Fig. 16.4).

An innovative element is added to these traditional information panels with the insertion of a QR code. This icon, which is linked to a website URL, brings the visitor to an extended illustrated article on the monument in question, coupled with a 3D model of the monument in the form of a digital terrain model (DTM) based on the available Ordnance Survey LiDAR data for the area. Some of the QR codes also relate to YouTube videos of unmanned aerial vehicle (UAV) video surveys of the monuments, which provide the visitor with a view of the archaeology from an angle which they cannot achieve on site themselves. It also provides an opportunity to 'virtually' visit monuments which cannot be accessed easily, as well as catering for patrons with limited mobility.

In future, we may explore the development of an app or website where we can further utilise the remote-sensing surveys in conjunction with the available LiDAR data. Georeferenced 3D LiDAR models are being used with draped remote-sensing data which present an interactive image of the subsurface archaeology. When these are displayed on a smart phone or tablet, it will be possible to create walking trails that will allow the visitor to walk over to a selected monument or part of the landscape and interactively 'see' the subsurface archaeology visualised by remote-sensing techniques as they move on or between the visible monuments.

These are our first steps in using LiDAR and remote-sensing technology as a resource for the visitor to interpret the visible and invisible Rathcroghan landscape as part of their own personal experience as they walk through the Outdoor Museum. Engagement with schools is being fostered by making subsets of the LiDAR data available for use in teaching and in projects to create simple 3D models of the principal monuments in the Rathcroghan landscape. In addition, the data lend themselves to the creation of interpretive

Fig. 16.4—(Left) Sawhorse frame with Tulsk Priory information panel; (above) Rathmore interactive information panel (courtesy of Rathcroghan Visitor Centre).

animations and to 3D printing of the monuments for the community to study and enjoy.

Complementary to the production of the interactive information panels, in 2016 the centre staff wrote and produced an archaeological trail booklet for Rathcroghan. The motivation behind this project was a desire to ensure that we could more fully assist the visitor to experience the monuments in the landscape here, regardless of time commitments. The booklet provides a detailed driving route and information on seventeen monuments. It incorporates recommended

viewing points for monuments that are not accessible to the public. The production of the *Rathcroghan Archaeological Trail* (Curley and McCarthy 2016) ties in with the information panels already on site and adds a further layer of detail to, as well as expanding the scope of the concept of, an interactive Outdoor Museum. One of the benefits of the booklet is that it caters for a section of the Rathcroghan visitor demographic for whom the use of digital formats may be a challenge. As the booklet was written and produced in-house, ownership remains with the centre and so provides a new revenue strand for the social enterprise.

Further to our completed projects relating to the public dissemination of the Rathcroghan landscape, centre staff are also submitting papers for publication in academic journals, with the current edition of *Emania* containing an article entitled 'Exploring the nature of the *Fráoch* saga—an examination of associations with the legendary warrior on Mag nAí' (McCarthy and Curley 2018).

IRONS IN THE FIRE

Encouraged by the success of the *Rathcroghan Archaeological Trail* and the information panels, the centre has undertaken a substantial Roscommon LEADER Partnership-funded project to produce two key additions to the visitor experience.

The centre has decided to embark on the acquisition of a number of locally provenanced artefacts from the National Museum of Ireland, bringing to fruition a conversation that began in 2015. To achieve this we commissioned the production of two museum-standard display cases, which serve as a new centrepiece to the interpretive rooms renovated in 2014. The motivation behind this project is to allow public access to aspects of material culture from pre-modern Rathcroghan and *Machaire Connacht*. The centre, having acquired 35 artefacts ranging in date from the Neolithic period (*c.* 4000 BC) through to the early modern period (*c.* seventeenth century), now displays this National Museum of Ireland loan collection of Roscommon's material culture in one of only two non-county museums in the Republic of Ireland, a feat that enables the centre to properly label itself a museum for the first time. The collection is complemented by an information booklet, produced in-house, entitled *Óenach Cruachain: gathering the elements of daily life in Connacht's ancient capital* (Conroy 2018).

The second case now houses a specially commissioned diorama representing, through figures and the construction of a landscape, a scene from the Irish epic *Táin Bó Cúailnge*. This now serves as a unique exhibit, particularly for the younger demographic, as we seek to bring the Rathcroghan story to as wide an audience as possible.

The second strand of the LEADER-funded project is the development of a new publication, *Rathcroghan: the guidebook* (Curley and McCarthy 2018), which provides the visitor with a comprehensive but accessible account of the multifaceted aspects of the Rathcroghan landscape, namely the archaeology, history and mythology of the area. This element of the project was inspired by a need to fill a gap in the information provided to the visitor on Rathcroghan. There are a number of academic publications more or less directly concerning Rathcroghan, but visitor feedback has identified the need for a publication geared towards public dissemination. The centre employed the same method of in-house production used for the archaeological trail, which carries the same ownership and benefits provided by this booklet.

This project represents the next phase of development at the Rathcroghan Visitor Centre and is geared towards the creation of the most rounded and enjoyable experience of an archaeological attraction in Ireland.

FARMING RATHCROGHAN INTO THE FUTURE

The importance of the Rathcroghan Visitor Centre goes beyond its role in community archaeology and in informing the visitor of this archaeological landscape. In November 2015 a meeting was called between the key stakeholders in the Rathcroghan Archaeological Landscape, bringing together local landowner representatives, the management of the Rathcroghan Visitor Centre, the Heritage Officer of Roscommon County Council, academics from the Department of Archaeology and the School of Humanities (NUI Galway) and community archaeology sectors. The intention of the meeting was to set out a road map for utilising the archaeology of Rathcroghan to positive ends for the present and future stakeholders. The group, thereafter called the Rathcroghan Resource Community (RRC), has since been exploring a number of avenues with this aim in mind.

One of the projects undertaken by the RRC in recent times, with the Rathcroghan Visitor Centre acting as the lead partner, has been the submission of a proposal for a five-year Department of Agriculture, Food and the Marine (DAFM) European Innovation Partnership (EIP-Agri) project entitled 'Sustainable Farming in the Rathcroghan Archaeological Landscape'.

The objectives of the Farming Rathcroghan Project are to manage, care for and conserve the internationally significant archaeological landscape of Rathcroghan by implementing a programme of economically sustainable and ecologically sound farming practices, whilst simultaneously facilitating visitors to the area via a series of dynamic access routes.

The project will develop and try out a suite of innovative management solutions designed to sustain a viable and vibrant farming community in the context of this culturally sensitive landscape. In so doing, the project will raise awareness and recognition among the general public of the significance of Rathcroghan as a farmed archaeological landscape and of the proactive role of farmers and farming in the care and maintenance of this living landscape in harmony with its rich cultural heritage and ecological assets. As part of this programme it will test and implement best farming and archaeological practice to proactively monitor, manage, maintain and enhance the ancient cultural landscape in an environmentally and ecologically friendly way. Through engagement with key stakeholders, archaeological expertise will be made available locally to the Farming Rathcroghan Project to support the proactive management of the archaeological landscape by Rathcroghan farmers.

This application has been the result of collaboration between the aforementioned members, as well as Teagasc and the National Monuments Service of the Department of Culture, Heritage and the Gaeltacht. This application, which has received the support to date of 48 Rathcroghan farmers, was approved; the second phase, which involved the creation of a detailed project plan, was submitted for approval with a view to gaining access to a five-year funding cycle. On 24 October 2018 the Department of Agriculture, Food and the Marine announced that the Farming Rathcroghan EIP-Agri project proposal has been selected for funding, with the approved amount totalling €984,000. We look forward very much to addressing the challenges posed by, and reaping the potential rewards of the success of, this innovative project, one that we hope might be implemented as a flagship project at other culturally sensitive landscapes throughout Ireland and the European Union.

CONCLUSIONS

The involvement of the staff in the upgrading of the interpretive rooms at the visitor centre reignited a sense of ownership over the Rathcroghan story, and provided a platform from which the centre could grow and evolve. This evolution was born out of a desire to ensure that Rathcroghan, the visitor centre and its services would once more become relevant to the communities that support them. The innovative ways in which the staff sought to achieve this relevance have led to the establishment of a successful annual community

archaeology conference, an increase in on-site interpretation of this archaeological landscape, and the development of a series of projects designed to sustain and build on the successes already achieved at the centre. This approach has been shown to be successful, as evidenced by the marked growth in service-users and the increase in revenues for the period 2014–18. The author believes that the approach taken at the Rathcroghan Visitor Centre engenders a pride and sense of ownership among the staff in all aspects of the running of this social enterprise. Moreover, it furthers the pride in ownership among the local community and the landowners of Rathcroghan, and can be the key to establishing and maintaining community-driven tourism projects in Ireland as a result.

REFERENCES

ArcLand (n.d.) *ArchaeoLandscapes Europe Project: Aims* (http://www.arcland.eu/about/aims).

Barton, K. and Curley, D. 2018 Archaeological remote sensing: some community engagement in Ireland. In L. Ciolfi, A. Damala, E. Hornecker, M. Lechner and L. Maye (eds), *Cultural heritage communities: technologies and challenges*, 20–37. Routledge, London.

Barton, K., Curley, D. and Hanlon, N. 2015 Rathcroghan and the role of remote sensing in interpreting a unique archaeological landscape. In A.G. Posluchny (ed.), *Sensing the past: contributions from the ArcLand conference on Remote Sensing in Archaeology*, 120–1. Habelt-Verlag, Bonn.

Calvi, L. and Vermeeren, A. 2015 DIY platform for innovative small museum experiences. Paper presented at the Communities and Technologies 2015 Conference, Limerick, 28 June 2015 (https://pure.buas.nl/en/publications/).

Carson, C. (trans.) 2009 *The Táin*. Penguin Classics, New York.

Conroy, E. 2018 *Óenach Cruachain: gathering the elements of daily life in Connacht's ancient capital*. Self-published.

Curley, D. and McCarthy, M. 2016 *Rathcroghan Archaeological Trail: Slí Seandálaíocht Ráth Cruachan*.

Curley, D. and McCarthy, M. 2018 *Rathcroghan: the guidebook*. Tulsk Action Group CLG, Ballinasloe.

Dooley, A. and Roe, H. 1999 *Tales of the Elders of Ireland (Acallam na Senórach)*. Oxford University Press, Oxford.

Gormley, M. 1989 *Tulsk parish in historic Magh Aí: aspects of its history and folklore.* County Roscommon Historical and Archaeological Society, Boyle.

Herity, M. 1984 A survey of the royal site of Cruachain in Connacht I. Introduction, the monuments and topography. *Journal of the Royal Society of Antiquaries of Ireland* **113**, 121–42.

Herity, M. 1985 A survey of the royal site of Cruachain in Connacht II. Prehistoric monuments. *Journal of the Royal Society of Antiquaries of Ireland* **114**, 125–38.

Herity, M. 1988 A survey of the royal site of Cruachain in Connacht III. Ringforts and ecclesiastical sites. *Journal of the Royal Society of Antiquaries of Ireland* **117**, 124–41.

Herity, M. 1989 A survey of the royal site of Cruachain in Connacht IV. Ancient field systems at Rathcroghan and Carnfree. *Journal of the Royal Society of Antiquaries of Ireland* **118**, 67–84.

Kinsella, T. (trans.) 2002 *The Táin: translated from the Irish epic Táin Bó Cúailnge.* Oxford University Press, Oxford.

McCarthy, M. and Curley, D. 2018 Exploring the nature of the *Fráoch* saga—an examination of associations with the legendary warrior on Mag nAí. *Emania* **24**, 51–60.

Waddell, J. 1983 Rathcroghan—a royal site in Connacht. *Journal of Irish Archaeology* **1**, 21–46.

Waddell, J. 1988 Excavation at 'Dathí's Mound', Rathcroghan, Co. Roscommon. *Journal of Irish Archaeology* **4**, 23–36.

Waddell, J., Fenwick, J. and Barton, K. 2009 *Rathcroghan, Co. Roscommon: archaeological and geophysical survey in a ritual landscape.* Wordwell, Dublin.

17. Creating communities: a local authority model

CHRISTINE BAKER

ABSTRACT

There has been an increasing thirst among communities to learn about their past and to share it with interested visitors. Community archaeology provides an opportunity for communities to engage with the archaeology, heritage and traditions of their local area. This can result in an increased awareness of and protection for the valuable archaeological resource, build engagement within and between communities and deliver economic benefits via tourism. This paper outlines the community archaeology experience as modelled by Fingal County Council.

INTRODUCTION

Fingal County Council has embraced the concept of community archaeology through its County Development Plan 2017–2023, its Heritage Plan 2018–2023 and the appointment of a Community Archaeologist as a core member of its staff. This has resulted in the development of a Draft Community Archaeology Strategy and the delivery of an innovative public programme that supports community archaeology groups and events. There are currently fourteen local authority (county/city) archaeologists in Ireland, distributed over six counties. The primary focus of local authority archaeologists is archaeology in the planning system, although they do support archaeological and heritage-based initiatives, which typically include signage, heritage trails, leaflets and local history publications. The prevalent heritage position within local authorities is that of the Heritage Officer, of which there are currently 27. The majority of Heritage Officers are ecologists by profession, although the remit is wide, ranging from graveyard projects, commemoration and oral history projects to implementing pollinator plans and biodiversity strategies. Approximately 22 local authorities employ Conservation Officers, who are responsible for the protection of the built heritage, the compilation of the statutory Record of Protected Structures and the development of Architectural Conservation Areas in towns and villages.

In 2007 the Heritage Council rolled out the Field Monument Advisor Scheme to local authorities. The remit of the Field Monument Advisor (which was a part-time position) was to visit landowners and advise them on their archaeological monuments, assess the condition of monuments and raise awareness of sites and monuments within both the community and the local authority. At the height of the scheme there were nine Field Monument Advisors, in counties Wicklow, Kilkenny, Clare, Louth, Meath, Galway, Fingal, Donegal and Sligo. In 2015 Fingal County Council, in conjunction with the Heritage Council, decided to pilot the position of Community Archaeologist, a position that then became full-time. The remaining part-time Field Monument Advisors were reframed as Community Archaeologists by the Heritage Council in 2016 and at the time of writing this scheme is ongoing with Galway County Council, Sligo County Council and with Burren Beo, Co. Clare, as part of a bespoke agri-environment scheme in the Burren. In 2019 a similar position, also with Heritage Council funding, has been initiated in the Rathcroghan archaeological complex in County Roscommon.

COMMUNITY ARCHAEOLOGY IN IRELAND

Access to cultural heritage (and by extension archaeological heritage) is a central tenet of international and European legislation and policy, which emphasise the value and potential of cultural heritage as a resource for sustainable development and quality of life in a constantly evolving society. The 'value of cultural heritage as a key component of, and contributor to, the attractiveness and sustainability of our cities, towns, villages and rural areas' is a National

Strategic Outcome in our *National Planning Framework: Ireland 2040* (DoHPLG 2018), while one of the central themes of the 2018 national Heritage Plan consultation was 'Communities and Heritage'. Community archaeology is therefore ideally placed to contribute to the national agendas for tourism, climate change, social inclusion, demographic change, health and well-being.

There are many definitions of, and even more arguments about, what constitutes community archaeology, especially whether a project is truly 'bottom-up' (community-led and designed) or is in fact 'top-down' (professionally designed with community participation). Recently the recognition that 'to define community archaeology—narrowly or broadly—serves little useful purpose' has been embraced, given the diversity of initiatives taking place under the banner of community archaeology (Moshenska and Dhanjal 2017, 1). This is especially true of Ireland, where the legal system for the protection of archaeology means that there must be professional partnership in any project based on excavation or geophysical survey. As can be seen elsewhere in this volume, community archaeology can therefore encompass a wide range of activities in addition to excavation, including building, geophysical, landscape and topographic surveys; oral history and school-based projects; graveyard conservation; archive research; heritage trails and signage; and citizen scientist projects.

Community archaeology in Ireland is as yet relatively unburdened by the levels of political and social responsibility that have been ascribed to it elsewhere. Simpson, in evaluating UK archaeology, makes the point that aspirational outcomes are often linked to political agendas, such as social issues like the integration of homeless individuals or the reduction of vandalism. These requirements are often externally perceived, controlled and promoted, yet in many cases may be the least successful element of community archaeology projects (Simpson and Williams 2008, 87). That said, the value of the archaeological heritage's contribution to well-being and society is beginning to be recognised. The Heritage Council 2018 survey found that 91% of the public agree that supporting and developing archaeology is important for Ireland (RedC Poll).

In contrast to other post-colonial countries, community archaeology in Ireland has not developed in order to express a national identity, nor as a means of empowerment for minorities. Unlike the highly politicised history of Australian archaeology, which has resulted in Aboriginal groups being positioned at the centre of the archaeological process, Ireland's community archaeology is more focused on local concerns. An impetus of some community-driven projects is tourism, with many groups drawn to the potential for the results of community archaeology projects to translate into a potential hook for attracting visitors and to highlight little-known historical stories and sites.

In many cases, community archaeology projects are driven by pride of place and a community's desire to find out more about their own past and traditions in times of constant change, economic downturn, urbanisation and a feeling of an increasingly disconnected society. The projects described in this paper have provided a means of gathering people together in a shared interest, whether it be a way of creating awareness around a mound in the open space of a housing estate, supporting works to save a degrading monument, giving children a practical means of linking to the past or simply recording what lies beneath and above before the memory is lost.

THE FINGAL MODEL

Fingal, which is contiguous with north County Dublin, was a territory set apart from earliest times—or, as Holinshed put it in 1577, 'an odd corner of the county'. The landscape ranges from coastal to rural, while its proximity to Dublin means increasing urbanisation, resulting in one of the fastest-growing, youngest and most diverse populations in the country. There are currently 1,015 statutorily protected Recorded Monuments in Fingal. Owing to the long history of agriculture in 'the bread basket of Dublin', at least 40% of known sites are subsurface. Thanks to weather conditions and increased use of geophysical survey techniques, the number of known archaeological sites is constantly increasing. Maintaining the links between communities and their surroundings in the face of extensive development remains an ongoing issue for the local authority. The approach pioneered has been one of reconnecting people with their past and ensuring that new communities connect with their localities, thereby creating awareness and ensuring the protection of the archaeological resource.

Although two community archaeology projects were undertaken within Fingal in 2014/15 (see Duffy, this volume, and Giblin and Mongey, this volume), in the absence of the established amateur tradition evident in Britain community archaeology was for the majority of people a new concept and experience (Fig.

Fig. 17.1—Enjoying community archaeology at Swords Castle.

17.1). The aim of Fingal's archaeology programme is primarily to give people access to their own past. To date, four community archaeology excavations have been undertaken—Swords Castle: Digging History (2015–17), the Bremore Castle Big Dig (2017), Digging Drumanagh (2018–20) and the Naul Community Dig (2019)—as well as the What Lies Beneath: Fingal Geophysical Survey project (2018) and Fingal Fieldnames project (2018/19). The research objectives of the excavation projects were based on the knowledge gaps identified in the various conservation plans and geophysical surveys undertaken as part of that process. All excavations were directed under Ministerial Consent or licence from the Department of Culture, Heritage and the Gaeltacht by the writer, alongside a team of professional archaeologists with community engagement experience (Stephen Johnston, Finola O'Carroll, Siobhán Duffy, Laura Corrway, Ian Kinch and Dr Kim Rice), who were contracted to train, explain, engage and record. Access to all three sites had also been restricted, in some cases for over a decade, owing to private ownership or institutional policies. From a local authority perspective, the community archaeology project is an innovative means of re-engaging people with the monument in their locality and of involving them in the plans for its future. The

concept is based on bringing the archaeological experience to new audiences and to those who had always wanted to try archaeology but never had the opportunity.

Swords Castle: Digging History

Swords Castle is a medieval episcopal palace, designated as a National Monument. The project encompassed several elements: Swords Archaeofest, which proved a fruitful opportunity to raise awareness of the project; collaboration with the National Museum of Ireland, who organised a 'Behind the Scenes' day at their Collections Resource Centre, also located in Swords; environmental, geological and post-medieval pottery days, where experts shared their knowledge and trained participants; and 'First Findings' seminars, wherein specialists involved in the post-excavation process shared results of the previous season's dig. The central element of the project was community excavation. The objectives of the archaeological excavation were manifold but primarily were to answer the archaeological research questions, to inform ongoing or planned works and to give both locals and visitors a means of engaging directly with the archaeology of each site. Interaction with visitors was encouraged, and volunteers enthusiastically explained

Fig. 17. 2—Sieving excavated soils for artefacts, Swords Castle.

the complexities of 'their' trench or showed 'their' find. The sieving stations proved popular, and not just with those not inclined towards the more physically demanding trench-digging (Fig. 17.2). The finds-washing tent allowed visitors, especially children, to see and touch what had been found.

Although Swords Castle is the best surviving example of a Dublin archbishop's palace and was an important administrative centre, there are limited historical records. Three seasons of community excavation have confirmed the presence of burials and settlement in the tenth and eleventh centuries, before the construction of the castle; previously unknown walls and kilns have been uncovered; storage pits and fish-gutting areas have been discovered; and one of the largest environmental assemblages outside medieval Dublin has been retrieved.

The award-winning Swords Castle: Digging History project has also incorporated interpretative elements, including 'Swords Castle: My Castle', a photographic exhibition curated by artist Andrew Carson, and two film pieces, also by Andrew Carson: Memories   (https://www.youtube.com/watch?v= Rnyz5ioOWmU), in which local people were interviewed about their memories of Swords Castle, and   a   companion   piece,   *Participation*

(https://www.youtube.com/watch?v= 1id9diAgPlM), which involved the filming of the excavation and interviewing the participants and supporters of the project. In 2017 the Fingal Arts Office commissioned artists to interpret the results of the analysis of the seeds and plants from the dig as part of the 'All Bread is Made of Wood' project (see Cowley *et al.*, this volume).

Bremore Castle Big Dig

Bremore Castle, a sixteenth-century fortified house, is located towards the northern limits of Balbriggan. This is one of the fastest-growing and most ethnically diverse towns in the state. The Bremore Castle Big Dig 2017 was developed as a way of re-engaging local people with Bremore Castle while restoration works remain ongoing. The site has been subject to significant rebuilding since the mid-1990s and has remained inaccessible to local people. Medieval Bremore was associated with a prominent Anglo-Norman family, the Barnewalls. Reginald de Barnewall acquired lands in Bremore in the early fourteenth century and by the close of that century the Barnewalls were described as the lords of Bremore, Balrothery and Balbriggan. Historical evidence records that Bremore Castle was attacked and burnt during the Confederate wars of the 1640s, was probably rebuilt in the early 1660s and had

Fig. 17.3—Community excavation within the walled garden at Bremore Castle, Balbriggan.

ceased to be a principal residence by the early 1700s. Almost 100 volunteers aged from eighteen to 90 years old established the presence of a previously unknown fifteenth-century ditch close to the surviving southern wall of the castle. Their work also revealed a seventeenth-century metalled yard surface that extended throughout what became the walled garden, as well as Victorian paths (Fig. 17.3). As the first excavation beyond the walls of Swords Castle, the Big Dig at Bremore demonstrated that the model could be successfully transferred to other communities.

Digging Drumanagh

Drumanagh promontory fort is a nationally important archaeological site and is of international significance in terms of Ireland's relationship with the Roman world. In private ownership until 2016, the site had been negatively associated with unauthorised metal-detecting, motorbike scrambling and public access issues. The Drumanagh Conservation and Management Plan demonstrated that despite its importance there has been little archaeological research carried out on the site. Digging Drumanagh was the first scientific excavation ever undertaken at the site and a means to engage positively with the site locally. The focus of Season 1 was the road leading to the

Fig. 17.4—Backfilling after Season 1 at Drumanagh promontory fort, Loughshinny.

Fig. 17.5—Geophysical survey, Rosepark, Balrothery, with John Nicholls.

nineteenth-century Martello tower and the excavation sought to examine the effect of the road construction on the layers below (Fig. 17.4). Most of the evidence and finds related to the Napoleonic period and the project succeeded in expanding knowledge of the occupants of the tower. The original ground level was established and the artefacts recovered included two decorated long-handled combs dating from the Iron Age. Local interaction with the site has focused on the schools, with a site visit from the nearby St Brendan's in Loughshinny and pop-up museums at both the national and secondary schools in nearby Rush. There has been an exhibition of the finds at Rush Community Centre, facilitated by Rush Tourism, and talks with the Loughshinny & Rush Historical Society.

What Lies Beneath

A significant number of archaeological sites in Fingal are preserved within the open space of housing estates, a consequence of development and the policy of preservation *in situ*. Most of these sites have no legibility, however, and are vulnerable to damage and to requests by new residents for playing pitches or tree-planting, which would have a detrimental effect. The What Lies Beneath project was a means of raising awareness of what is literally on people's doorsteps, demonstrating the technology involved in archaeological prospection and informing the Council's various departments of the archaeological resource within Fingal's open spaces and parks. Six sites—Corduff Park and St Catherine's Park, Dublin 15, Rosepark Estate, Balrothery, the Chapel Farm estate, Lusk, Swords Glebe and Newbridge Demesne, Donabate—were surveyed by volunteers working with John Nicholls of Target Geophysics and Cian Hogan and Ursula Garner of Earthsound Archaeological Geophysics under licence (Fig. 17.5). While the results were mixed, with a high level of disturbance identified within open spaces, a new enclosure site was uncovered in Newbridge Demesne. The results were displayed in an exhibition in Blanchardstown Library and an accompanying booklet.

WHO DOES COMMUNITY ARCHAEOLOGY?

It is important for participants to have a means of anonymous feedback into the projects, in order to develop the Fingal model further and also to give participants an opportunity to voice concerns or

Table 17.1—A selection of comments from Fingal community archaeology participants.

- Great community project. Great excitement in the village about what's going on here. Raises the interest locally in archaeology.

- A fun experience once again. As usual the archaeologists were always willing to answer our questions and always made us feel our efforts were worthwhile. It was good to see the school kids visiting the site. Hopefully there will be another dig here next year.

- Great for the community to allow access to this part of our heritage. For all people.

- What a great experience! This is community archaeology at its very best. It's very enjoyable project with a lovely atmosphere and high standards.

- I'd give my eyeballs to do it again!

- Very enjoyable and informative. Lovely to do something for community and chance to meet like-minded people.

- This is a fantastic project. Great to have the local community engaged with and enjoying archaeology. You need more community digs in various areas to give people an opportunity and break down the feeling archaeology is only for professionals.

- Great experience. It is usually difficult to get involved in an archaeology dig so this is a great idea.

- I liked to have the chance in this project to come in contact with Irish people and Irish culture.

suggestions. An average of 55% of participants filled out feedback sheets. Evaluations of community excavation projects in the US and UK have shown that the reality of the community archaeology experience routinely does not match expectations. This stems in part from the public perception of what archaeology is, but also from the profession's idea of what the community *should* want. In contrast, each Fingal project experience lived up to expectations for 100% of those who replied (Table 17.1).

As previously stated, giving people access to their own past is a central concept of the Fingal community archaeology model. A fundamental aim is that of opening up archaeology to non-traditional heritage audiences—to those who may never have thought of archaeology as being for them, as well as those who had always wanted to try it (Fig. 17.6). Other than being over eighteen years of age there were no constraints on taking part, and efforts to reach new audiences and socio-economic groups included signing up volunteers at community open days and sports clubs; having a Heritage tent at the county show and at the local festivals; linking with the local tourism organisations and community groups, latterly through the Fingal Public Participation Network; notifying local newspapers; and via social media. The results on all projects have encompassed locals and people from the wider Fingal area; members of new communities; family groups; couples; Fingal County Council staff members; members of the National Learning Network,

the Dublinia Training programme, Tourism Ireland and Men's Sheds; members of other community archaeology groups; and several heritage professionals and students. Tourists from Germany, the USA, Switzerland, Britain, France and Italy have also taken part, with several returning in consecutive years. While the majority of participants have been immediately local or from the greater Fingal area, some have travelled from surrounding counties such as Kildare, Louth and Meath, and some from further afield, including Galway and Cork.

A notable contrast to perceptions of participation in heritage-based events and Fingal community archaeology is that of the age profile of participants. While the primary audience for heritage events is generally accepted as being of retirement age and above, the core age groups of community archaeology participants in Fingal is 30–49 (34%) and 50–65 (35%), with similar smaller percentages of younger (15%) and older (16%) participants. This is a demographic who are generally juggling family commitments, elderly parents and full-time jobs but who perhaps also have harboured long-held ambitions to take part in an archaeological excavation. While there is weekend access available for participating in the excavations, it still means taking holidays and making domestic arrangements in order to take part. The flipside is that entire families often come to visit their loved ones—granny brings the kids, dad brings the folks, a brother will come along to see what the fuss is about or a sister

Fig. 17.6—Participants in Season 2 of Digging Drumanagh.

is dragged down to keep someone company. Often this leads to the sharing of unique snippets of local knowledge about the place or requests to visit schools to share the results. It also means that the community archaeology experience becomes embedded throughout society.

CREATING COMMUNITIES

Successful delivery of community archaeology projects supports the broader aims of the Council in relation to heritage, tourism and community. Community archaeology is an example of national agency partnership between the Heritage Council and Fingal County Council that delivers policies and objectives with local benefits. The results of the community excavations have not only made significant contributions to national research agendas but have also succeeded in raising awareness of the value of the archaeological resource for communities and have created connections by giving citizens direct access to, and experience of, their heritage.

The development of the Fingal Community Archaeology Strategy 2019–2023 (Baker 2019) has been undertaken in two phases as the community archaeology programme has developed. A total of 632 people contributed their views, with a strong preference for increasing the visibility of the archaeological heritage through trails, signage and awareness, education and family-based activities, including excavation, field-walking, geophysical survey etc. (Fig. 17.7). One of the primary aims of the strategy is to foster collaboration between communities, agencies, networks and individuals through the medium of heritage, in order to build strong and cohesive communities in Fingal.

To date, community archaeology initiatives have allowed over 600 people to realise their ambition to take part in digs, learn new skills alongside professional archaeologists and connect with their local archaeological sites and monuments. From the outset, participants were encouraged to make choices as to when, how and to what level they wished to engage in the project. For many the opportunity just to

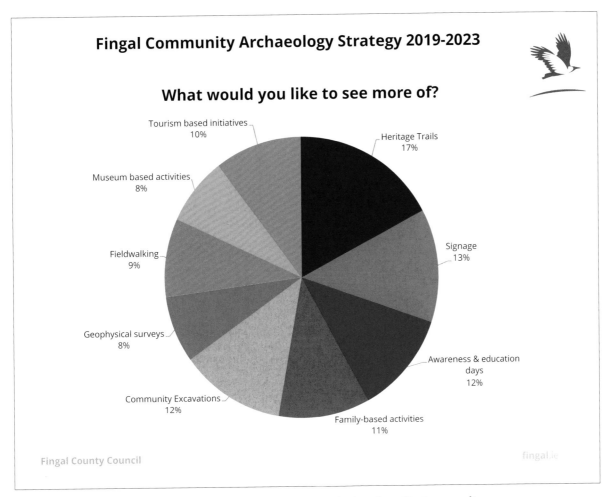

Fig. 17.7—What do people want more of? Fingal Community Archaeology Strategy results.

experience an archaeological dig was enough; others have taken the experience further—returning to college to study archaeology, volunteering at the National Museum of Ireland, or developing art projects or Irish-language pieces in response to the dig. It has also empowered individuals to engage with their local archaeological sites and monuments and to commission their own exhibitions, and has created a confidence to interact with those who had hitherto been perceived as 'the experts'. Equally, participants have contributed to each project with local knowledge and a range of skills and experience, ideas and perspectives that have enriched and enhanced the totality of the experience for all.

One of the outstanding outcomes of community archaeology in Fingal has been the building of a community with an interest in archaeological heritage that is diverse, committed and connected. Just 21% of participants in the 2015 first season of Swords Castle: Digging History had previous excavation experience. By 2018's Digging Drumanagh, 80% of participants

had previous experience, most of it garnered from previous Fingal events. In Britain the 'Gross National Happiness' agenda has resulted in an exploration of the relationship between well-being and the historic environment. Historic England (2019) found that cultural engagement—visiting archaeological and historical sites, sharing memories, handling archaeological objects and empowering people to reclaim a sense of place—can contribute to social cohesion, positive interactions and self-esteem and counter environmental degradation. Similarly, a study on archaeological excavations using quantitative methodological well-being measures found that 'voluntary archaeological excavations, i.e. those done in a community centred framework, can increase wellbeing' (Sayer 2015, 21). While such measures have yet to be applied to Fingal, it is clear that social bonds have been formed between strangers who may otherwise not have interacted, friendships have been made and an enthusiastic and increasingly experienced digging community has emerged.

REFERENCES

Baker, C. 2019 *Fingal Community Archaeology Strategy 2019–2023*. Fingal County Council, Swords.

DoHPLG 2018 *Project Ireland 2040 National Planning Framework*. Department of Heritage, Planning and Local Government, Dublin.

Historic England 2019 Wellbeing and historic environment: why bother? *Historic England Research* **11**, 7–15 (https://historicengland.org.uk/images-books/publications/historic-england-research-11/).

Moshenska, G. and Dhanjal, S. 2017 Introduction: Thinking about, talking about, and doing community archaeology. In G. Moshenska and S. Dhanjal (eds), *Community archaeology: themes, methods and practices*, 1–5. Oxbow Books, Oxford.

Sayer, F. 2015 Can digging make you happy? Archaeological excavations, happiness and heritage. *Arts and Health* **7** (3), 247–60.

Simpson, F. and Williams, H. 2008 Evaluating community archaeology in the UK. *Public Archaeology* **7** (2), 69–90.

18. *All Bread is Made of Wood: This Dirt*—a public art intervention at Swords Castle

CAROLINE COWLEY, FIONA HALLINAN, SABINA MacMAHON,
DR MERIEL McCLATCHIE AND ANNE MULLEE

> *Lift these ashes*
> *into your mouth, your blood;*
> *to know what you devour*
> *is to consecrate it,*
> *almost. All bread must be broken*
> *so it can be shared. Together*
> *we eat this earth.*
> —Margaret Atwood, *All Bread is Made of Wood* (1978)

ABSTRACT

Heritage sites can be interpreted in new ways thanks to collaborations between artists, archaeologists and historians. Exploring a recent project around the production of food in north County Dublin, artists Fiona Hallinan and Sabina MacMahon worked with Christine Baker (Fingal County Council's Community Archaeologist) and Dr Meriel McClatchie (UCD School of Archaeology) to devise speculative explication around the use of carbonised grains and seeds excavated at Swords Castle. McClatchie has analysed environmental samples from the excavation, which reveal the presence of a large granary, indicating the storage and possible distribution of grain from Swords in the medieval period. Using this research as a starting point, Hallinan and MacMahon devised conceptual works, drawing on the often-speculative nature of archaeological interpretation, to suggest alternative histories and methods of engaging with our heritage.

INTRODUCTION

This article describes the art project *All Bread is Made of Wood* and its collaboration with Fingal County Council's 'Swords Castle: Digging History' community excavation project. As part of the project's annual Environmental Day, Caroline Cowley, the Council's Public Art Co-ordinator, commissioned *All Bread is Made of Wood: This Dirt*, which was curated by Anne Mullee. Artists Fiona Hallinan and Sabina MacMahon were invited by Mullee to contemplate bread and its elements as a vehicle for the transference of knowledge and memory as embodied in its production. *All Bread is Made of Wood: This Dirt* was developed through a combination of research, speculation, making and analysis of archaeological material collected at Swords Castle. The group collaborated with Fingal County Council's Community Archaeologist, Christine Baker, and with Dr Meriel McClatchie (UCD School of Archaeology) to present the project's first public iteration, which took place on 29 August 2017.

FOOD AS ART

Drawing on principles of socially engaged art practice (Bishop 2012), the project seeks to investigate the cultural, social and ceremonial significance of food and food production in north County Dublin, looking at both the medieval and the contemporary. The core aims of the project are to provide space for the artists to engage with the broader concept, to develop working relationships with the community of the area, including older residents and an African women's group, and to devise temporary, site-specific artworks drawing on the diverse body of research that emerges. Food has been co-opted into art practice for centuries, from appearing as the subject-matter of seventeenth-century Dutch Golden Age painters to the work of contemporary research-based projects, including 'the food thing'[1] and the experimental culinary creations of the Domestic Godless.[2]

In *All Bread is Made of Wood*, 'bread' acts as a catalyst for personal cultural perspectives in an Ireland that is cleaving to a romanticised idealised past while in metamorphosis, becoming complex, richer and trickier to navigate. Bread is viewed as the constant, an anchor to moor us in times of turmoil. In working with Ireland's transfigured population, bread becomes a metaphor and vehicle for the advocacy of a range of interpretive practices, especially those that can enhance and communicate meanings to the wider community. This principle is set out in the International Council on Monuments and Sites *International Charter for the Conservation and Restoration of Monuments and Sites* (ICOMOS 1964), to assist in safeguarding the tangible and intangible values of heritage sites.

The ICOMOS charter also encourages communities to interpret sites from their own individual cultural perspectives. The grains discovered at Swords Castle, and their historical production and possible use, resonate with how food is central to the Nigerian women of the *Nwannediuto*[3] networking group, who have also participated in *All Bread is Made of Wood*, taking part in a non-public recipe salon at Newbridge House in August 2017. The bread we speak of is similarly the Nigerian *akara* (fritter) or *moin moin* (bean pudding), where the bean is an essential basic foodstuff. Beans and peas were also discovered in abundance at Swords Castle, providing a link between a different cultural heritage and our shared present.

SWORDS CASTLE: INTERPRETING A HERITAGE SITE THROUGH PUBLIC ART

Swords Castle is not a castle in the accepted sense but rather a medieval episcopal residence. It is attributed to the first Anglo-Norman archbishop of Dublin, John Comyn (*c*. 1150–1212), and was founded in the late twelfth century as the administrative centre of an extremely wealthy manor. Here lands were granted, weights and measures were inspected, rents collected and petitions from tenants and traders heard. By the sixteenth century it was a ruin, albeit one that then housed 40 Protestant families fleeing persecution in the Low Countries. It was purchased in 1830 by the Cobbe family of Newbridge House, Donabate, who grew a number of apple and soft fruit varieties there for some years (Baker 2017). Excavations carried out during the community archaeology and research excavation project Swords Castle: Digging History (2015–17) revealed the history of the castle as the important site of a granary storing barley, bread wheat and oats, possibly grown in north County Dublin. These grains likely provided the medieval inhabitants with porridges, stews and breads.

Fingal Arts Office has always been cognisant of the value of its local tangible and intangible heritage, and the role that public art can play in providing the opportunity to deeply connect people with place. Contemporary art theorist Lucy Lippard reflects in her book *Undermining* that 'archaeology is time read backwards' (Lippard 2014). In this view, then, the layers of *This Dirt* are metaphorical towns turned upside down. The archaeological work or 'mining' at Swords Castle continues to derive new meaning from its almost 1,200-year history.

These excavations are expertly led by Fingal County Council's Community Archaeologist, supported by specialist expertise, including collaboration with UCD's School of Archaeology, and energised by a host of voluntary local participants, many experiencing their first archaeological excavation. In the context of *All Bread is Made of Wood*, the multiple interpretative propositions made by the project allow the emergence of a sense of the castle's long existence, of journeys taken, food prepared and meals shared. Each layer of archaeology that is revealed represents a new body of knowledge about the site, its use and its transformations.

ON IRISH FOOD HISTORY

While Ireland is not generally noted for its cuisine, elements of food production in Ireland are associated with the country's characterisation as an agricultural economy. Food forms part of a nation's intangible cultural heritage, which can include practices or activities such as the construction of musical instruments, pilgrimage routes or the protection of national cuisines and foodstuffs (UNESCO 2003). This notion of the 'intangible' is salient to *All Bread is Made of Wood*, as both an abstract notion and its relationship to the ephemeral artefacts of social history.

Prior to the fifteenth and sixteenth centuries, certainty around Irish food history is scant. Records of handwritten and printed cookery books and 'recipts', or recipes, illustrate the food culture of the landed gentry, documentation that allows us glimpses of the diet of the élite but not that of the ordinary person. Cookery books grew from an informal tradition of gathering and exchanging recipes, a practice that grew in popularity from the sixteenth and seventeenth centuries (Shanahan 2015), where ideas for food preparation were collected by gentlewomen to be shared with contemporaries or added to a family culinary archive.

Fig. 18.1—Meriel McClatchie shows visitors some of the seeds and grains at the Environmental Archaeology Day at Swords Castle (© Anne Mullee, 2017).

Shanahan notes that this material evidence of cooking and foodstuffs reflects the diet of the wealthy rather than that of the 'ordinary' impoverished Irish populace, which was likely supplemented by foraging and gathering in addition to subsistence farming (Clarkson and Crawford 2001). It is fair to infer, then, that the nuanced diet of the non-gentry may not be adequately reflected by this source material. In order to collate an accurate picture of what the average diet of the ordinary Irish person was like prior to the routine gathering of social histories, we turn to what archaeology can tell us.

In referring to Dr Meriel McClatchie's analysis of grains and seeds found at Swords Castle (Fig. 18.1), Fiona Hallinan and Sabina MacMahon have devised works that employ speculation and unconventional interpretation. Collaboration between artists and archaeologists at heritage sites, including Swords Castle, has huge potential for illuminating and presenting the full range of interpretive possibilities from culturally diverse demographics and from local perspectives.

This approach is already under way as part of the NEARCH Programme (New Scenarios for Community Involved Archaeology 2013–18)[4] in the Netherlands. In 2017, 35 artists were invited to participate in an exhibition held at three venues in Maastricht. *The Materiality of the Invisible* acknowledged that both artists and archaeologists not only share a passion for probing what lies beneath the surface but also endeavour to reveal things that were formally disregarded but yet have the potential to change our views of our past, present and future against the backdrop of rapid change and shifting cultural positions. During Dr McClatchie's demonstration and insights at Swords Castle at the Environmental Day, participants and public were able to marvel at the minutiae of these ancient grains, the accident of their preservation and the uses they may have had. It was this latter question that informed the work imagined and created by artist Fiona Hallinan, who used reference images of the grains and seeds to make nail transfers and composed a meal made from the grains, seeds and foraged foods that could have been familiar to the castle's medieval inhabitants.

ARCHAEOLOGICAL EVIDENCE FOR PLANTS AT SWORDS CASTLE

As previously noted, during the medieval period Swords Castle was a manorial centre that controlled significant agricultural production in the region (Murphy and Potterton 2010). It was hoped that remains of the actual plant foods associated with this agricultural activity might be uncovered during the excavation. It often comes as a surprise to people that the delicate remains of plants can survive when buried in the ground for hundreds of years. One would expect these fragile remains to rot away, but in certain conditions plant components can survive for hundreds and even thousands of years. At archaeological excavations across Ireland, ancient plant remains are often discovered when buried deposits are closely inspected. The study of these plant remains enables important insights into what past communities were eating and how local environments might have appeared. This type of investigation is known as 'archaeobotany', combining expertise in both archaeology and botany. At Swords Castle, an archaeobotanist—Dr Meriel McClatchie, UCD School of Archaeology—worked closely with excavation director Christine Baker to develop a strategy for recovery and analysis of plant remains.

Specific conditions are required to ensure long-term preservation of organic remains such as plants. In the case of Swords Castle, the plant remains survived because they were burnt, and in many cases then placed into features that helped protect them, such as storage pits and rubbish pits. Perhaps cereals, for example, were dried over a fire before storage or were cooked over a fire as part of a meal, and some of the cereal grains inadvertently came into contact with the fire. In the open flame, where there is plenty of oxygen, the grains usually combust and turn to ash, leaving little trace in the archaeological record (other than their silica skeletons). In areas of the fire where there is restricted oxygen, however, plant components can become 'charred', being converted to a chemically inert carbon. This means that the plant components do not break down and rot away but instead remain hidden underground until their discovery by archaeologists. Although they change in colour, becoming blackened, these charred plant components often retain many elements of their shape and appearance, and they can be identified when examined under a microscope, revealing people's interactions with plants in the past.

Careful excavation and laboratory analysis enabled the discovery of thousands of charred plant components from Swords Castle, providing scientific evidence for the types of plants that were being used here in the centuries before, during and after the main period of castle occupation. Many of the deposits dated from the eleventh to thirteenth centuries, the transition between the early medieval and medieval periods in Ireland. The material consisted mainly of cereal grains—predominantly bread wheat, with some oats

Fig. 18.2—Meriel McClatchie demonstrates how archaeological botanical material is collected on site at Swords Castle (© Brian Cregan, 2017).

and barley (Fig. 18.2). Other cultivated crops included peas and beans. Occasional fruit and nut remains were present, including hazelnut, bramble and sloe, as well as other wild plants. The plant remains discovered at Swords Castle are typical of the types of plants growing in early medieval to medieval Ireland, particularly in the east of the island. The quantity of material recovered is, however, unusually large: more than 16,000 plant components have been found to date, emphasising the important role that food played in activities at Swords Castle.

Bread wheat was the main cereal type recovered at Swords Castle. It is considered one of the primary crops of medieval Ireland (Murphy and Potterton 2010), particularly in eastern and south-eastern regions. While bread wheat was present in early medieval Ireland, it became much more important following the arrival of the Anglo-Normans (Monk 1986), owing in part to the introduction of new farming techniques better suited to the demanding requirements of bread wheat. The medieval period in Ireland therefore witnessed not just the arrival of new peoples but also the emergence of new food preferences, such as bread wheat. A significant increase in food markets and fairs, as well as the emergence of new trade routes, further expanded the variety of foods available to Dublin's citizens, thereby creating new food traditions in the city and its surroundings.

Wheat was used in the production of luxury bread. The superior quality of wheaten flour, when carefully processed, produces pleasant, light and fine-textured bread, compared to the heavy, coarse and dark breads of oat and barley flours (Sexton 1998). Wheat was also consumed in the form of the other foodstuffs, including gruels and ale. Oat and barley grains were also found at Swords Castle, representing cereals that could have been used in the production of broader, flatter breads, in addition to porridge, pastes and ales, as well as being an ingredient in stews (McClatchie 2003). While cultivated plants were certainly important at Swords Castle, a wide variety of wild plants were also recorded. Nowadays we may regard many of these as 'weeds', but in the past some may have been gathered as leafy greens and condiments. They may not all have been important in terms of nutrition, but in conjunction with other foods they could have been vital for palatability.

Gerard's *Herball* (1633) described how common sorrel, for example, provided a 'profitable sauce in many meats' and was 'pleasant to the taste'. Fat hen is now commonly regarded as a weed but it was sold by hawkers and eaten as a leafy vegetable in Dublin until the eighteenth century (Geraghty 1996). Plants may also have been gathered for other uses, such as for medicines and textile dyes. Excavations at Swords Castle provide new insights, therefore, into lost food and plant traditions, reminding us of the central role that plants played in many aspects of people's lives.

FIONA HALLINAN—*SEED CARRIERS*

Seed Carriers [food truck menu]
Oat bread, sloe and apple jelly, *crème fraiche,* **blackberry**
Barley porridge with fat hen, sorrel, broadbean gremolata, hazelnut
Lemon barley water

This pair of works responded to the activity of the community archaeological dig at Swords Castle, providing alternative entry points for a public audience to the findings and research of the archaeology team. In devising this work, Hallinan was drawn to images from the *Digital seed atlas of the Netherlands* (Cappers *et al.* 2006), to which she was introduced by Dr Meriel McClatchie, and its macroscopic illustrations of plant remains, including specific examples of grains and seeds found at Swords Castle. She became interested in the inter-relationship between people and these remains. Seeds managed to survive through multiple generations of humans, to be discovered and categorised by us, and drawn upon to build an image of the societies of a different time. Hallinan speculated about the agency of the seeds and their use of humans as a means of transporting the information they held through time and space. This led her to develop the pair of works *Seed Carriers*. In this project, plant macro-remains such as seeds previously found in archaeological deposits at Swords Castle were made visible in two ways: in one instance, figuratively, as illustrations on nail transfers applied to the nails of participants, and in another, constitutively, as ingredients used in the menu of an on-site food truck (Fig. 18.3).

Both of these means of display were conceived of as gestures of hospitality on the Environmental Day of the archaeological dig at Swords Castle. Applying nail transfers depicting images of the seeds to the hands of the volunteer participants was a way of making visible the results of the archaeological activity, celebrating the social aspect of the day out and underlining its participatory nature by ornamenting the hands that have been involved (Fig. 18.4). The food truck, serving a menu that included ingredients found during the

Fig. 18.3—Fiona Hallinan's *Seed Carriers* food truck at Swords Castle on 29 August 2017 (© Brian Cregan, 2017).

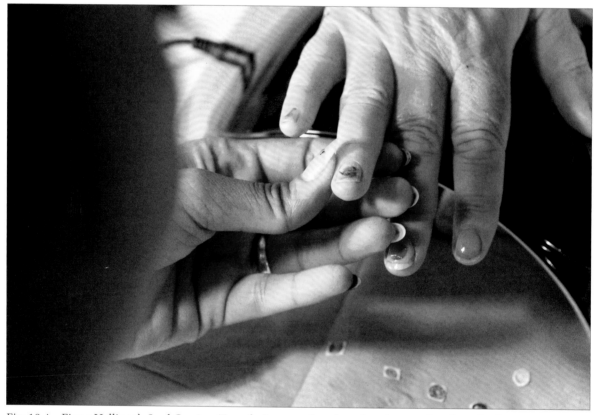

Fig. 18.4—Fiona Hallinan's *Seed Carriers*. Transfer images of seeds and grains are placed on the fingernails of the community archaeologists and visitors (© Brian Cregan, 2017).

excavations on the site, acted both as an embodied point of engagement with knowledge gained from the archaeological digs and as a means to nourish the participants involved.

SABINA MacMAHON—*ANTI-ANTI-PASTA*

MacMahon's contribution to *All Bread is Made of Wood: This Dirt* took the form of a day-long pop-up museum-style exhibition in the Archbishop's Chapel at Swords Castle on 29 August 2017. Entitled *Anti-anti-pasta*, the exhibition marked the culmination of an extensive research project exploring the fascinating life of a little-known Italian Futurist artist named Ermenegildo Cervi (1879–1966). Born in Naples, Ermenegildo Cervi relocated to north County Dublin in 1930, following a disagreement with his Futurist contemporaries over the social and artistic movement's call for a widespread ban on pasta in Filipino Marinetti's (1930) *Il Manifesto della Cucina Futurista* ('The Manifesto of Futurist Cooking'). Futurism celebrated speed, light, technology—everything that was modern and dynamic—but in this widely publicised manifesto on food its leaders declared that *pastasciutta* (dried pasta) induced pessimism, nostalgia

and lethargy in ardent *mangiamaccheroni* (pasta-eaters) and denounced the consumption of this long-standing, versatile and nutritious staple of the Italian diet. Horrified at this denigration of his national dish, Cervi decided to distance himself from the Futurists and join family members who had previously emigrated to Ireland, where they established what would become the country's first traditional Italian chip shop. They assured him of their adopted homeland's fondness for complex carbohydrates, and so he planned to attempt to establish a new community of pasta-eaters in Dublin to ensure the foodstuff's endurance. Upon his arrival in Ireland, Cervi was impressed by Irish people's strong connection to a shared past through their cultural heritage, and he set about researching the possibility of adopting a uniquely 'Irish' way of cooking pasta in order to encourage the natives to adopt it as an everyday staple alongside bread and potatoes. Somewhat bizarrely, he decided that the Bronze Age *fulacht fiadh* presented the most suitable means of achieving his goal, and to this end he held several public pasta cook-outs between 1932 and the beginning of the Emergency at a cooking pit that he constructed in his back garden. Little documentation of these events survives, but it has been noted that he presided over proceedings in full Celtic Revival dress.[5]

Fig. 18.5—Sabina MacMahon's *Anti-anti-pasta* exhibition in the Archbishop's Chapel (© Brian Cregan, 2017).

Fig. 18.6 —'Ermenegildo Cervi', Sabina MacMahon's *Anti-anti-pasta* exhibition in the Archbishop's Chapel (© Brian Cregan, 2017).

While his endeavour to promote pasta as a ready alternative to the potato in the twilight years of the Free State ultimately failed, he produced numerous innovative new pasta forms influenced by both his Futurist leanings and membership of what was then the largest 'foreign' community in Ireland—the Italians, who in the 1930s numbered over 1,000. He continued to paint in an idiosyncratic Futurist style until his death in 1966, but dedicated most of his time to making abstract sculptures from a specially formulated bread dough similar to that used in traditional Neapolitan pizzas.

MacMahon's research into Cervi's life and work resulted in an exhibition consisting of five roll-up banners acting as portable information panels and a small collection of personal artefacts from Cervi's estate, accompanied by object labels. Shown in a vitrine and on a plinth-like display table, the artefacts consisted of photographs of Cervi on holiday in Italy, a dough-scraper, a pasta-strainer, three wooden rolling-pins and a metal cooking pot used to make his special *macaroni* tomato sauce. In look and feel the display was similar to other information-heavy temporary exhibitions of the kind frequently encountered in libraries, regional museums, heritage centres and other civic spaces (Fig. 18.5).

But one thing separated the material—both textual and physical—included in *Anti-anti-pasta* from its earnestly informative brethren: its subject was entirely fictional. Ermenegildo Cervi has never existed outside of the imaginary biography created for him from an amalgamation of real (true?) histories of the lives of members of the Futurist movement and that of MacMahon's partner's maternal great-grandfather, Giuseppe Cervi; the discovery of the archaeological remains of wheat and other grains at Swords Castle; the various and ongoing waves of migration to north County Dublin; the cultural significance of food; and the interest in blurring the already vague line that exists between fact and fiction which has informed the artist's art practice for the past decade. The photographs of Ermenegildo are those of an unknown Italian stranger (Fig. 18.6), bought online along with his pasta-making equipment. His cooking pot, long retired from daily use, was borrowed for the day of the exhibition from her grandmother's garage. McMahon's art practice is largely research-based and concerned with a multidisciplinary investigation of credibility, plausibility and parafiction, as defined by Carrie Lambert-Beatty (2009) in relation to art critic and theorist Rosalind Krauss's (1980) applications of the associated term 'paraliterary'. In contrast to the imagined fact-based world of fiction, the parafictional allows for real and/or imaginary people, places and things to intersect with the work as it is lived. In parafiction the truth-likeness or quality of realism in something, combined with the manner in which it is presented to the viewer, the completeness of its stylistic mimicry, can lead to its acceptance as true or real because of the likeness of the proposition to the truth and its exploitation of the pragmatics of trust.

The artefacts, texts and primary sources presented in the simulated museum and fine art exhibition environments she creates, as well as the speculative narratives and histories they reveal, are simultaneously real, not real and not not-real. They can be interpreted as a species of 'fictive' art, whereby a fiction is presented as fact and subsequently attains a truth status for some people some of the time. Viewers can take the work at face value or, finding subtle inconsistencies or improbabilities contained within it, begin to question its factualness and, by extension, the factualness of the historical record at large—essentially learning something true through untruthful means.

Archaeological finds that provide physical evidence of our material culture—the minute burnt remains of seeds and grains at Swords Castle as much as the Pyramids or Stonehenge—are ripe for interpretation, not only by archaeologists, scientists and historians but also by creative practitioners, artists and writers. Like all objects, archaeological remains, big and small, are generous, accommodating the multiple meanings, histories and biographies that we project onto them. Why should a medieval grain of wheat in north County Dublin and the tradition of food production to which it belonged not form part of the story of an idealistic Italian immigrant to mid-twentieth-century Ireland who easily could have existed? Why should it be restricted only to always telling the truth when there is much to be learned from telling stories instead?

CONCLUSION

The challenge of interpreting historical sites—and, indeed, archaeological findings—asks how we can allow for a range of diverse perspectives. *All Bread is Made of Wood*'s work with Fingal's Community Archaeology project and UCD School of Archaeology and the inviting of artists to become part of speculative discourse permit us to engender valuable multiple viewpoints. By sharing ideas about and making food, we become complicit in deeply embedded gifting practices that exist to create social cohesion and acceptance (Hastorf 2016), while strengthening bonds of community. Current approaches to readings of intangible cultural heritage invigorate discursive enquiry, exploring the potential of alternative, historical hypotheses which may have their origins in local stories or traditions. So it is not without plausibility that Sabina MacMahon's exhibition *Anti-anti-pasta* offers us a real account of the invention of pasta in north County Dublin, while there is potential for the food presented by Fiona Hallinan in *Seed Carriers* to catapult us into the past with flavours very much enjoyed in our present. Through these interventions, we can remove ourselves from engrained notions of history while manifesting possible divergent paradigms.

REFERENCES

Atwood, M. 1978 *All Bread is Made of Wood. Selected poems II: poems selected and new 1976–1986.* Oxford University Press, Toronto.

Baker, C. 2017 *Swords Castle. Archaeology Ireland* Heritage Guide No. 77. Wordwell, Dublin.

Bishop, C. 2012 *Artificial hells: participatory art and the politics of spectatorship.* Verso, London/New York.

Cappers, R.T.J., Bekker, R.M. and Jans, J.E.A. 2006 *Digital seed atlas of the Netherlands.* Groningen Archaeological Studies 4. Barkhuis Publishing, Eelde.

Clarkson, L. and Crawford, M. 2001 *Feast and famine: food and nutrition in Ireland 1500–1920.* Oxford University Press, Oxford.

Doyle, J. 2013 *The food thing.* New Writing for Public Art (Publicart.ie, https://bit.ly/2qyQJ6i; accessed 14 April 2018).

Geraghty, S. 1996 *Viking Dublin: botanical evidence from Fishamble Street.* Royal Irish Academy, Dublin.

Gerard, J. 1633 *The herball or generall historie of plantes: very much enlarged and amended by Thomas Johnson.* Islip and Norton & Whitakers, London.

Hastorf, C. 2016 *The social archaeology of food: thinking about eating from prehistory to the present.* Cambridge University Press, Cambridge.

ICOMOS 1964 *International Charter for the Conservation and Restoration of Monuments and*

Sites. International Council on Monuments and Sites, Venice.

Krauss, R. 1980 Poststructuralism and the 'paraliterary'. *October* **13**, 36–40.

Lambert-Beatty, C. 2009 Make-believe: parafiction and plausibility. *October* **129**, 54.

Lippard, L.R. 2014 *Undermining: a wild ride through land use, politics, and art in the changing West*. Newmarket, New York.

McClatchie, M. 2003 The plant remains, Cork city excavations. In R.M. Cleary and M.F. Hurley (eds), *Cork City excavations 1984–2000*, 391–413. Cork City Council, Cork.

Marinetti, F.T. 1930 *Il Manifesto della Cucina Futurista*. Gazzetta del Popolo, Turin.

Monk, M.A. 1986 Evidence from macroscopic plant remains for crop husbandry in prehistoric and early historic Ireland: a review. *Journal of Irish Archaeology* **3**, 31–6.

Murphy, M. and Potterton, M. 2010 *The Dublin region in the Middle Ages: settlement, land-use and economy*. Four Courts Press, Dublin.

Sexton, R. 1998 Porridges, gruels and breads: the cereal foodstuffs of early medieval Ireland. In M.A. Monk and J. Sheehan (eds), *Early medieval Munster: archaeology, history and society*, 76–86. Cork University Press, Cork.

Shanahan, M. 2015 *Manuscript recipe books as archaeological objects: text and food in the early modern world*. Lanham, Lexington.

UNESCO 2003 *Convention for the Safeguarding of the Intangible Cultural Heritage*. UNESCO, Paris.

Ward, A. 2017 Dress and national identity: women's clothing and the Celtic Revival. *Costume* **48** (2), 193–212.

NOTES

[1] 'The food thing' is an ongoing, open-ended, collaborative project that emerged from GradCAM, the Graduate School of Creative Arts and Media, Dublin. The project centres on the production, preparation, consumption, exchange and discussion of foodstuffs, and, critically, the politics and economic conditions which determine and are determined by food production (Doyle 2013).

[2] The Domestic Godless was founded by artists Stephen Brandes and Mick O'Shea (later to be joined by Irene Murphy) under the Cork Artists' Collective banner at the exhibition Artists/Groups at the Project Arts Centre, Dublin, in 2003. Since then the project has explored the potential of food (its taste, its presentation, its history and its cultural values) as a vehicle for irreverent artistic endeavour and experimentation. Through recipes, installations and public presentations, it employs food as both a concept and a medium through which to convey humour, empathy and other qualities that distinguish art from purely craft (www.thedomesticgodless.com).

[3] *Nwannediuto* is an African women's group founded in 2004 by Lauretta Igbosonu in order to provide community and support and promote development and integration in Fingal. *All Bread is Made of Wood* is collaborating with *Nwannediuto*, exploring intimate histories of food and hospitality.

[4] Over the last 25 years, archaeology and cultural heritage management have undergone significant scientific and professional developments. Conducted by the French National Institute for Preventive Archaeological Research, the NEARCH project, supported by the European Commission for five years (2013–2018) in the framework of the Culture programme, is a European-wide cooperation network of sixteen partners from ten countries willing to explore these changes and their consequences. NEARCH aims to explore the various dimensions of public participation in contemporary archaeology and bring to the field, which is strongly influenced by economic and social developments in society, new ways of working and collaborating (www.nearch.eu).

[5] Celtic Revival dress was a contrived Irish national costume devised in the late nineteenth/early twentieth century. It was intended to be a visual symbol of Irish renaissance, one that would help in the effort to counter British influences and establish a strong cultural identity. Celtic Revival clothing was worn by both men and women as a signifier of cultural and political sympathies (Ward 2017). It often featured symbols drawn from Ireland's medieval ecclesiastical past, such as the Celtic cross.

19. Bust to boom: an inverse equation?

PAUL DUFFY

ABSTRACT

This article reflects on the significant growth of community archaeology in Ireland since 2012, both in terms of participatory heritage projects and as a recognisable concept/subdiscipline in itself. The rapid pace of development of community archaeology is discussed in the context of wider developments in archaeological practice and a brief examination of the possible causes for this boom is presented, followed by a non-exhaustive summary of projects and initiatives that the author feels have been instrumental in this growth. The question is posed as to whether self-reflection and accountability with regard to models of community archaeology are needed or desirable. The final section comprises a speculative look ahead to what directions community archaeology may take over the coming decades. This is framed in the context of the current funding streams available and how these may develop in future, as well as the part that planning and contract specifications may play in the growth and sustainability of community archaeology projects.

INTRODUCTION—RINGING IN THE CHANGES SINCE 2012

Writing in early 2019, I believe it is fair to say that there has been little substantive change in the field of archaeological practice in the Republic of Ireland since 2012. There has, however, been some rearranging of the department with responsibility for archaeology and the National Monuments Service. In 2016 the Department of Arts, Heritage, Gaeltacht and the Islands (DoAHGI) became the Department of Arts, Heritage, Regional, Rural and Gaeltacht Affairs before the advent of the current Department of Culture, Heritage and the Gaeltacht in 2017. There have been several changes in the ministerial office, with Mr Jimmy Deenihan TD handing over to Ms Heather Humphries TD in 2014, and Ms Josepha Madigan TD taking on the role in 2018.

While an overhaul of the National Monuments legislation is in progress, there has been little change since 2012, the most significant exception to this being the European Union (Environmental Impact Assessment of Proposed Demolition of National Monuments) Regulations 2012 (http://www.irishstatutebook.ie/eli/2012/si/249/made/en/print, accessed 10 April 2018). This regulation, however, is relevant only to sites deemed to be National Monuments that have been discovered on infrastructure projects. Any other changes have been cosmetic or due to large-scale governmental housekeeping (i.e. the implications for the National Monuments Act under the Local Government Reform Act 2014: http://www.irishstatutebook.ie/eli/2014/act/1/enacted/en/html, retrieved 10 April 2018).

The licensing system—the mechanism that controls and vets the processes of archaeological excavation in the Republic of Ireland—has changed slightly with the introduction in 2017 of a new application form. This now requires a written statement from the developers to the effect that they are in a position to, and fully acknowledge their obligation to, fund all on-site and post-excavation works necessitated by the development.

A more conspicuous change regarding the public institutions has arisen from several high-profile retirements within the public sector, with many long-standing members of the National Museum of Ireland and the National Monuments Service stepping down since 2012 and being replaced with highly experienced and dynamic appointments.

At an academic level, while some research paradigms have come to prominence since 2012 (notably experimental archaeology), I would suggest that there has been no sea change in how courses are structured and delivered, with content adjusted no more than in the past to allow for recent developments and new thinking (though this is not to detract from the number of seminal and ground-breaking publications that have emerged in this time).

Posterity may well judge that the emergence of a trade union for archaeologists employed in the private sector proved to be the defining characteristic of the last six years in Irish archaeology. While organised representation for archaeologists represents a seismic shift in the workplace dynamic, at the time of writing it is too early to fully gauge the implications of this movement.

In my opinion, however, the most obvious and visible change in the field of archaeology in Ireland since 2012 has been the explosion in what are termed community archaeology projects, which in the main have sprung from a grass-roots level, often nurtured by local authorities, public bodies such as the Heritage Council and other organisations such as the Irish Archaeological Field School and Grassroots Archaeology. As the Adopt-a-Monument experience has shown, every county can now boast community archaeology or community heritage projects of one shape or another. This explosion has been most readily charted in the pages of the quarterly magazine *Archaeology Ireland*, which has its finger squarely on the pulse of trends and currents in the industry and sector as a whole. A scan of the contents listing for the past six years shows that articles detailing community projects occur with increasing frequency from 2012, until by 2014/15 it is rare to find an issue without at least one article on a project or aspect of community archaeology. Community archaeology modules are now taught at undergraduate and postgraduate level in several universities in Ireland. Entire conferences are dedicated to this phenomenon and grant schemes are structured around it.

The emergence of 'Community Archaeologists' in some local authorities in recent years is of great significance in terms of this development and shows just how much the subdiscipline of community archaeology has advanced from a time in the recent past where such a thing was not only beyond aspirational but also unimaginable in the truest sense of the word. How did we get here?

DIFFERING PERSPECTIVES—BOOM OR REBRAND?

Before blindly accepting the statement that 'community archaeology in Ireland has seen an unprecedented boom since 2012' we should examine the history of the matter. From the perspective of a more recently qualified archaeology graduate/practitioner, it might seem clear that for decades the community archaeology paradigm evidenced elsewhere (particularly in the UK and the USA) had passed Ireland by.

On the face of it, the narrative seems clear: the entire modern archaeological industry in Ireland was born of development-led projects, particularly those post-dating Ireland's ratification of the Valletta Convention. The devastation of the commercial archaeology sector in 2008 and the years following the

economic crash resulted in a period of crisis and confusion for practitioners, many of whom were made unemployed or forced to seek employment outside the industry. Once the dust settled, an organic and uncoordinated shift of focus towards archaeology in the community occurred. This was a direct result of a preponderance of trained, experienced and time-rich (unemployed) or dispossessed (employed in other fields) archaeologists turning their attention to their own locales. Notice was taken of the international situation and the multitude of projects and models in existence elsewhere and the realms of possibility engendered by such efforts. Some observers viewed this phenomenon circumspectly: 'it is hard not to see this Damascene conversion as a job preservation strategy' (Horning and Brannon 2012). While there may have been an element of this at play in some cases, it nevertheless does not negate the positive results achieved; nor is there anything wrong with 'job preservation', which could just as easily be termed proactive or innovative approaches to heritage employment.

With the recalibration of the industry following several years of modest economic recovery, diverse and *ad hoc* models of community archaeology were carried into the mainstream of archaeological practice, lodging within local authorities, university modules and commercial consultancies.

While this narrative would seem to be correct in many particulars, a graduate/practitioner of an older generation might take exception to this generation's claims to have invented community archaeology! Take, for example, Kells Priory, Co. Kilkenny, an iconic medieval abbey excavated in the 1970s and '80s (Fanning and Clyne 2007). The excavation team on this dig were, in the main, local unemployed labourers who had been offered seasonal work through a FÁS (national employment agency) initiative. This team assisted with excavation, survey and recording during work on the site (Manning 2007). This was generally how excavation was conducted in Ireland from the 1930s into the 1980s: academics supervising excavations with labour sourced through local employment schemes. The same model was in widespread use across the country, as would be attested by anybody involved in the Wood Quay excavations or, indeed, on urban digs throughout Dublin into the 1990s.

This local focus offered work in difficult times while providing a real way for the community to engage and to interact with excavations. While it must be noted that such engagement was circumstantial (the people—largely men—involved had no agency in deciding whether they worked on an excavation or on roadworks, for example), could these types of models be considered to represent community archaeology in the most basic sense? This trend ceased definitively in the 1990s and can be linked to the roll-out of the 'developer pays' principle in Ireland, initially under local government regulations before being enshrined in the government publication *Framework and principles for the protection of the archaeological heritage*, which followed the aforementioned Irish ratification of the Valletta Convention in 1997 (DoAHGI 1999, 24–5, 33; Ciuchini 2010, 19). While public outreach and dissemination of results remained at the core of archaeological best practice across the State agencies, opportunities for community participation dwindled.

This 'developer pays' principle contributed to the subsequent and sharp rise in construction-led excavations, the poorly regulated growth in construction that followed and the resulting increase in commercial archaeological consultancies. In short, the demand for archaeological resources outstripped supply in the country, leaving little scope for community considerations … bringing us back to our starting point.

So, in some ways, the rise of a commercial archaeological sector associated with booming development drew attention and resources away from the community coalface throughout the years of the Celtic Tiger. With the derailing of this economic progress, archaeologists, passionate about their profession though without a viable opportunity to pursue it as a career, were freer to engage with archaeology and heritage at a local and fundamental level. And here we are faced with evidence of inverse equation. Construction bust means community boom …

BUST TO BOOM—THE INVERSE EQUATION

Moving on, therefore, with full cognisance taken of those who have ploughed this furrow before, it remains clear that community archaeology has increased by an order of magnitude in the last six years, both for practitioners engaging in this type of work and for groups identifying as community archaeology groups or carrying out community archaeology projects. When looking for a cause or catalyst for this growth, several factors present themselves: (i) the rise of the armchair archaeologist (it was around this time that back-to-back bingeing on *Time Team* episodes on

certain television packages became possible for many!), with coverage of archaeology and archaeological processes increasingly featuring in television documentaries; (ii) the launch by the National Monuments Service of the updated and more user-friendly www.archaeology.ie, which came online in 2011, allowing people easier access to a rich mine of data on monuments in their locality; and (iii) the proliferation of open-access archaeology courses at many universities, which have seen an increased uptake from members of local history groups from across the country.

Added to this, the work of local authority archaeologists and Heritage Officers, Heritage Council grant funding and the National Museum's education and outreach programmes have been instrumental, as has the huge peak in public awareness of archaeology occasioned by sustained public outreach and dedicated dissemination of results by the archaeology section of the National Roads Authority (now Transport Infrastructure Ireland—TII) in the immediate wake of the expansive motorway construction projects of the 2000–8 period (http://www.tii.ie/technical-services/archaeology/). As outlined above, the reconfiguration of the relationship between archaeologists and, to a lesser extent, archaeological consultancies with local communities immediately following the crash has been a contributing factor.

As the contents of this volume illustrate abundantly well, these factors have manifested themselves in communities through a rich variety of models, group compositions, motivations, backgrounds and research agendas.

To illustrate the *ad hoc* and uncoordinated growth, there follow some select examples of notable projects, initiatives and drivers of community archaeology in Ireland since 2012. These various projects have been chosen to illustrate the varied ways in which groups have been conceptualised, formed and realised, and how the landscape of community archaeology has evolved. The selection no doubt reflects my own bias, arising from my personal experience and geographical location, and does not claim to be either exhaustive or evenly spread throughout the country (I have omitted mention of initiatives from Northern Ireland, as I believe that these are adequately represented elsewhere in this volume).

The Historic Graves Project
Possibly the first project within our study time-frame to emerge with an awareness of fostering an active role for communities in the curating, recording and

safeguarding of their own heritage, the Historic Graves Project was ahead of the curve in terms of what was to follow. The project focuses on training community groups in the use of 'low-cost, high-tech survey of historic graveyards and recording of their own histories. They build a multi-media online record of the historic graves in their own areas and unite to a national resource' (www.historicgraves.com). The project provides a model that could prove to be exceptionally useful in terms of interlinking and cross-promoting community archaeology and heritage activities from around the country—namely the hosting of an open-source multi-media resource.

LEADER-funded projects, 2007–13

The LEADER scheme is an EU rural development fund to which several groups in Ireland have successfully applied for funding to carry out remedial works to heritage sites or enhancement of setting/access etc. in the interest of promoting tourism or local awareness (https://www.chg.gov.ie/rural/rural-development/leader/). This is perhaps the most significant funding stream available to groups in Ireland hoping to carry out community archaeology projects relating to upstanding features. Funding is administered by Local Action Groups (LAGs), which are partnerships of both public and private entities from a defined geographical area. They are responsible for selecting and approving projects in their respective areas in accordance with local development strategies developed specifically for their area. The National Monuments Service has been heavily involved in facilitating projects involving built heritage. A community-led structure is one of the core criteria (at LAG level) for qualification for funding. The definition of a community-led group is contained within article 32 of the EU Common Provision Regulation (https://eur-lex.europa.eu/legal-content/EN/TXT/?uri=celex:32013R1303) and, given the general unfamiliarity of practitioners in Ireland with its content, it bears reproducing here in part:

> 'Community-led local development shall be:
> (a) focused on specific sub-regional areas;
> (b) led by local action groups composed of representatives of public and private local socio-economic interests, in which, at the decision-making level, neither public authorities, as defined in accordance with national rules, nor any single interest group represents more than 49% of the voting rights; (c) carried out through integrated and multi-sectoral area-based local

development strategies; (d) designed taking into consideration local needs and potential, and shall include innovative features in the local context, networking and, where appropriate, cooperation.'

Fingal County Council Heritage Office

As Ian Doyle of the Heritage Council pointed out during his chairing of the community archaeology session of the Irish Conference of Medievalists in 2016, there is one local authority that crops up time and again in any discussion on community archaeology in Ireland—Fingal County Council. The flourishing of projects initiated *and* facilitated by the Council since 2012 has been a significant driver of the growth of community archaeology in the country (Baker, this volume). Some of the landmark developments pioneered by the Heritage Office include the 2012 Adopt-a-Monument scheme, the 2014 'Fingal's Heritage Supporting Communities' conference and the metamorphosis of the Field Monuments Advisor position into the first dedicated role of Community Archaeologist in the country in 2016. This transition reflects the reality of a role that has pioneered large-scale excavation projects at Swords Castle and Bremore Castle, enabling local community members and interested members of the public to actively participate in excavation and research on a scale never seen before in this country (http://fingal.ie/planning-and-buildings/heritage-in-fingal/communityarchaeology/).

Grassroots Archaeology/Resurrecting Monuments

The Grassroots Archaeology Project came into being in late 2012 and was designed to be an archaeological research and excavation project embedded within the local community of Baldoyle, Co. Dublin (Duffy 2014). The decision of the Royal Irish Academy Standing Committee for Archaeology to allocate funding to this project resulted in three seasons of survey and excavation within residential gardens and Fingal County Council park space in the Seagrange Housing Estate. The project generated a lot of interest locally and in the surrounding communities, and unearthed artefacts and features dating from the ninth century to the twentieth century. The success of the project led to an expansion of the project model into a wider area, with amendments to foster a more 'bottom-up' approach. This resulted in Irish Research Council funding under the 'New Foundations scheme in association with Professor Gabriel Cooney of UCD. A successful season of research, lectures, survey and excavation followed in 2015, as detailed elsewhere in this volume. The Resurrecting Monuments Group, though formed initially with input from professionals/academics, now operates consciously as a self-governed, community-led entity, which (save for complying with any relevant statutory obligations and obtaining any necessary approvals) has complete control over its research agendas and outputs (Duffy 2016; Giblin and Mongey, this volume).

Landscape and Geophysical Services

From 2012, Landscape and Geophysical Services have been pioneering an inclusive model of participatory research in community geophysical survey. This model provides initial training and induction for community groups commissioning surveys, leading to direct participation in fieldwork and some input into the processing of the data. Through active participation in the data-gathering, this model engenders a real sense of ownership of the geophysical results in communities. Following participation in this kind of project, community members are more likely to feel comfortable presenting the results in conference or open-day scenarios (see Reynolds, this volume; Duffy 2016; Giblin and Mongey, this volume).

Rathcroghan 'Above & Below' conference, 2012 to present

Beginning in 2012, the 'Archaeology Above and Below' two-day conference has evolved into a crucial outlet for community-orientated projects to present their work. The conference provides opportunities for teams and practitioners to meet in an energising, collaborative and supportive atmosphere, and often draws speakers from abroad to come and make presentations on experiences and models of community engagement that they have experienced. In 2015 the organisers began to publish abbreviated proceedings online in an open-source document (http://www.rathcroghan conference.com/uploads/1/4/4/6/14467310/abstracts_ 2015_above_and_below_conference_.pdf). This online publication constitutes the first collaborative volume in Ireland to be dedicated to providing a publishing outlet for community archaeology projects and, as such, marks an important milestone (Curley, this volume).

Glendalough Heritage Forum

An evolved solution to a complex situation, the Glendalough Heritage Forum is a response to tensions arising from nationally significant archaeology with World Heritage status potential inhabiting a space that is also of intrinsic cultural and economic value to an active, modern community. Management of the site

presents massive challenges with regard to tourist numbers and complex above-ground and below-ground archaeology, compounded by the continuation of its use into the modern era for farming and as a graveyard for the local community. Marrying academic input with public sector archaeology as well as a dedicated and considered approach to devolving control of some aspects of the project to the community, the Glendalough Heritage Forum (GHF) consists of a wide range of stakeholders, including local residents, landowners, State agencies, County Council representatives and researchers from a variety of institutions. The stated aim of the forum is to 'increase communication, collaboration and understanding between those with an interest in the cultural heritage of the famous valley of Glendalough and surrounding settlements'. Output to date has included survey, talks, expositions and excavations:

- The GHF have raised money from a variety of sources to employ John Tierney to train a local volunteer group to produce a graveyard survey (http://irserver.ucd.ie/bitstream/ handle/10197/7261/GVAP_Newsletter_5-Graveyard_Survey.pdf?sequence=1). This has included the production of a guide to a walk through the graveyard, all done by members of the survey team.
- Excavations in close partnership with UCD, which included the delivery of a highly successful community-focused dig at the monastic site.
- Exhibitions are organised by the GHF each year, e.g. 'An Age-Old Attraction' (http://www. countywicklowheritage.org/page/laragh_phot os?path=0p2p32p) and 'Art & Atmosphere' (http://www.countywicklowheritage.org/page /glendalough_art_and_atmosphere?path=0p2 p32p). These exhibitions brought together wonderful images and provide a very rich archive, all freely available online.

The Adopt-a-Monument scheme

In the 'big bang' and rapid expansion of community archaeology there has been the danger of a somewhat directionless expansion, with groups and initiatives operating individually or in a vacuum. Into this breach stepped the Heritage Council with the progressive Adopt-a-Monument model pioneered in Scotland and Finland over the previous decade. The Adopt-a-Monument project has begun to corral the existing and, in some cases, rudderless projects and to elicit new applications (Jackman, this volume). As a pilot scheme it has proved to be very effective, and has generated a lot of interest and positive engagement from communities across the country. The scheme has also occasioned the production of the Adopt-a-Monument *Guidance for community archaeology projects* (https://www.heritage council.ie/content/files/Guidance_for_community_arch aeology_projects.pdf). This publication marks a watershed in community archaeology practice in Ireland, as for the first time groups have access to a standardised roadmap to bring them through the process of engaging locally with their heritage.

Buttevant Heritage Guide

As Rónán Swan (pers. comm.), head of TII archaeology, has recently put it, 'the public is no longer the audience' in terms of archaeology. This comes on the back of a very interesting recent work carried out by Abarta Heritage on behalf of the TII in Buttevant, where the local community were involved in the synthesis and communication of archaeological results in their town. TII and Abarta worked with the local community to create a guide that showcases the town's heritage for visitors. The archaeological information in the guide was based on the discoveries made in Buttevant during recent street enhancement works. This information was incorporated into a series of texts that formed a narrative for an audio guide for the town. The local knowledge and insights provided by the community helped to place the discoveries in context, and the level of collaboration in this project is demonstrated by the fact that the guide is narrated by members of the community themselves (https://www.abartaheritage.ie/creating-buttevant-heritage-trail/).

CLASSIFYING COMMUNITY PROJECTS—YES OR NO?

In the past, questions about framing community archaeology projects within the wider context of international best practice and current theoretical approaches have been lacking in Ireland. As seen, projects have evolved in an *ad hoc* way, falling into several ill-defined categories. This situation is perhaps inevitable, given that in the last decade archaeology in Ireland has been coming up the curve in terms of community-based projects, and initiatives across the spectrum of 'bottom-up'–'top-down' models have been welcome additions to the landscape (Baker 2016).

Searching for a model of community archaeology

best practice and project design in 2012, while a very short time ago in terms of private sector archaeology, the would-be community archaeologist had to look beyond what was happening in Ireland to the international stage, where a variety of models could be seen (Duffy 2014, 198–9). Community archaeology, driven in the beginning by post-colonial backlash, entered the consciousness of communities at large in the UK, France, Australia and the United States from the 1980s onwards (Atalay 2012, 38–40). One of the initial push factors in its development arose in the context of wresting control from a dominant 'Authorised Heritage Discourse' (Smith and Waterton 2009, 29–30) that was in some cases linked to a colonial power and that had dictated the direction of research and dissemination in archaeology. Community archaeology at this level provided an outlet for populations such as Indigenous Australians, Native Americans and African Americans to reclaim ownership of their heritage. These somewhat confrontational origins have resulted in rigorous and exacting definitions being applied at different times to what is and what is not 'Community Archaeology'.

Applying such rigours to community archaeology groups that are attempting to find a route towards engaging with their heritage or to practitioners finding their way in this emerging subdiscipline is not helpful. Discussion of and education concerning the different available models, without judgement or prejudice, are essential for the future development of the subdiscipline. The differing models of community archaeology have been addressed in the academic literature in an Irish context (Baker 2016; Baker *et al.* 2019; Doyle 2018, 53–5; Duffy 2014, 193–6; Kador 2014, 34–6), but this discussion has yet to percolate down to community level. For a healthy development of community archaeology into the future, knowledge of these different models needs to be embedded in communities, local authorities and funding bodies engaging with community archaeology/heritage projects.

THE WAY FORWARD—OPPORTUNITIES AND PITFALLS

The future seems bright for community archaeology in Ireland. It is now a recognised subdiscipline of archaeological practice; it is viewed as a desirable output for local authorities and as a crucial element of research projects, and is firmly on the agenda for many funding streams and development plans. As briefly explored above, however, the time to take stock and appraise directions and definitions is at hand.

As discussed above, there are three main drivers of community archaeology projects in the Republic of Ireland. They include funding from the Heritage Council, who, either through their Adopt-a-Monument scheme or through other funding avenues, have supported numerous community groups in past years; LEADER funding, obtained at a European level; and local authorities (i.e. county and city councils), who may allot discretionary funding to 'bottom-up' projects or design their own projects from within.

While great work is being facilitated by each of these funding streams, only a fraction of applicant communities are ultimately successful in obtaining project funding through these avenues. Successful projects often receive funding for a maximum of three years, after which time it becomes very difficult to sustain group activities.

There is something of a disconnect here, given the scale of commercial archaeological projects which take place from year to year across the country. There are three ways in which archaeological initiatives that engage with a community as stakeholders (i.e. invested with some control over a project) could be promoted within the commercial archaeology sector.

Licensing requirements

While dissemination of results and engagement with communities constitute the ethical core of archaeological practice, there are no specific requirements to this effect under the excavation licences issued by the National Monuments Service. With the long-anticipated overhaul of the National Monuments Act, an opportunity presents itself to inscribe a licence condition stipulating some form of community engagement during the lifetime of larger archaeological excavations.

Planning conditions

The nature and extent of archaeological works on a given development are often dictated by planning conditions attached to a grant of planning. While dissemination and public reporting can be conditioned to a grant of planning, there is opportunity here for the planning authorities to specify some form of community engagement from the outset of larger projects. These could include initial consultations, community research programmes to run concurrently with fieldwork and/or site visits, where health and safety conditions allow. An element of this work is already being carried out by a network of local authority archaeologists, whose remit includes dissemination and community inclusion. For example,

during the redevelopment of a large site in Dublin City, planning conditions ensured preservation *in situ* and display of certain archaeological structures, to include extensive interpretation of the excavation results within the final build. Whilst this model can only work in a scenario where significant archaeology is known to exist on a site, it illustrates how strong, public-facing stipulations can be attached to development.

TII contracts

As the largest procurer of archaeological services in Ireland, TII have long been active in promoting and pioneering novel community engagement (as per the Buttevant project detailed above). TII contracts generally require the Archaeological Consultant to 'facilitate any school or organised visits that may be arranged throughout the course of the on-site Services'. Further, job specifications for Stage (iv) work (post-excavation stage) can include all or some of the following:

- Public lecture
- Popular archaeological article(s)
- Peer-reviewed academic article
- TII monograph
- Leaflet/brochure
- Museum exhibition
- Site visits—schools and general public

There is huge potential for these specifications to be rolled out more generally across State procurement bodies and, specifically with larger excavations, to be made more proscriptive in terms of community involvement in some aspect of the project.

THE FUTURE IS A FOREIGN COUNTRY

To finish, here is a reflection on a future that is less plausible-seeming and very distant but which may arrive on our doorstep with very little warning in what seems like no time at all. In reading Yuval Noah Harari's bestselling *Homo Deus* recently, one of the few comforts to be had was in the following lines:

'[…] there is a 99 per cent probability that by 2033, human telemarketers and insurance underwriters will lose their jobs to algorithms. There is a 98 per cent probability that the same will happen to sports referees, 97 per cent that it will happen to cashiers and 96 per cent to chefs.

Waiters—94 per cent. Paralegal assistants—94 per cent. Tour guides—91 per cent. Bakers—89 per cent. Bus drivers—89 per cent. Construction labourers—88 per cent. Veterinary assistants—86 per cent. Security guards—84 per cent. Sailors—83 per cent. Bartenders—77 per cent. Archivists—76 per cent. Carpenters—72 per cent. Lifeguards—67 per cent. And so forth. There are of course some safe jobs. The likelihood that computer algorithms will displace archaeologists by 2033 is only 0.7 per cent, because their job requires highly sophisticated types of pattern recognition and doesn't produce huge profits. Hence it is improbable that corporations or government will make the necessary investment to automate archaeology within the next twenty years' (Harari 2017, 379–80).

The book is a level-headed and inexorable exploration of how technology has and likely will affect our society, ethical framework and physical selves in the very near future. The above quote occurs within a chapter detailing the widely accepted predictions that by 2033 a dominant percentage of jobs will be carried out by a combination of artificial intelligence and robotics. The fact that 'archaeologist' is singled out by the author, however, seems to be based largely on economic grounds. While he outlines how research and development will be able to (and already has in many cases) create algorithms and technology to automate even the most 'human' of jobs (including teaching, policing and novel writing!), he concludes that the massive input of funding that would be required to develop such technology for an archaeological context would not be warranted on economic grounds.

Thinking about this after reading, my initial optimism was replaced with a sinking rational realisation—the author is writing from a North American perspective. He is more than likely not *au fait* with the bottom-line cost of archaeologically resolving 100km of a motorway or of excavating an urban site with deep stratification in Europe. If Mr Harari is even partially correct, the future is not bright for archaeological practitioners. While this is not the place to ponder the wholesale ramifications of technology for our society, it is nonetheless reassuring to consider that archaeology within the community may provide the antidote to such mechanisation of the job in a way not available to many other professions. It

is hard to imagine someone finding an outlet as a community steel-fitter or a community quantity surveyor, for example. Then again, perhaps I'm lining the nest for some job preservation strategies down the line …

To finish on a more pertinent note, the future-proofing of community archaeology is by no means assured. Once again, the strain on archaeological resources has reached a tipping point, as construction in urban areas has reached pre-bust proportions. With 'build more houses' the only discernible solution being espoused in the current housing crisis (accommodation crisis might be a better term), it appears that this strain will once again push the industry to breaking point in coming years. Commercial sector archaeology needs to be sure that it does not, once again, lose sight of the community behind its hoardings.

REFERENCES

Atalay, A.S. 2012 *Community-based archaeology: research with, by and for indigenous and local community.* University of California Press, Berkeley.

Baker, C. 2016 Community archaeology: more questions than answers. *Archaeology Ireland* **30** (3), 37–40.

Baker, C., O'Carroll, F. and Duffy, P. 2019 Creating opportunities and managing expectations: evaluating community archaeology in Ireland. In J.H. Jameson and S. Musteata (eds), *Transforming heritage practice in the 21st century: contributions from community archaeology*, 15–29. One World Archaeology series. Springer, Cham.

Ciuchini, P. 2010 Archaeology funding in the Republic of Ireland. Unpublished MA thesis, University College Dublin (https://www.academia.edu/364098/Archaeology_funding_in_the_Republic_of_Ireland; accessed 5 January 2018).

DoAHGI 1999 *Framework and principles for the protection of the archaeological heritage.* Stationery Office, Dublin.

Doyle, I.W. 2018 Community archaeology in Ireland: less mitigator, more mediator? In V. Apaydin (ed.), *Shared knowledge, shared power: engaging local and indigenous heritage*, 45–60. Springer, New York and London.

Duffy, P. 2014 Grassroots Archaeology—an experiment in monument resurrection and suburban identity in north Dublin. *Journal of*

Community Archaeology and Heritage **1** (3), 193–209.

Duffy, P. 2016 Resurrecting Monuments—a year in the life of a community archaeology group. *Archaeology Ireland* **30** (1), 11–14.

Fanning, T. and Clyne, M. 2007 *Kells Priory, Co. Kilkenny: archaeological excavations*. Stationery Office, Dublin.

Harari, Y.N. 2017 *Homo Deus: a brief history of tomorrow*. Vintage, London.

Horning, A. and Brannon, N. 2012 Irish archaeology 25 years on—upwards, downwards and onwards. *Archaeology Ireland* **26** (2), 14.

Kador, T. 2014 Public and community archaeology—an Irish persepctive. In S. Thomas and J. Lea (eds), *Public participation in archaeology*, 35–48. Boydell Press, Woodbridge.

Manning, C. 2007 The Kells Priory excavations: personal memories of working on the site. *Archaeology Ireland* **20** (4), 13–15.

Smith, L. and Waterton, E. 2009 *Heritage communities and archaeology*. Bloomsbury Academic, London.

20. 'Little concerted effort' or the 'tyranny of participation'? Thoughts on community archaeology in Ireland

IAN W. DOYLE

ABSTRACT

'… [T]here is no groundswell of amateur involvement in archaeology. Local societies are largely focused on historical periods, and of those that profess archaeological intent, only a few … are at all active in field-survey. Interested individuals do exist, but rarely is their information harnessed by the professional archaeologist … Unlike Britain and many parts of Europe, few mechanisms exist to collate the efforts of these local workers … There is little concerted effort to inform the layperson of his or her potential contribution to our subject' (Reeves-Smyth and Hamond 1983, 384).

So wrote Reeves-Smyth and Hamond in a polemical piece on the state of Irish archaeology in 1983. Their ire was directed not only at the lack of opportunities for community participation but also at the performance of the State's archaeological service and prevailing academic frameworks. Looking back after an interval of some 35 years, their comments on the role of communities and 'the layperson' did have some validity. Yet has this changed? This paper takes the view from 1983 as a starting point and will examine current practice and policy using a number of frameworks.

PUBLIC ARCHAEOLOGY?

The concept or practice of public archaeology is taught increasingly in Irish universities at present. This is positive in that it places what were ongoing practices into an academic framework, as the suspicion has been that outreach activities were something that archaeologists instinctively carried out but did not think about extensively. Yet, what is public archaeology? There are many definitions and discussing these is not the central aim of this paper; indeed, in many ways definitions are problematic (Richardson and Almansa-Sánchez 2015, 205). For brevity, the definition set out by Matsuda and Okamura (2011, 4) is a helpful start, delineating public archaeology as 'a subject that examines the relationship between archaeology and the public, and then seeks to improve it'.

Given, however, that archaeology is always either publicly funded or carried out as a requirement of a planning process that seeks to uphold the common good, the term could be seen as a tautology, and in this case the comments of Francis Pryor (1989, 51) on public archaeology are worth bearing in mind: 'I am often asked by visiting scholars why I believe so fervently in Public Archaeology, and I could reply … that the alternative, Private Archaeology, has been practised for far too long'. In this vein, this writer has argued that during the economic boom of the early

years of this millennium archaeological practice typically had a three-point relationship between the developer, the regulator in the form of government and the professional archaeologist, whether as practitioner or private company. Since then, the years of the financial crisis (2009–14), which were a challenging period for the Irish archaeological profession, saw a growing interest in community involvement in archaeological heritage projects, in particular from archaeologists previously employed in pre-development-funded projects (Doyle 2018). One practitioner (by way of verbal comment) cites the 2008 World Archaeological Congress in Dublin as a personal turning point that revealed the potential of community-based approaches.

Obviously, the concept of public archaeology contains a multitude of practices that would be helpful to examine. To begin this, Table 20.1 presents an eight-part typology of public archaeology as devised in the United Kingdom (Moshenska 2017, 5–11). This framework takes the breadth of what is normally referred to as public archaeology and seeks to map out the various elements of archaeological practice that contribute to this activity. As can be seen, there are many strands with varying degrees of community involvement, yet this is not exhaustive and there are many areas of overlap.

Starting at the top left, in an Irish context there

Table 20.1—Some common types of public archaeology (after Moshenska 2017).

Archaeologists working with the public: community archaeology and heritage projects run by museums, universities or commercial units	**Archaeology by the public**: local archaeological societies, amateur interest groups, independent scholars	**Public sector archaeology**: heritage resource management work carried out on behalf of national, regional or local government
Archaeological education: formal and informal learning about archaeology and the ancient world in schools, museums, online and otherwise	Some common types of public archaeology (after Moshenska 2017)	**Open archaeology**: archaeological work that is made publicly accessible through viewing platforms, webcams, guides or interpretation materials
Popular archaeology: television shows, museum exhibitions, books, magazines and websites about archaeology and the ancient world	**Academic public archaeology**: 'The study of archaeology in its economic, political, social, cultural, legal and ethical contexts'	

are many examples of projects that have an outreach element, open day or public-facing aspect that allows for participation. As set out by Kador (2014) and Doyle (2018), there is a spectrum of community involvement which extends from projects with an outreach element to public archaeology examining how the public interacts with archaeology and towards community archaeology designed with the central involvement of the public and community-based archaeology. The activities encompassed in this part of Moshenska's framework are in the public archaeology range of this spectrum, with professional and governmental institutions firmly in the driving seat. Nonetheless, a range of community-initiated archaeological projects are carried out in Ireland, as detailed in this volume, many of which are supported by Heritage Council community-focused grant schemes or through LEADER-type local funding programmes. A feature of these projects to date has been partnerships between archaeologists and communities.

Archaeology by the public in the Irish context remains something of a chimera owing to the particular culture of our archaeological tradition (Doyle 2018), which ensures the need for licences and permits and in many cases the need for technical knowledge. Metal-detecting is strictly controlled and it is illegal to search for archaeological objects. Despite some vocal objections to this regulatory regime from a small metal-detecting lobby, there has not been a large-scale call for a relaxation of such controls. A recent survey of public attitudes to archaeology commissioned by the Heritage Council found that only 30% of those surveyed were aware of these controls, but when this situation was explained 69% believed that this was to ensure that archaeological objects did not fall into private collections (Heritage Council 2018).

As argued elsewhere, this overall tradition and regulatory regime have resulted in a particular hybrid type of community archaeology in Ireland whereby simplistic models of top-down or bottom-up forms of practice do not suffice; instead, in many cases what has developed is a positive partnership approach between professionals and communities. This situation echoes the comments of Simpson and Williams (2008), who have argued that for community archaeology to be seen as 'being initiated and controlled by the people, for the people, is something of a naïve fantasy'. Nonetheless, in an Irish context community archaeological practice overlaps both of these elements of this framework, i.e. archaeologists working with the public and archaeology by the public.

Projects by local historical or archaeological societies are generally non-invasive and more typically consist of field trips and lecture series, which for many members of the public fully meets their needs. The development of an Adopt-a-Monument scheme in Ireland and the presence on the calendar of Heritage Week provide a focus for many heritage groups and communities to undertake and present projects, but the need to develop capacity and confidence in local heritage groups remains critical. The matching of groups with heritage experts has been one of the main ways of overcoming this and of helping communities to navigate the hurdles of best practice. Similarly, the work of historicgraves.ie with local community groups in recording and uploading data to an online database offers a model for training in both heritage and digital skills that is building into an important national resource. The growing role of voluntary and not-for-profit civil society groups who have undertaken the running of visitor sites, e.g. at Lough Gur, Co. Limerick, is also a point of note.

In this framework, public sector archaeology refers to all of the activities of public sector organisations and may include heritage management, regulation and communication carried out by national and local government. In the Irish context, national government has a particular regulatory role that it undertakes, but activities aimed at communication, including exhibitions, publications, lectures and conferences, are strongly ingrained in the organisational cultures that prevail. The more recent development has been the increasing role of local government through a small but growing number of archaeologists, heritage officers and conservation officers. At the time of writing there are fourteen local authority archaeologists, albeit with eight of them based in one single local authority.

Archaeological education is a broad category, including the higher educational institutes, schools, field schools and some historical and archaeological societies. Night courses for certificates and diplomas, some of which are run as online programmes, can act as gateways to draw students into formal degree courses in archaeology. A new trend in heritage has been the development of free MOOCs or Massive Online Open Courses, and it is hoped that this will continue (e.g. Trinity College Dublin on the Book of Kells). Yet another new development has been the resurgent interest in experimental archaeology as an academic exercise. This offers an appeal to new audiences thanks to its sociability and the tactile nature of its practice, involving the reconstruction and occupation of houses and the replication of crafts such as textile- and pottery-manufacturing as well as food-processing. Finally, the growth of archaeological field schools has also been a notable development in recent years, where experienced practitioners offer field training generally to students, many of whom are from overseas. An estimate of current field school operations in Ireland at present is five, with a focus varying from prehistoric to post-medieval periods. The longer-running examples have become deeply engrained in their local host communities and make a contribution to their economies. A hybrid model is perhaps the Glendalough excavations project, which involves a third-level training excavation (the School of Archaeology, UCD) opening up to community volunteers for part of its duration. The recent Heritage Council survey of public attitudes to archaeology found that 25% of those surveyed would like to take part in an excavation; it is not surprising, therefore, that the Glendalough project and others like it are frequently over-subscribed.

Moshenska's category of open archaeology represents practice that is available to visit either in person or online. Viewing platforms or windows in hoardings have a long history, and the tradition of a ceremonial turning of the sod at excavations in Ireland appears to be a long-established tradition, certainly going back as far as 1952, when An Taoiseach Éamon de Valera cut the first sod at the Rath of the Synods on the Hill of Tara (Cahill 2018). Leaving aside the political symbolism of this, such acts draw media attention and provide legitimacy, but on more typical excavations viewing facilities, guided tours and open days are an invaluable way to communicate the act of excavation. The process of interpretation is perhaps the most specialised aspect of this.

A key achievement in terms of popular archaeology was the creation of the quarterly magazine *Archaeology Ireland*. Since 1987 this has brought news of discoveries and research to a broad audience. Moreover, advancements in digital technology now mean that locational details of monuments can be examined online, while there is also a wealth of aerial photographic and cartographic resources freely available. Perhaps the area where ground has not been gained in the time since Reeves-Smyth and Hamond commented is that of television and media. It is hard to identify sustained archaeological programming on traditional media, and much coverage of archaeological issues in recent years has concerned pre-development projects that experienced delays, cost over-runs or controversy. Yet there is a strong public appetite for knowledge of the past, and there are opportunities through social media and podcasts to provide channels of communication. In 2018 the discovery of a Neolithic passage tomb in the Boyne Valley through well-designed excavation and of a new crop-mark enclosure by judicious use of a photographic drone in drought conditions were very encouraging. These discoveries received worldwide coverage and were very beneficial for the profile of archaeological practice in Ireland. Notably, the 2018 Heritage Council survey of public attitudes to archaeology found that 71% of those surveyed received archaeological knowledge from documentaries and from news reports on television and radio. Publications such as books accounted for 28%. Ironically, print is the traditional publication medium for the profession, owing to a relatively low cost and the place of the book as the normal output.

Academic public archaeology has developed as a respectable area of research, with courses in this area taught in numerous institutions across the island of Ireland. It is, however, unclear how many of these modules are mandatory for students. On a different note, the commitment of many academic researchers to open-access publications is important, as many of the typical fora for archaeological publications remain inaccessible to communities or are priced beyond their means.

BUT WHY THIS FOCUS?

Internationally there has been a strong and growing appreciation of the need for inclusivity and greater participation in cultural heritage (Hudson and James 2007). There are numerous reasons why this has happened, including the rise of the concept of multi-vocality and the identification and challenging of an Authorised Heritage Discourse (AHD), the influence of heritage practice from places like Australia where there has been a long-standing realisation that mainstream practice had marginalised indigenous communities, the role of heritage in the idea of place-making and of giving a sense of time depth and identity in a changing world, as well as a need across western Europe to demonstrate greater social return and relevance in the allocation and spending of scarce public resources.

Since the 1980s this shift has been represented in documents such as the Australia ICOMOS Burra Charter or the Council of Europe Faro Convention on the Value of Cultural Heritage to Society (Table 20.2). Both of these documents highlight the need for greater public involvement in the opportunities and challenges which cultural heritage presents and represent a move away from an expert-dominated view. In particular, the Burra Charter articulates a set of values that recognise that different individuals and groups might perceive cultural heritage in different ways. Equally, there is a recognition that such charters were written explicitly with disenfranchised local groups (indigenous peoples) in mind and, while such groups are not immediately obvious in Europe, local communities were similarly often ignored about decisions relating to heritage which were taken by government bureaucracies (Willems 2014, 109). The Burra Charter is not a key element of the archaeological curriculum, yet participation, communication and public engagement are becoming more and more understood as basic elements of practice.

It was not always this way, however. Looking at the ICOMOS 'Lausanne' Charter of 1990 for the protection of archaeological heritage, there is an impression that the professional remains clearly in control, that ceding control only happens if dealing with the heritage of indigenous people and that 'local … participation should be actively sought' rather than any initiative coming from local communities. The Council of Europe Valletta Convention for the protection of archaeological heritage continues in this vein, with signatories committing to carry out educational activities to develop public awareness and to promote public access to monuments and collections. In many ways Valletta is very much a product of its time and its provisions are very much what could be seen as 'hygiene factors' seeking to protect archaeological heritage in the face of development pressures. Looking at it after an interval of a quarter of a century, it does seem dated in approach and there are frequent discussions on the need to update it at European Association of Archaeologists annual conferences (e.g. at Maastricht in 2017; see Olivier 2014).

The 2005 Council of Europe Framework Convention on the Value of Cultural Heritage for Society (or Faro Convention) marked a step change in this regard. The very idea that cultural heritage is a right for communities to participate in and a source of identity builds upon the achievements of Valletta. The deficit model of cultural heritage whereby professionals retain all knowledge and remain in control of communication has now been replaced by a call for the public to 'participate in the process of identification, study, interpretation, protection, conservation and presentation of the cultural heritage'. Ireland has yet to ratify Faro but we are not alone in this, as at the time of writing only eighteen countries out of the 47 members of the Council of Europe have ratified this convention. The relatively low level of formal acceptance suggests that aspects of this convention are challenging or unclear for many State administrations. By way of comparison, the Florence or European Landscape Convention of 2000 has been ratified by 39 countries.

Two further, more recent, documents at European level continue this trend of encouraging participation. The Italian EU presidency of 2014 finalised conclusions that seek to promote greater involvement in the governance and decision-making of cultural heritage and continue this theme of cultural heritage as a shared resource. This document emerged in the context of a growing interest at EU level in cultural heritage, which also saw the appearance of a paper examining the place of cultural heritage in the EU's research programme Horizon 2020. In the same year, the European Commission adopted a communication entitled *Towards an integrated approach to cultural heritage for Europe*. This continued to advocate for the continued development of 'more participative interpretation and governance models that are better suited to contemporary Europe, through greater involvement of the private sector and civil society'. In December 2018 the EU Commission published the European Framework for Action on Cultural Heritage, which deepens the interest of the EU in these matters, in particular by identifying a pillar of actions devoted to participation and access for all.

Finally, the latest document cited in Table 20.2, that of the Council of Europe European Cultural Heritage strategy for the 21st century, strengthens the articulation of cultural heritage as a focus for social cohesion and as a means for positive societal development. In this vein, it seeks to 'reposition cultural heritage policies, placing them at the heart of an integrated approach focusing on the conservation, protection and promotion of heritage by society as a whole—by both the national authorities and the communities which are the custodians of that heritage'.

The obvious question that follows on from the excerpts presented in this survey is: where is the national policy context? To date, much of the focus on community participation has taken place in this international and professional disciplinary context but with little in terms of a national formal government policy other than successive strategic plans from the Heritage Council. A promising start was made in the government's *National Heritage Plan 2002*, which contained an objective to 'Increase community ownership of heritage by empowering local communities to become more involved in heritage issues' (DAHGI 2002, 12). Unfortunately, shortly after its publication there was a reconfiguration of government portfolios and departments and this plan lost currency.

At the time of writing in late 2018, national government has signalled a willingness to create a foothold in policy through its public consultation document *Heritage Ireland 2030*. This states that it 'will listen to and respect the voices of communities and help and support them in taking care of their valued heritage', and then sets an objective to provide 'better supports for communities working to care for and promote their local heritage' (DCHG 2018, 14). This is a welcome and timely development and the shift in empowerment is visible. While the 2002 plan talked about communities becoming more involved, the 2018 consultation document talks about communities taking care of their heritage.

SO, IS IT ALL GOOD, THEN? TOWARDS A CONCLUSION

Looking at the developments above in terms of a rapid survey of Irish archaeology using the Moshenska framework, one could be forgiven for thinking that all is well and dramatically improved since Reeves-Smyth and Hamond commented in 1983. There have undoubtedly been improvements in much of the practice and many of the structures of Irish archaeology, in the sheer volume of data and knowledge, in the training and qualifications of the practitioners and, as the focus of this paper, in the contribution that communities can make to heritage management. While resources (or rather the lack of) remain a constant issue, as do concerns about the career paths of archaeological professionals and how fieldwork contributes to archaeological knowledge, these are issues that archaeological practice faces across Europe. Looking at some of the literature on community archaeology, one of the key concerns seems to be the extent to which it meets objectives not only in terms of engaging people with the past but also in terms of social engagement. In many ways there almost seems to be a dip in confidence as to whether this practice is meeting its own objectives—or, to phrase it more simply, 'is it working'? Yet, despite this doubt, for many heritage professionals and volunteers who engage with community archaeology it is a positive experience (Sayer 2015). That said, for Moshenska (2017, 13) such projects need to be more proactive and consistent in the gathering of data and in evaluating their impact. For Simpson and Williams (2008, 87) this is a matter of self-reflexive and qualitative forms of evaluation, but with an ultimate question that community archaeology must 'provide the public service it claims to provide … meeting and adapting to the wants of the community—and must prove its broader values'. In a world where resources to support such archaeological projects are scarce, it is difficult to argue with the idea that what gets measured gets managed—or, perhaps more correctly, gets funded—and this is an issue that deserves far greater priority as community-based approaches to heritage develop.

There are, however, other issues worthy of consideration. There is a growing sense of discord about participation as a practice within other disciplines, and elements of this thinking need to be reflected in the heritage context. Perhaps the most significant contribution in this area is the idea of 'participation as the new tyranny'. This phrase was coined by Cooke and Kothari (2001), who examined

Table 20.2—Conventions, charters and strategies pertaining to community involvement.

Name	Status/origin	Relevant to community and stakeholder participation (direct quotations in italics)
Charter for the Protection and Management of the Archaeological Heritage, signed in Lausanne	ICOMOS charter (1990)	*Local commitment and participation should be actively sought and encouraged as a means of promoting the maintenance of the archaeological heritage. This principle is especially important when dealing with the heritage of indigenous peoples or local cultural groups. In some cases it may be appropriate to entrust responsibility for the protection and management of sites and monuments to indigenous peoples* (Article 6).
The European Convention for the Protection of the Archaeological Heritage (revised) (ETS No. 143), signed in Valletta	Council of Europe Convention (ratified by Ireland) 1992	*Each Party undertakes: to conduct educational actions with a view to rousing and developing an awareness in public opinion of the value of the archaeological heritage for understanding the past and of the threats to this heritage; to promote public access to important elements of its archaeological heritage, especially sites, and encourage the display to the public of suitable selections of archaeological objects* (Article 9).
The Council of Europe Framework Convention on the Value of Cultural Heritage for Society (CETS No. 199), signed in Faro	Council of Europe Convention 2005	*The Parties undertake to: encourage everyone to participate in the process of identification, study, interpretation, protection, conservation and presentation of the cultural heritage* (Article 12).
Burra	ICOMOS Australia Charter (revised 2013)	*Participation: Conservation, interpretation and management of a place should provide for the participation of people for whom the place has significant associations and meanings, or who have social, spiritual or other cultural responsibilities for the place* (Article 12).
Conclusions on the Participatory Governance of Cultural Heritage	Council of the European Union 2014	*Invites the member states to: develop multilevel and multi-stakeholder governance frameworks which recognise cultural heritage as a shared resource by strengthening the links between the local, regional, national and European levels of governance of cultural heritage, with due respect to the principle of subsidiarity, so that benefits for people are envisaged at all levels* (Article 13).
European Cultural Heritage Strategy for the 21st Century	Council of Europe strategy 2018	Numerous sections including: *The 'social' component harnesses the assets of heritage in order to promote diversity, the empowerment of heritage communities and participatory governance.*
European Framework for Action on Cultural Heritage (Commission Staff working document)	European Commission 2018	

the emergence of participatory development. This practice emerged from a recognition that top-down developmental approaches were not working and sought instead to make people central to development. In examining this area, the authors identified three sets of tyrannies: (1) tyrannies of decision-making and control, (2) the tyranny of the group and (3) the tyranny of the method. Given that archaeological practice is typically driven by professionals who adhere to specific methodologies recognised as best practice, it may be timely to pause on projects and reflect on whether decision-making is distributed equally or is concentrated or vested in a single individual. Similarly, how strong is the power of the group and how much appetite is there for engagement and decision-making? While there are projects driven by communities with strong vested interests in how they should develop, it is worth considering Moshenska's (2017, 9–10) comments that much of the public support for archaeological heritage is based on what is referred to as shallow engagement, in so far as the vast majority of the public do not want huge amounts of information or responsibility. Motives for individual engagement in heritage projects may be wide-ranging: a recent Swedish study on community involvement in the management of a relict mining cultural landscape identified issues like 'individual and collective well-being and place identity', and in some cases opportunities to spend time with partners. Other answers identified tourism and recreational opportunities (Fredholm *et al.* 2017, 8).

A second paper worthy of consideration derives from the healthcare sector and sought an answer as to whether the user was a 'friend, foe or fetish'. Against the backdrop of changes in the delivery of health and social care under the UK's New Labour government, the authors raised the question of whether or not '... the voice of the User becomes a fetish—something which can be held up as a representative of authenticity and truth, but which at the same time has no real influence over decision making' (Cowden and Singh 2007, 15–16). They point to a lack of clear guidelines on what user involvement is, and also signal the need for caution regarding which social groups tend to dominate participatory fora and systems. Clearly, there is food for thought here as regards the development of archaeological heritage projects, and the key point is that archaeology is not the only discipline that has to think about its public and how it participates. Conversely, borrowings from other disciplines on these issues are infrequent in much of the writing on public and community archaeology. That said, there may be a

key difference in that, unlike in the healthcare context, where the use of services may not be voluntary, most participants in heritage projects are self-selecting, i.e. they volunteer. Such volunteerism can probably be best seen as on a spectrum ranging from wanting to take part or wanting to be informed to seeking a role in analysing material, seeking funding and making decisions. The challenge is to read and understand this involvement spectrum so as not to overburden some or underutilise the skills of others.

Finally, a thought on knowledge and the generation of new archaeological information about the past. During the years of frenetic archaeological activity necessitated by meeting the needs of development, there were ongoing concerns that, amidst all the excavation work involving the destruction and recording of archaeological deposits, new data were being gathered but were not being transformed into knowledge (Reeners 2006). While many community archaeological projects are non-invasive, they still generate data. Moreover, for many people there is still a strong cognitive association that excavation is what archaeology is all about, and because of this very resilient perception several community projects have moved to excavation by working in partnership with professional archaeologists and the regulatory authorities. In terms of equity and practice, such projects need to be held to the same standard as those necessitated by the needs of development, i.e. there should be a presumption of a research output, be it in the form of a publication or journal contribution above

Fig. 20.1—A basic model showing the need for overlapping issues of archaeological knowledge, the creation of social benefits and good practice in terms of governance and sustainability.

the level of an unpublished 'grey literature' report. Perhaps one way to consider this is to see three circles of concern that should overlap. Such a model is presented in Fig. 20.1, which sets out the priorities of producing archaeological knowledge, the creation of social benefits and, finally, good practice in terms of governance, administration and sustainability. Perhaps the ultimate in good practice is represented by the intersection of all three overlapping circles, yet this is a model that needs greater development and refinement based on case-studies.

To conclude, stronger frameworks do prevail at present for community participation than at the time quoted at the beginning of this paper, but that is not to say that all is perfect. In many ways this is still an evolving form of practice, and ongoing training and supports are needed. Nonetheless, among communities across Ireland there exists a strong interest in becoming involved in heritage projects, whether it be conservation and recording of a local historic cemetery, participation on an excavation or taking part in or learning about various forms of survey. How we as a profession sustain this remains a critical question.

REFERENCES

Cahill, M. 2018 The first sod. In J. Fenwick (ed.), *Lost and found III: rediscovering more of Ireland's past*, 1–4. Wordwell, Dublin.

Cooke, B. and Kothari, U. 2001 The case for participation as tyranny. In B. Cooke and U. Kothari (eds), *Participation: the new tyranny?*, 1–15. Zed Books, London.

Cowden, S. and Singh, G. 2007 The 'user': friend, foe or fetish? A critical exploration of user involvement in health and social care. *Critical Social Policy* **27** (1), 5–23.

Department of Arts, Heritage, Gaeltacht and the Islands [DAHGI] 2002 *National Heritage Plan 2002*. Government of Ireland, Dublin.

Department of Culture, Heritage and the Gaeltacht [DCHG] 2018 *Heritage Ireland 2030: public consultation*. Government of Ireland, Dublin.

Doyle, I.W. 2018 Community archaeology in Ireland: less mitigator, more mediator? In V. Apaydin (ed.), *Shared knowledge, shared power: engaging local and indigenous people*, 45–60. Springer, New York.

Fredholm, S., Eliasson, E. and Knez, I. 2017 Conservation of historical landscapes: what signifies 'successful' management? *Landscape Research* (July 2017), 2–14.

Heritage Council 2018 Public perceptions of archaeology. Unpublished survey by RedC.

Hudson, J. and James, P. 2007 The changing framework for the conservation of the historic environment. *Structural Survey* **25** (3–4), 253–64.

Kador, T. 2014 Public and community archaeology— an Irish perspective. In S. Thomas and J. Lea (eds), *Public participation in archaeology*, 35–48. Boydell Press, Woodbridge.

Matsuda, A. and Okamura, K. 2011 Introduction: New perspectives in global public archaeology. In K. Okamura and A. Matsuda (eds), *New perspectives in global public archaeology*, 1–18. Springer, New York.

Moshenska, G. 2017 Introduction: Public archaeology as practice and scholarship where archaeology meets the world. In G. Moshenska (ed.), *Key concepts in public archaeology*, 1–13. UCL Press, London.

Olivier, A. 2014 The Valletta Convention: twenty years after—a convenient time. In V. van der Haas and P.A.C. Schut (eds), *The Valletta Convention: twenty years after—benefits, problems, challenges*, 11–16. EAC Occasional Paper No. 9. Archaeolingua, Budapest.

Pryor, F. 1989 'Look what we've found': a case study in public archaeology. *Antiquity* **63**, 51–61.

Reeners, R. (ed.) 2006 *Archaeology 2020: repositioning Irish archaeology in the knowledge society: a realistically achievable perspective*. UCD, Dublin.

Reeves-Smyth, T. and Hamond, F. 1983 Conclusions: landscape archaeology in Ireland. In T. Reeves-Smyth and F. Hamond (eds), *Landscape archaeology in Ireland*, 379–89. British Archaeological Reports, British Series 116. Oxford.

Richardson, L.J. and Almansa-Sánchez, J. 2015 Do you even know what public archaeology is? Trends, theory, practice, ethics. *World Archaeology* **47** (2), 194–211.

Sayer, F. 2015 Can digging make you happy? Archaeological excavations, happiness and heritage. *Arts and Health: An International Journal for Research, Policy and Practice* **7** (3), 247–60.

Simpson, F. and Williams, H. 2008 Evaluating community archaeology in the UK. *Public Archaeology* **7** (2), 69–90.

Willems, W.J.H. 2014 The future of World Heritage and the emergence of transnational heritage regimes. *Heritage and Society* **7** (2), 105–20.